NUCLEAR PROLIFERATION IN THE 1980s

This book analyzes the viewpoints of a diverse group of younger scholars on the dilemma of nuclear weapons in a world of endemic conflict. In particular, the problem of the spread of nuclear weapons to other countries is examined. Incentives to and disadvantages of the acquisition of nuclear weapons are analyzed, along with the responsibility of existing nuclear weapons states for the potential proliferation of these weapons. Original proposals for coping with proliferation are advanced.

As a study on non-proliferation it is unique in that it represents the work of young specialists from the very countries which will be most concerned with the issues in the current decade and the next.

The editors

William H. Kincade is executive director of the Arms Control Association, Washington, DC.

Christoph Bertram is director of the International Institute for Strategic Studies, London.

The contributors

Cynthia Cannizzo is assistant professor of Political Science at Ohio State University in Columbus, Ohio, and a research associate of the Mershon Center.

Fergus Carr is a doctoral candidate in International Relations at the London School of Economics.

Gloria Duffy, former communications director of the Arms Control Association, Washington, DC, and a consultant to the Rand Corporation, is now a Hubert H. Humphrey Doctoral Fellow in the Arms Control and Disarmament Program at Stanford University.

Jo L. Husbands is a staff associate of CACI, Inc., a Washington, DC, consulting firm.

Zalmay M. Khalilzad is assistant professor of Political Science at Columbia University in New York City and a consultant to Pan Heuristics, Los Angeles, California.

Pierre Lellouche is a research fellow at the Institut Français des Relationes Internationales in Paris and a candidate for the doctor of laws degree at Harvard Law School.

Richard K. Lester is a doctoral candidate and Hugh Hampton Young Fellow in the Department of Nuclear Engineering at the Massachusetts Institute of Technology, Cambridge, Massachusetts.

C. Raja Mohan is a doctoral candidate in Disarmament, Arms Control and International Relations at Jawaharlal Nehru University, New Delhi.

Bijan Mossavar-Rahmani is a visiting research fellow in the International Relations Division of the Rockefeller Foundation, New York City.

Harald Müller is a doctoral candidate in International Relations at Johann Wolfgang Goethe University, Frankfurt, and a research fellow at the Frankfurt Peace Research Institute.

Robert A. Strong is a doctoral candidate in Political Science at the University of Virginia, Charlottesville, Virginia.

Theodor Winkler is associated with the Programme for Strategic and International Security Studies of the Graduate Institute of International Studies, Geneva.

NUCLEAR PROLIFERATION IN THE 1980s

Perspectives and Proposals

Edited by
William H. Kincade
and
Christoph Bertram

St. Martin's Press   New York

Library of Congress Catalog Card Number: 82–42602

ISBN 0–312–57975–6

Contents

Introduction

Ten years ago, the Nuclear Non-proliferation Treaty took effect. There was widespread concern, even among adherents to the pact, about the viability of the distinctions it created between the rights and duties of nuclear weapon states and non-nuclear weapon states and between signatories and non-signatories. At the time, however, it was hoped that the Treaty's inherently discriminatory character could be mitigated or managed, if it attracted widespread support and adherents lived up to the obligations and the spirit of the Treaty.

In the decade since 5 March 1970, only India, in addition to the five nuclear weapon states existing at that time, has overtly exploded a nuclear device, thus crossing the threshold usually considered to mark attainment of the status of a nuclear weapon state. Israel, thought by many to possess nuclear weapons, has given no unequivocal sign of its capability, nor has South Africa, also considered a candidate nuclear weapon state. Meanwhile, 110 countries have signed or ratified the Non-proliferation Treaty (NPT), leaving some 33 nations, including France, China, and India, outside its network of obligations.

Though in these superficial terms international efforts to prevent the spread of nuclear weapons appear to have been fairly successful, a number of developments in the intervening years have cast grave doubt on whether the 1980s will pass with as few additions to the nuclear club as the 1970s. Indeed, so strong and numerous are the pressures for developing the capacity to make explosive nuclear devices that the proliferation of nuclear weapons and efforts to prevent or retard it have already emerged as one of the issues likely to dominate international relations in the 1980s. Long a lively but frequently abstract topic for diplomatic discussion, nuclear proliferation and non-proliferation policy increasingly determine the ways in which nations in particular regions relate to each other, how rivalries and alliances operate (Soviet-American cooperation and Western disagreement over non-proliferation strategies), and the challenge of nuclear events (the aborted South African nuclear test of 1977 and a possible nuclear event in that region in 1979) to international crisis-management.

The significance of the problem is indicated by the degree to which nations are adjusting more traditional foreign and domestic policy objectives to cope with nuclear weapons proliferation. The desire to acquire, or to prevent the acquisition of, the ability to make nuclear weapons increasingly influences policy decisions in the areas of economic development, energy, trade security, science and technology, and foreign assistance. For a growing number of nations, foreign relations cannot be conducted, nor foreign, and often domestic, policy formulated, without recognition of their implications for nuclear proliferation. The domestic impact of nuclear non-proliferation or proliferation is greatest in the areas of energy and environmental policy. It is already being felt in the United States, where non-proliferation considerations increasingly drive policies relating to commercialization of new nuclear technologies and storage of spent nuclear fuel. Its effect can also be seen in the delays attending the operation of nuclear fuel reprocessing plants in France and England, where weapons-grade material is recovered from spent nuclear fuel rods for return to the using country.

The developments which have led to the present situation are disparate and complex:

Advances in the technology of peaceful nuclear energy which increase the fuel efficiency of nuclear reactors but also produce higher-grade fissile or weapons material (plutonium or enriched uranium) were foreseen but perhaps not fully appreciated during the negotiation of the NPT. (See Figure 1). Obtaining the indigenous capability to enrich uranium before it is placed in a reactor and to extract plutonium and unused uranium from the spent fuel when it is removed have promised to make nuclear energy more economically competitive with other energy sources and more immune to fuel supply disruptions. Breeder reactors for countries investing in nuclear power soon expected to move from the experimental to the commercial stage, would, if successful, reduce fuel costs and vulnerability still further, while increasing the availability of weapons-grade material.

A growth in many nations of a significant nuclear technology base – both in terms of facilities and trained manpower – has paralleled advances in nuclear technology. The development of this expertise was partly a result of Western non-proliferation policies which heavily promoted nuclear energy as a means of reducing economic inequality, and thus economic and security incentives to obtain an indigenous capacity to build nuclear weapons. At the same time, the number of

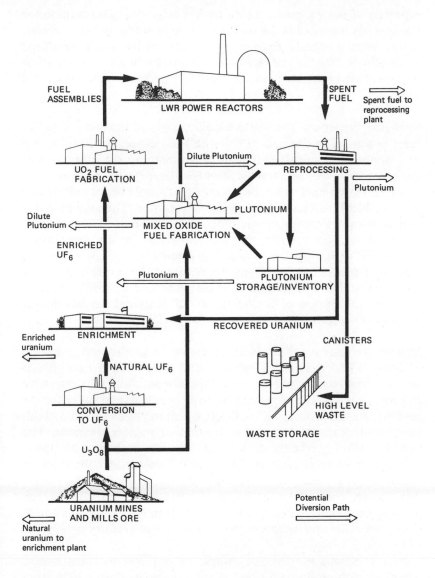

Source: Office of Technology Assessment, United States Congress.

FIGURE 1   Light-water reactor fuel cycle (showing path for diversion of materials)

exporters of nuclear power hardware has expanded. Competition for markets has increased in the search for foreign trade, prestige, access, and economies of scale. Existing suppliers are redoubling their efforts – sometimes offering the most advanced technologies – while some importers are beginning to export hardware or know-how in a limited way.

Increased fuel costs. The world-wide increases in the price of petroleum beginning in the mid-1970s, with their especially crushing impact on the economic development programmes of the Third World, strongly reinforced these trends. Steeply rising petroleum prices led to demands for cheaper sources of energy that would be more insulated from political manipulation or other disruptions. The uneven distribution of known natural uranium, (concentrated in the United States, Soviet Union, South Africa, Sweden, Australia, Canada, and Spain), and actual or anticipated changes in exporters' policies encourage fears of a producers' cartel and doubt about the future availability and price stability of uranium. These fears and uncertainties have increased the appeal of fuel-efficient self-contained nuclear power technologies which promise virtual energy self-sufficiency.

Structural change in the international system. A gradual redistribution of power is underway in the international system. The rise and fall of new regional actors and often abrupt discontinuities in interstate relations, has aggravated regional security problems and suggested the need for greater security self-reliance, which might be served by both energy independence and the acquisition of nuclear weapons. The volatility and uncertainty of alliances coexists with growing interdependence in areas such as the monetary system and the trade in foodstuffs, raw materials, and manufactured goods. This interdependence, contrary to the hopes of some in the early 1970s, has produced as much friction as cooperation. It thus provides additional risks of conflict and heightens the importance of security problems.

Shift in US non-proliferation policy. In response to these trends, American non-proliferation policy abruptly shifted after 1975 from promoting all forms of nuclear power short of processes directly capable of producing nuclear weapons material domestically and abroad. The Ford and Carter administrations undertook to slow the commitment to new, proliferation-prone technologies, recommended that spent fuel not be recycled but instead stored indefinitely as part of a 'once-through' fuel system, and imposed conditions on nuclear-power-related exports, including uranium fuel. Formerly the world's largest supplier of nuclear facilities and training and still a major nuclear fuel exporter, the United States was widely accused of reneging on provisions of the Non-proliferation Treaty which mandated nuclear technology transfer. Exporters and importers of nuclear power technology, apprehensive about supply disruptions of just this kind, responded to the turn-about by insisting firmly on developing the new nuclear technologies which appeared to promise relative energy independence.

Limitations of preventive measures. The pressures for energy and security independence cast in sharp relief the inherent limitations of the 'safeguard' and inspection programs of the International Atomic Energy Agency, designed to deter or provide 'timely warning' of the use of nuclear power reactors for weapons manufacture. The IAEA has an uneven record in obtaining adherence to the safeguards and is further limited by its conflicting role as an international promoter of atomic energy. Two efforts were mounted in the 1970s to remedy deficiencies to prevent diversions. In addition to reactor safeguards, 'full scope' safeguards were proposed for associated fuel rod fabrication, enrichment, and reprocessing facilities. These proposals met considerable resistance from both exporters and importers. Secondly, a Nuclear Suppliers Group, meeting in London and now numbering 15 nations, was established to coordinate policy on the transfer of sensitive technologies and to establish conditions for exports. Although it succeeded in developing a 'trigger list' of sensitive technologies which automatically invoke safeguards, the suppliers group has been hampered by the diverging perspectives and interests of its members. The limitations of earlier non-proliferation measures were perhaps most dramatically exposed when India detonated a 'peaceful' nuclear explosive in 1974. India's action led to the belated proposals for full scope safeguards and to formation of the suppliers group. But neither the original safeguards nor these latter developments have had a decisive effect on the steady growth in countries like South Africa and Argentina of the capacity to make similar devices. Threats by individual suppliers, chiefly the United States, of nuclear, economic, and security penalties, and occasionally the promise of rewards, have met with success in some cases. These sanctions and rewards can never permanently forestall a nation from going nuclear. Ironically, offering rewards may make their author liable to a form of continuous nuclear blackmail, if near-nuclear nations continue to maintain ambiguous postures between having and not having the bomb.

Delays in superpower arms control. The United States and the Soviet Union are already suspected by non-nuclear weapons nations of seeking to perpetuate a nuclear condominium. Despite a decade of negotiations, they have been able to make good on their pledges in the Limited Test Ban Treaty and the NPT to reduce their own arsenals of nuclear weapons. Their failure has had several negative consequences for proliferation. The trebling of superpower nuclear inventories since the Strategic Arms Limitation Talks (SALT) began in 1969 has underlined the apparent utility of nuclear forces, especially for the threshold nuclear weapon states. The apparent bad faith of the original negotiators of the NPT has cast in doubt the existing non-proliferation regime, prejudiced the atmosphere for future progress, and provided an excuse for any nation deciding to go nuclear.

The apparent cost-ineffectiveness of nuclear explosions, compared to conventional methods, for peaceful purposes like oil and gas production and major earth-moving projects, raises questions about the need to develop peaceful nuclear explosives (PNEs). Unresolved problems surrounding disposal of nuclear wastes, plant siting and system operating and security procedures are creating doubts about the future of nuclear power for some governments. These doubts are increased by the growing capital costs of nuclear power plants, compounded by construction delays and, in some cases, the inability to achieve designed performance levels. The growth of an anti-nuclear power movement in the United States and Europe, and scepticism within the Soviet bureaucracy, casts a shadow over the promise of cheap, reliable energy supplies from nuclear power. The general spread of nuclear science, and gradual dispersion in the United States and abroad, of information on nuclear weapons design fosters fears that terrorists or other sub-national groups could acquire nuclear devices.

*   *   *   *   *

Amid the uncertainties, pressures, and conflicting trends of the 1970s, concern about the potential increase in the number of nuclear weapon states was inadequate to produce a consensus on how to address this problem, or even whether it was soluble or a problem. Complicating the issue still further, the neat distinction drawn by the NPT between a nuclear weapon state and non-nuclear weapon state dissolved in the ambiguity of various levels of, and routes to, nuclear weapons capability. The 'Nth' country problem (used to refer to the *next*, unknown nuclear state – not indefinite quantity) of predicting the next nuclear weapon state was supplanted by the question of knowing how to determine when a country achieved this status.

Despite an Indian explosion with no known peaceful application and a Pakistani quest for an enrichment plant for which it has no civilian use, these bitter regional rivals nevertheless stoutly affirmed the peaceful nature of their respective nuclear programmes, the lack of any intent to acquire or produce nuclear weapons, and their willingness to accept safeguards or other measures on a non-discriminatory basis, contingent on the other's acceptance. An equivocal, intermediate position, between having the capacity to make weapons and actually making them, has thus begun to take shape. This raises questions as to whether such a posture is designed to ward off sanctions and penalties while work on usable weapons and delivery systems goes forward, to increase bargaining leverage on other security issues, or to obtain a nuclear deterrent without nuclear weapons.

The development in the 1970s of ambiguity about nuclear weapons means that non-proliferation policy has subtly changed character, not only in relation to other global issues, but in its own thrust. Nuclear weapons technology has not proved as easy to confine by diplomatic and technical means as the framers of the NPT hoped. Nor have other levers against proliferation – such as the US offer of military aircraft to Pakistan or subsequent termination of economic assistance or even tight Soviet control of fuel supplies for its nuclear clients – provided workable, durable and guaranteed solutions. The experience of the last decade appears to confirm publically the private fear of many diplomats that the task of the 1980s may be less to prevent nuclear proliferation than to retard the spread of nuclear weapons while learning to live in a 'nuclear-armed crowd' or at least a crowd with a growing number of potential bomb-makers.

In the face of these dangers, there is an urgent need to reconsider the issue, to reassess the approach of the past and to develop new instruments to cope with the problem. This is the purpose of this book.

It is unique in two respects.

First, it is the work of young scholars who won an international competition to participate in a conference devoted to the problems and prospects of nuclear proliferation for which these papers were prepared; if anyone can point toward useful answers for the problem, this group has a chance to qualify. Second, contrary to most studies on nuclear proliferation, this collection is marked by the deliberate effort to include in the argument those views which all too often have been the object but not the subject of non-proliferation studies: the views from the 'Third World'. Indeed, unless an international regime can be developed that accommodates these views, there is little hope for an effective non-proliferation policy. Equally, unless Third World countries themselves recognise the proliferation of nuclear weapons as a threat to their own security, rather than merely as an inconvenience to the policies of the nuclear 'haves', this threat will not be met.

Few human enterprises succeed without common effort. The editors of this volume owe a debt of gratitude, in the first instance, to the Rockefeller Foundation, which has supported the conference series and made available its conference facilities on Lake Como, Italy, so hospitable to thought, inquiry, and the exchange of ideas. We are also deeply indebted to the conference participants: those who wrote and then revised their papers, and those whose papers do not appear here but whose contributions to the value of the book, if less evident, are nonetheless real. To Jeffrey Porro and Gloria Duffy, successive editors of the Arms Control Association's monthly publication, *Arms Control Today*, who reviewed and provided valuable comments on the book at different stages, and to Marilyn Dickey and John Herzberg of the Carnegie Endowment for International Peace, who, respectively, provided editorial assistance and the bibliography on nuclear proliferation, our thanks are also due. We are grateful, as well, to Rashna Writer, who served as the Institute's conference coordinator, to Amanda Cadle of the Arms Control Association, who was instrumental in both the administration of the conference and the production of this volume, and to the other members of the staffs of IISS and ACA who, in less obvious but vital ways, contributed to this endeavour.

William H. Kincade   Christoph Bertram
Washington   *London*

'Billion' is used in this book in its US sense of a thousand million.

Part I
Why Nations Go Nuclear:
Three Perspectives

1 The Nuclear Weapon States: Why They Went Nuclear

ROBERT A. STRONG

The literature on the problem of nuclear proliferation has expanded in the last few years in proportion to the increased salience of the problem. Preventing the spread of nuclear weapons – an important item on the international agenda in the 1960s – receded somewhat from public attention after the successful negotiation of the Non-proliferation Treaty (NPT) in 1968. It re-emerged as a critical issue in the mid-1970s following the Indian nuclear test and the Arab oil embargo, which increased the economic and political incentives for the rapid development of proliferation-prone nuclear energy technologies.

The assumption that the use of nuclear material for energy production could be safely isolated from its use for military purposes, an idea at least as old as President Eisenhower's Atoms for Peace proposal, was challenged by these events. The use of international safeguards to prevent the diversion of reactor fuel and by-products proved to be an inadequate solution because many countries, including important potential proliferators, were not parties to the NPT and therefore were not obliged to submit to effective international inspection. More important, the movement toward a plutonium-based fuel cycle meant that easy access to weapons-grade nuclear material would exist for all nations investing in advanced nuclear technology, and perhaps for terrorist groups who would find it possible to steal or buy the more readily available plutonium. The approaching proliferated world, once discussed in the abstract terms of changing polarities in the international system, became a more immediate and frightening prospect.

As disturbing as it is to contemplate nuclear weapons in the hands of many nations, or a single fanatic organization, it is important to remember that the history of the nuclear age has not been as disastrous as might have been expected. To date, there are only six acknowledged nuclear powers – the United States, the Soviet Union, Great Britain, China, France, and India.[1] Each of these countries has exploded a nuclear device which, according to the language of the NPT, is the definition of a nuclear weapon state.[2] Other nations have had the ability to 'go nuclear' for some time and have elected not to do so.[3]

Nations do not automatically build nuclear weapons as soon as they have the knowledge, raw materials, and facilities that make weapon production feasible. A logical starting point for a reconsideration of the problem of proliferation, therefore, is the known actions of the six nations that have clearly decided to become nuclear powers. Their decisions constitute the primary political data for understanding why proliferation takes place, and may provide some guidance for policy makers who want the spread of nuclear weapons to be halted or inhibited. It must be acknowledged, however, that the history of nuclear decision making may prove to be largely unimportant; the problem of proliferation in the 1980s may not be the same problem faced in other decades by other countries. But, even if that is true, knowing why past nuclear decisions are different from current and prospective ones might well be of value. In the imprecise and imperfect business of making foreign policy, both the analogies and the fallacies to be found in history are lessons worth learning.

THE NUCLEAR DECISION

It is considerably easier to say that the study of decisions to go nuclear is important than it is to say why those decisions were made. It can even be difficult to find the point at which a nuclear decision occurs. The convention of labelling a nation as a nuclear power following a test explosion is a convenient and diplomatically important way of distinquishing between nuclear and non-nuclear states. But the decision to conduct a test can be a relatively automatic step in a long chain of events that begins years before. Except in the case of India, the timing of nuclear tests has tended to be a technical rather than a political consideration.[4] If deciding to test a nuclear weapon is not always the crucial step, when does a nation become a nuclear power?

Did Great Britain go nuclear when it initiated uranium research in 1941, when it established an independent nuclear programme in 1945 as a response to American post-war secrecy, when the first atomic bomb was tested in 1952, or the first hydrogen bomb was tested in 1957, or when a modest deterrent was finally deployed in the early 1960s?[5] During the two decades in which Britain's nuclear force emerged, its purposes and justifications changed significantly because of development in strategic thought and fluctuations in party politics. To concentrate analysis on the 1945 decision or the 1952 test or the ultimate deployment would not do justice to the complexity and contradictions in British nuclear politics. Alternatively, considering all of the stages in Britain's nuclear decision forces us to confront a confusing and sloppy reality that defies precise description.

To some extent, the same problem is encountered in the study of all nuclear powers whose current possession of nuclear weapons is the result of a series of decisions and actions. Each series has its own dynamic, if not its own logic, and each suggests a variety of consequences for the problem of proliferation.

Nuclear decisions, whenever they are made, are characteristically the product of secret consultations and deliberations. Very little is known about Joseph Stalin's decision to acquire atomic weapons for the Soviet Union except that he apparently wanted them in a hurry.[6] Speculation is often made about Chinese and Soviet nuclear decision making, but it is rarely possible to confirm conclusions. Even in the West, secrecy prevails. Congress never officially approved the Manhattan District Project, and Vice President Truman knew nothing about the programme until after Franklin Delano Roosevelt's death. The British Parliament did not publicly debate nuclear armaments until 1952, and, although the leaders of the French Fourth Republic openly supported nuclear research, they avoided public discussion of the crucial strategic and diplomatic issues implied by the creation of French atomic power.[7] Secrecy surrounding nuclear facilities in Israel and South Africa makes the status of these non-nuclear nations ambiguous.

Even if we could comprehend the chronology and penetrate the secrecy of nuclear decision making, it would still be difficult to establish a single explanation for a decision to go nuclear. Forces in domestic politics, qualities of national leaders, distributions of bureaucratic power, misperceptions about the past, and assumptions concerning the future would all have their part in the decision process. The study of decision making naturally involves a large number of variables that force the analyst to consider the interplay of reasons, interests and perceptions and make most conclusions tentative. The study of comparative decision making only multiplies these complications.

These problems – the existence of multiple decision points, the secrecy surrounding discussions of nuclear policy and the inherent complexity of decision-making analysis – do not, however, preclude meaningful observations about why nations go nuclear. Even a cursory examination of available historical evidence dealing with nuclear decisions reveals recurring themes, arguments and circumstances. It is, nevertheless, useful in reviewing these common characteristics to keep in mind the limitations involved in the evaluation of nuclear decision making. These limitations, it is hoped, make the conclusions cautious, without rendering the analysis vacuous.

FEAR

During the Second World War, atomic research was conducted by the United States (in cooperation with Great Britain and Canada), Germany and the Soviet Union.[8] According to the leaders and participants in the American Manhattan Project, the primary motivating force for enormous US efforts to develop an atomic bomb was the fear that Germany was making the same effort. Albert Einstein's letter to Roosevelt in 1939, which initiated American interest in atomic weapons, suggested that the Germans were taking steps to stockpile uranium and duplicate recent critical atomic experiments.[9] When Truman announced the Hiroshima bombing, he described allied scientists as having been in a 'race of discovery against the Germans', and thanked providence that the Germans had not won the race.[10] The Manhattan Project scientists, who protested the Hiroshima bombing, agreed with Truman about the original intent of American nuclear research:

> The compelling reason for creating this weapon with such speed was our fear that Germany had the technical skill necessary to develop such a weapon and that the German government had no moral restraints regarding its use.[11]

In more abstract terms, the Maud Committee, which reported to the British government in 1941 on the feasibility of atomic weapons, concluded that 'no nation would care to risk being caught without a weapon of such decisive possibilities.'[12] The advantages of possessing nuclear weapons seem to have been a secondary matter that the United States did not fully investigate until after the war in Europe had ended; our first concern was with the more obvious disadvantages of confronting a Nazi regime armed with atomic bombs.

Today, apprehension that an enemy has, or will have, nuclear weapons is perhaps the most important motivation for proliferation. The intense public debate in India over the development of nuclear weapons began immediately after the Chinese atomic test in 1964. According to Sampooran Singh, director of India's ballistic research laboratory, national security was the dominant theme in the arguments of nuclear proponents.[13] Pakistan reacted to the Indian nuclear test by making substantial commitments of limited resources in order to acquire nuclear weapons.

Fear of nuclear enemies is not, however, universal or abstract and does not mean that all nations will eventually be compelled to seek nuclear arms, or that every instance of proliferation will start a regional chain reaction of more proliferation. Fear among nations is particular, based on long-standing conflict and reasonable expectations of future hostilities. Pakistan is worried about India's nuclear weapons in a way that Burma is not. What is more, Pakistan is more worried about India's nuclear capabilities than about the much larger capabilities of China or Russia. Nations are only apprehensive about their nuclear neighbours under particular conditions. It follows that almost every case of proliferation will vary with the specific security problems faced by the nation seeking nuclear weapons. There is, therefore, no 'Nth' country, there are only specific countries afraid of existing or prospective nuclear powers.

Ideally, prevention of proliferation should be accomplished by reduction of world and regional tensions. In some cases, like the Middle East, this may even be happening. Ironically, preventing proliferation more often involves alleviating regional apprehensions by supplying rivals with conventional arms in recognition of the fact that fear provides a powerful inducement to go nuclear. This was attempted by the Ford Administration when the then US Secretary of State, Henry Kissinger, visited Islamabad and offered sophisticated aircraft in exchange for cancellation of the French contract to build a reprocessing plant in Pakistan. A similiar policy was recommended to the Carter Administration by senior members of the House Foreign Affairs Committee.[14] The relationship between conventional arms sales and the nuclear option no doubt affects American dealings with Taiwan and South Korea, and the rearming of West Germany in the

1950s was accompanied by French insistence that West Germany renounce possession of nuclear weapons.

For many, this trade-off between conventional arms and proliferation constitutes a dilemma. In the aggregate, conventional weapons may be just as destructive as a few crude atomic bombs and, some would argue, may be more likely to be used.[15] But, even if conventional arms in large quantities can produce the same death and devastation that would result from a nuclear explosion, the two events are not equivalent. International interest in preventing proliferation is based on the assumption that the use of even one nuclear weapon anywhere in the world would have dangerous consequences beyond the immediate damage it would cause. Not only would fallout cross international boundaries, but the widely held belief that the use of nuclear weapons is unthinkable and futile would be challenged. At the very least, it can be said that the use of nuclear weapons would have consequences that cannot be accurately predicted.

Even more ironic than the practice of using conventional arms to prevent proliferation is a proposal for the nuclear weapon states to reduce the incentive to acquire nuclear weapons in advance of a country's need by offering to provide them when clearly required.[16] In this way, a deterrent effect is created without actual possession of weapons. Thus, for example, the United States and the Soviet Union would announce their intention to sell nuclear weapons to the non-nuclear victims of regional nuclear attack. This strategy would be a complete departure from the principles of the NPT and would be problematic for certain possible proliferators, such as Japan and West Germany, who are concerned about Soviet nuclear power. Yet the interesting aspect of this policy alternative is that it assumes that fear is the motivating force for proliferation, and it argues that a balance of apprehension about the acquisition of nuclear weapons is better than a balance of terror with the possession of nuclear weapons.

VICTORY

Despite American wartime concern about the possible German atomic programme, the final construction and testing of the first atomic bomb did not occur until the status of Germany's nuclear research became irrelevant. The issue in the summer of 1945 was the use of the new weapon in the Pacific. The conclusion reached by the Truman Administration was that the destructive capacity and psychological impact of a few atomic explosions would shorten the war with Japan. In other words, they would have a decisive effect. The familiar justification for the Hiroshima and Nagasaki bombings is that they precluded the need for large-scale invasions of the Japanese home islands that would have cost many more Japanese and American lives. 'General Marshall told me [Truman] that it might cost half a million American lives to force the enemy's surrender on his home grounds'.[17] Revisionist historians claim that both the atomic explosions and the proposed invasions were unnecessary since Japan was ready to negotiate a surrender by July of 1945; but they admit that Japan was forced to cease hostilities as soon as the devastation of Hiroshima and Nagasaki was fully reported to Tokyo.[18] Nuclear weapons were clearly useful in ending the Second World War, either months or days before it would have ended without their use.

In many ways, the American situation in 1945 was unique. At the end of a long and costly total war, facing a determined enemy, having a monopoly on atomic weapons, believing that monopoly would last for some time, and not fully realizing the secondary effects of atomic warfare, American leaders were easily convinced that the newly developed bombs should be used to accelerate a Japanese surrender. Since 1945 no nation has tested a nuclear explosive during a war, and, of course, no nation could ever again have exclusive control over nuclear technology or remain ignorant about radiation dangers. Yet it is conceivable that in the future, nations engaged in a conventional conflict would be tempted to acquire nuclear weapons in order to have a decisive capacity for ensuring victory or preventing defeat. Some of the speculation about Israel's nuclear capabilities considers the effect that the various Middle East wars fought with conventional arms have had on the movement toward an Israeli nuclear option.[19] Perceiving itself surrounded by potential enemies, South Africa may be subject to similar considerations.

Until recently, the development of nuclear weapons has been such a difficult task that its accomplishment during war would have been possible only for advanced countries in a protracted conflict or as a result of extensive pre-war preparation. In the near future, this may no longer be true. Nuclear reactors that use or produce plutonium or highly enriched uranium place within the borders of many countries the materials necessary for easy acquisition of a small nuclear arsenal. Even if using reactor fuels for weapons involved violations of international and bilateral agreements, knowledge of the violations might come too late to prevent the construction or use of the illegal weapons. The widespread development, then, of plutonium-based nuclear energy systems would place a number of nations in the status now commonly attributed to Israel and South Africa: they would be on the verge of going nuclear and, in the event of a war or a desperate security threat, could readily obtain a decisive weapon in a very short period.

Several policies now in effect are designed either to remove the temptation of ready access to weapons-grade material, or to impose some sanction making it harder for potential proliferators to give in to that temptation. The United States, for example, has encouraged the development of new, less dangerous nuclear fuel cycles, protested the sale of reprocessing and enrichment technology to nations with obvious security problems (Pakistan, South Korea, and Taiwan), and attempted to use nuclear trade policy as a lever to control the marketing of new nuclear energy technologies.

It is too soon to say whether any of these steps will be successful in eliminating the temptation to acquire a possibly decisive weapon. At present, the International Nuclear Fuel Cycle Evaluation has produced more scepticism than enthusiasm about proliferation-resistant technologies, but diplomatic pressure has brought the cancellation of some nuclear development agreements, and the US Congress has passed potentially strict nuclear trade legislation. The Nuclear Non-proliferation Act of 1978 requires the United States to suspend technical assistance and fuel shipments to any country substantively breaking the regulations contained in international or bilateral agreements but allows the President to resume trade if he believes it will promote non-proliferation objectives.[20] Sanctions against nations that break international agreements in the construction of nuclear weapons have also been discussed but not imposed. The NPT has no provision for action in the event of treaty violations and permits a signatory to withdraw from treaty obligations after giving a three-month notification. Sanctions that go beyond suspension of bilateral nuclear trade would have to be negotiated. While it is easy to conceive of a punishment that would prevent a nation from carelessly crossing the nuclear threshold, it is much more difficult to imagine widespread agreement on invoking such a penalty or a sanction that would be effective against a nation in a struggle for its existence. The temptation of a potentially decisive weapon is likely to remain a strong motivation for proliferation, especially where the component of fear is high and other military 'equalizers' seem inadequate.

DETERRENCE

In the evolution of American justifications for going nuclear and 'being nuclear', fear of Germany and victory over Japan were followed by deterrence of Russia. Deterrence remains the principal purpose of the American nuclear arsenal and potentially a significant factor in decisions to acquire nuclear weapons.

The American monopoly over nuclear technology was short-lived, more so than most American leaders had expected. The fact that the world had two nuclear antagonists meant that the calculations justifying Truman's Hiroshima decision would no longer be possible. Use of a large number of atomic bombs, and later thermonuclear bombs, against an enemy that would retaliate in kind meant that victory in any meaningful sense was unattainable in a large-scale nuclear war. Winston Churchill's description of this reality remains eloquent and chilling:

> Then it may be we shall by a process of sublime irony, have reached a stage in this story where safety will be the sturdy child of terror and survival the twin brother of annihilation.[21]

While the logic of deterrence suggests that proliferation is not a problem, since a nuclear-armed world would be deterred on all sides, in practice the strategic relationship between the United States and the Soviet Union has involved substantial dangers that make the desirability of proliferation doubtful. The delivery systems that carry nuclear weapons are, to varying degrees, vulnerable to attack, and the maintenance of a credible deterrent requires either a policy of launching an immediate counterattack on receiving warning of an incoming assault, of investing in sophisticated and relatively invulnerable weapon systems, or both. The first alternative is dangerous since it means that there would be very little time to interpret a military situation, no flexibility in the response to be made, and more chances that nuclear weapons would be used through accident or miscalculation. The second alternative is expensive and perhaps beyond the capacity of some potential nuclear weapon states.

The United States and the Soviet Union have found that the maintenance of their strategic balance has required the construction of large and elaborate forces that are almost always criticized as insufficient. In the late 1950s the balance of terror was thought to be precarious because of the advent of the missile age and the increased vulnerability of bombers. Subsequent technical innovations have frequently been heralded as new sources of strategic destabilization. Even today, speculation that the Soviets are arming to wage and win a nuclear war against the United States at some future date is taken seriously by some Americans. Mutual deterrence is not easily achieved or maintained, and, of course, if it ever fails, the consequences could be disastrous beyond imagination. By the early 1960s both super-powers were convinced that small nuclear forces should be discouraged because they would be even more unstable and inflexible than American and Soviet strategic forces were proving to be.[22]

Not all nations have agreed, or now agree, with these conclusions. In the 1950s the British believed that they were building a viable deterrent force that could be used against the Soviet Union, if need be, independently of American strategic power. The testing of thermonuclear bombs reinforced this belief. Churchill explained to Parliament the need for Great Britain to build a hydrogen bomb by pointing out both its supplemental and independent deterrent value:

> The broad effect of the latest developments is to spread almost indefinitely and at least to a vast extent the area of mortal danger. This should certainly increase the deterrent upon Soviet Russia by putting her enormous spaces and scattered population on an equality or near-equality of vulnerability with our small densely populated island.[23]

A decade later French strategists, particularly Pierre Gallois, argued that a moderate French nuclear force could independently deter a Soviet invasion of Europe since the ability to destroy even a few Russian cities might be sufficient to make a Soviet-initiated European war unlikely.[24] French nuclear power did not need to be equal to that of the Soviet Union, only proportional to the interests at stake between the two nations.

Indian military strategists took up the debate about the utility of small nuclear forces after the Chinese atomic test in 1964; many adapted Gallois' theories of deterrence to Indian defence problems. According to Raj Krishna, 'the risk of war in Asia is much greater at the present [1969] when China has a nuclear monopoly in Asia as well as the largest conventional army. This risk will diminish if one or more Asian nations which possess large conventional forces also develop some nuclear capability.[25] Colonel R. D. Palsokar of the Indian army has argued that even a small deterrent force would be adequate to prevent a new border war with China.[26]

Deterrence has figured in many nuclear decisions, not only because small nuclear forces are thought to have significant deterrent value, but also because the large nuclear forces of allies are thought to lack transferable deterrent credibility. Though the Soviet and American strategic forces became ever larger and more lethal, their ability to deter anything except attacks on the territories of the two superpowers became questionable. Alliance guarantees that involved commitments of strategic power have been strained in the 1950s and 1960s and again today as the populations of the United States and the Soviet Union became increasingly open to massive levels of destruction. Thus, the superpowers might be reluctant to exercise their nuclear power on behalf of allies out of fear of escalation and hence damage to their own territories.

Shortly after returning to power, Charles De Gaulle argued that Russia's growing missile capability and its threat to American security would prohibit the United States from giving nuclear assurances to Europe indefinitely. In his Ecole Militaire speech announcing the French *'force de frappe'*, De Gaulle asked:

Who can say, for example, whether some sudden advance in development – particularly in the field of space rockets – will not provide one of the two camps with such an advantage that its peaceful inclinations will not hold out? Who can say whether, in the future, if basic political facts should change completely, as has already occurred on the earth, the two powers that would have a monopoly of nuclear weapons might not make a deal with each other to divide the world between them?[27]

De Gaulle concluded that Europe, and especially France, needed its own deterrent.[28] The Chinese were equally frustrated in their alliance with the Soviet Union when the Soviets refused to guarantee nuclear support for Chinese confrontations with the United States in the Taiwan Straits. Alice Hsieh suggests that China's decision to go nuclear was made when the Chinese leaders in the late 1950s concluded that American atomic bombs were not 'paper tigers' and that the availability of Soviet nuclear power for Chinese initiatives would be limited.[29] By 1963 Chen Yi, a Chinese military leader and foreign minister, could openly say, 'How can any one nation say that they will defend another – these sorts of promises are easy to make, but they are worth nothing. Soviet protection is worth nothing to us'.[30]

Controlling the spread of nuclear weapons through the use of security guarantees or alliances to provide protection for potential nuclear powers in exchange for commitments to non-proliferation may run afoul of the uncertainty of such guarantees and the appeal of an independent deterrent force. It should be remembered that even the strongly-worded commitments of the North Atlantic Treaty Organization (NATO) alliance did not prevent the French from building their own deterrent force. As long as tensions between the superpowers are high and their basic interests are at issue, their promises of support to other nations will be tempered by their own global strategic calculations. Recognition of these basic facts of intentional life may suggest to others, as it did to Britain and France, the value or necessity of an independent nuclear deterrent.

ECONOMY

For almost two decades after the Second World War it was widely thought that basing defence on nuclear weapons would reduce the size of defence budgets. Even before the Eisenhower administration introduced its 'New Look' in defence, the British Conservative government in 1952 reduced military manpower, NATO commitments, and non-strategic weapon development because of economic pressure to control military spending and because of confidence that nuclear weapons could provide adequate defence at less cost than large modern armies. Both American and British leaders insisted that nuclear weapons were a good buy and Secretary of State John Foster Dulles boasted that they provided a 'bigger bang for a buck'. This claim was based on two propositions. Deterrence was thought to prevent both attacks on the homeland and less serious confrontations that could escalate to general nuclear war. Strategic nuclear forces, therefore, reduced the need for conventional armies. In addition, the development and deployment of tactical nuclear weapons in the mid-1950s implied that nuclear technology could compensate for inferior conventional strength, even if strategic nuclear weapons were never used.

The argument that nuclear weapons were economical was eventually rejected for two reasons. The rising costs of delivery systems and the rapid obsolescence of some of those systems began to eat away at the savings produced by reductions in conventional forces. An invulnerable strategic capability gradually came to require solid-fuel rockets, hardened silos, radar warning systems, and nuclear-powered submarines, all of which were expensive to develop and deploy. After failing to produce its own missile system, Britain was forced to purchase sophisticated technology from the United States; and de Gaulle abandoned his plans for a '*tous azimuts*' nuclear strategy in the late 1960s because of its immense cost and demands for domestic programmes.

Even without the rising costs of delivery systems, the claim that nuclear weapons were economical was challenged by the evolution of strategic thought. The wisdom of a predominantly nuclear defence with its frequent threats of massive retaliation began to be criticized by military strategists and political leaders in both Great Britain and the United States.[31] When the Kennedy administration rejected the doctrine of massive retaliation and adopted a strategic policy of graduated deterrence, defence spending necessarily increased. The new policy required larger and better equipped conventional forces, improved command and control capabilities, more accurate missiles, and the maintenance of a variety of strategic delivery systems. These changes were designed to give the President greater control in crisis situations and reduce the likelihood that he would ever have to choose between surrender and suicide. Nations desiring similar capabilities would not find that nuclear defence comes cheap.

Throughout the nuclear age the cost of building nuclear warheads has dropped, while the cost of building more capable and less vulnerable delivery systems has risen. For a nation with a strong nuclear energy programme, such as India, the expense of producing weapons-grade plutonium is very small. Should India decide to develop missiles capable of reaching Peking, or nuclear submarines, or even thermonuclear bombs and tactical nuclear warheads, the cost would be significantly higher and would constitute some strain on scarce national resources. But, of course, India may not feel compelled to take all of these steps, or any of them. There is a misleading presumption in some of the proliferation literature that each nuclear nation will be required to copy the strategic doctrine and technical sophistication of the superpowers. Any nation wishing to achieve military equality with the United States and the Soviet Union, at least in quantitative or qualitative terms, would probably have to imitate American and Soviet strategic forces and pay a substantial price to do so. But a regional nuclear power might well be able to keep its strategic budget low by designing its weapons to be carried by today's advanced military aircraft.

The question of how economical nuclear weapons are is clearly linked to the earlier question of whether small nuclear forces have a significant deterrent value. It is also linked to the question of whether nuclear energy is a cost-effective alternative to other energy sources. If it is, then the cost of going nuclear by using the materials, facilities, and technical expertise of a nuclear energy programme will continue to be small and within the reach of a long list of nations. Without proof that nuclear energy is uneconomical for some or all countries, and without effective sanctions that threaten to impose diplomatic penalties and domestic energy costs (e.g., through denial of nuclear fuel) on potential proliferators, the building of small nuclear arsenals from a nuclear energy base is likely to revive Dulles' alliterative description of the cost-effectiveness of nuclear weapons.

PRESTIGE

If small nuclear forces have debatable military value, going nuclear may nevertheless be justified by the international recognition it commands. This prestige may result from real or imaginary military power, from the demonstration of scientific and industrial strength associated with nuclear power status, or from the increased superpower attention that nuclear or near-nuclear nations may receive.

President Truman described the Manhattan Project in his memoirs as an 'achievement of the combined efforts of science, industry, labor and the military' without 'parallel in history'.[32] The construction of the first atomic bomb was in many ways a remarkable enterprise, but American experts have tended to underestimate the speed and sophistication of Soviet and Chinese nuclear programmes, in part because they could not imagine any other nation easily duplicating their efforts. In the last 30 years it has become considerably easier to enter the 'nuclear club' and will likely become even easier if the use of nuclear energy for power generation continues to expand. The very image of a nuclear club, still used in discussion of proliferation, suggests some achievement or special status for its members. Even if this status is increasingly undeserved, it may be desirable to a developing nation whose 'great leaps forward' or 'green revolutions' have failed to produce significant economic progress. Or it might be desirable to a country, such as Brazil, which has achieved remarkable economic growth without receiving commensurate attention from major world powers.[33] Nuclear weapons may serve as either a substitute or a symbol for general technological development.

Among the acknowledged nuclear powers, the political prestige of appearing to be militarily equal to the United States and the Soviet Union has probably been more important in proliferation decisions than demonstrating technological accomplishment. De Gaulle insisted in the late 1950s that France must have an independent military capability and global political responsibilities. He wrote:

> There is no France of worth, notably in the eyes of Frenchmen, without worldwide responsibility. That is why she does not approve of NATO, which does not allow France her proper role in decisions and which is limited to Europe. That is also why she is going to provide herself with an atomic armament. By that means, our defense and foreign policy will be able to be independent, on which we insist above all.[34]

The Chinese also complained that the Soviets 'do not treat with us on a basis of equality,' and justified their nuclear programme on the need for recognition of their national greatness.[35] Shyam Bhatia, writing a year before the Indian nuclear test, argued that 'the strongest case for going nuclear now rests . . . on the foreign policy considerations that only a nuclear India can extract political, military, and economic advantages from the two Superpowers'.[36]

The ability to convert nuclear status into influence in the policy decisions of the superpowers is a questionable proposition, but nuclear weapons do make their possessors something to be reckoned with. Chinese nuclear power was in some sense a factor in the reversal of American policy toward that country, while, on the other hand, De Gaulle's *'force de frappe'* and NATO policies alienated many American political leaders and alone did not bring about automatic recognition of France as a world power. Nevertheless, French nuclear forces have presumably aided its claim to a special international role; the question is whether the benefits justified the costs or were achievable by other means. The Anglo-American 'special relationship' may be mentioned as evidence that allied nuclear weapon states treat each other in some ways as equals, but there is a long history of American-British cooperation in foreign policy, and Great Britain's special relations and nuclear status were insufficient to produce American support or Soviet acquiescence during the Suez crisis. Nor has Britain's nuclear force offset a more general decline in its prestige stemming from other causes.

The prestige sought from nuclear weapons is not always related to influence in alliances or international recognition of any kind; the benefits of becoming a nuclear nation are sometimes found in domestic politics. In the British parliamentary debates over the 1957 Defence White Paper, which made heavy commitments to strategic forces, Denis Healey called the proposed nuclear programme a 'virility symbol to compensate for the exposure of . . . military impotence at Suez'.[37] De Gaulle's *'force de frappe'* was intended, in part, to restore military pride and purpose to a nation defeated in the Second World War and forced to surrender considerable colonial territory. Even if the French people were not convinced that the *'force de frappe'* would restore power and glory to the republic, the army needed the prestige and status of nuclear weapons, and de Gaulle certainly needed army support for his government and for his Algerian policy.[38]

Preventing nations bent on going nuclear primarily to enhance their prestige is a subtle and difficult task. The existence of a nuclear club, the inequality of nuclear weapon and non-nuclear weapon states in the provisions of the NPT, and even the attention given to the problem of proliferation suggest that there is already considerable international recognition attached to the possession of nuclear weapons. If that recognition cannot be eliminated, perhaps the creation of alternative sources of prestige would ease the proliferation pressures on some nations. Creating new international forums, or expanding old ones, to acknowledge the economic power of Japan, West Germany, Brazil, and other established and emerging non-nuclear nations might reduce incentives for their proliferation. Ensuring that new nuclear powers are not given favourable treatment or new diplomatic attention would also be helpful. Unfortunately, almost any policy to divert or minimize the recognition accorded to nuclear powers may have the effect of reducing concern about the dangers of proliferation; depreciating the significance of nuclear weapons will make it that much easier for nuclear threshold states to justify acquiring them.

Nations that acquire nuclear arms for international recognition or great power influence or domestic political advantage are probably less likely to use those weapons than nations that are motivated by pressing security problems. Terrorist groups, however, could conceivably explode a nuclear device merely to attract world attention to their cause. This version of the recognition problem is the most difficult to address. Beyond denying terrorists access to nuclear material, there appears to be no way to prevent desperate attempts to get recognition from possession or use of nuclear explosives.

MOMENTUM

Domestic political considerations may also enter into nuclear decision making because going nuclear may serve the interests of particular individuals or groups. It has frequently been observed that, in the twentieth century, technology and bureaucracy have pre-empted significant amounts of the decision-making power formerly held by political leaders.[39]

The construction of nuclear weapons and their delivery systems, and the establishment of a significant nuclear energy capacity, inevitably involves large numbers of people in complex organizations for considerable periods of time. The decision to go nuclear requires preparations that may take months or years and resources that represent substantial portions of a national or military budget. After those preparations are undertaken, it may be difficult to resist the final acquisition of nuclear weapons, even if the preparations were only intended to keep options open. Admiral William D. Leahy, Truman's military adviser, suggested in his memoirs that some of the scientists and managers of the Manhattan Project may have favoured the use of the atomic bomb in Japan in order to justify the billions of dollars spent on their programme.[40] France, at least under the Fourth Republic, left the direction of its nuclear policy to the military and bureaucratic agencies interested in making France a nuclear power.[41] When de Gaulle returned to office, the preparations for a 1960 atomic test were already being made, and he merely added doctrine to an established programme. India has made substantial investments in atomic energy since 1948 and Prime Minister Nehru, who publicly opposed any Indian manufacture of nuclear weapons, conceded that, 'so long as the world was constituted as it was, every country would have to develop and use the latest scientific devices for its protection'.[42] The history of recent Indian nuclear politics suggests to some observers that Prime Minister Indira Ghandi, like Nehru, was against going nuclear and resisted pressure from Parliament, public opinion, and government officials for several years. Gradually during a period of political weakness, she acquiesced in the series of decisions that resulted in a nuclear test.[43]

In addition to the pressure that may develop from certain groups for going nuclear, the gradual character of many nuclear decisions may mean that the pressure of events goes unnoticed. Churchill reported that when he and other senior British officials were informed at Potsdam of the plans to end the Japanese war, they hardly discussed the matter:

The historical fact remains, and must be judged in the after time, that the decision whether or not to use the atomic bomb to compel the surrender of Japan was never at issue. There was unanimous, automatic, unquestioned agreement around our table, nor did I ever hear the slightest suggestion that we should do otherwise.[44]

When the British decided after the war to undertake independent nuclear research, they saw themselves continuing a wartime project, not embarking on a new venture. There was apparently no concern for how their actions might affect future proliferation; they did not even realize they were proliferating.[45] Concerns and consequences that seem crucial to us today may never have entered into some nuclear decisions. Beneath the complexity and secrecy of nuclear politics is the discouraging prospect that nations sometimes become nuclear by the force of events and not the force of argument.

De Gaulle once wrote, 'It seems as if the political paths which the various nations tread must lead them, so far as war is concerned, to the same conceptions, exactly implied by the material progress of the time'.[46] He was discussing tanks and the need for the pre-war French army to build modern equipment and learn mobile tactics. Unfortunately, his observations may also apply to nuclear weapons. Nations may be doomed to follow the same path of military development, moving at various speeds but always leading to the acquisition of the best available equipment and strategy. The very word 'proliferation' implies that the spread of nuclear weapons has a natural and organic character that may be impossible to arrest.

What is here called momentum is really three separate problems – the political influence of individuals and organizations favouring the development of nuclear weapons and energy, the inability of political leaders to recognize fully the consequences of their actions, and the existence of a technological determinism.

The first problem is difficult to deal with by any international strategy. Foreign interference in the domestic or bureaucratic politics of other governments is usually illegal and often ineffective. But some things may be done to reduce the momentum for going nuclear. Proposals have been made to suspend or re-evaluate American training of foreign nuclear technicians since these individuals often lead pro-nuclear forces when they return home.[47] The use of nuclear trade sanctions against future proliferators may alter the calculations of nuclear energy lobbies in developing countries whose programmes could be destroyed by a decision to test a nuclear weapon. In addition, the growth of environmentalist opposition to all phases of nuclear power may mean, at least in democratic countries, that the proponents of nuclear energy, whether they favour the building of nuclear weapons or not, will have a powerful political force with which to contend.

The second source of momentum, ignorance of long range consequences, is likely to be less important in future cases of proliferation than it was in the past. The NPT, even for those nations that have chosen not to sign it, has produced international awareness of the problem of proliferation. The treaty may be opposed, but it can hardly be ignored.

It is the third meaning of momentum that raises the most serious policy questions. If political decisions are dictated by the 'material progress of the time', then it appears that there is very little to be done about proliferation. In the broad view of history, technological determinism may describe our destiny, but De Gaulle's statement, quoted earlier, was addressed to a generation of political and military leaders who obstinately (or ignorantly) opposed the material progress of their time and failed to prepare France for the Second World War. The force of technology can be resisted for significant periods of time, and nations follow the path of progress at varying speeds. What is more, if De Gaulle is correct that all nations eventually adopt the same concepts 'as far as war is concerned', that would not necessarily mean that all countries will build nuclear weapons. If all nations shared the superpower perception that small nuclear arsenals are dangerous and destabilizing, there would be less, not more, incentive for proliferation. It is controversy about the meaning of technological advancements, not the advancements alone, which has been important in political decision making throughout the nuclear age.

CONCLUSIONS

Why nations go nuclear is clearly a complicated question. The factors that have played a part in nuclear decisions are relatively easy to identify. It is much harder to determine which of those factors was crucial in any particular decision, and still harder to develop appropriate strategies for the prevention of future proliferation.

The first three reasons for going nuclear – fear, victory, and deterrence – grouped together as national security would seem to be the most important explanation for nuclear decisions. All of the current nuclear nations have had some reason to be apprehensive about the actions of other nuclear powers. Even India, the most ambiguous member of the nuclear club, has had cause to worry about Chinese nuclear forces. Whether the possession of nuclear weapons alleviates these security apprehensions may well be the central question for the problem of proliferation. If it does, then very little can be done about the problem. If it does not, then the task will be to convince prospective proliferators that nuclear weapons produce more danger than security. That will be a difficult argument to make as long as the superpowers simultaneously claim that their own large and sophisticated nuclear arsenals contribute to a stable deterrence and a partial detente.

If controversy persists about the utility of small nuclear arsenals, as is likely, it may still be possible to reduce or slow proliferation by addressing the security problems of various potential proliferators. In some cases, negotiated settlements of international disputes may be initiated or supported by nations interested in preventing proliferation; in other cases defensive alliances, sales of conventional arms or strong sanctions against proliferators could be effective. In some instances, nothing will work or the goal of inhibiting proliferation will be in conflict with other equally important policy objectives. No single or guaranteed solution is possible to the many security situations that exist or are imaginable in the current international system, and any attempt to prevent proliferation by increasing the security of apprehensive nations will require a complex and flexible foreign policy.[48]

The remaining reasons for going nuclear are a mixture of international and domestic forces, including the prestige attached to nuclear status; the influence that may accompany membership in the nuclear club; the pressure exerted by political parties, public opinion, or bureaucratic interests. Obviously, these forces will vary from country to country, but a few general observations can be made.

For almost all of the existing nuclear powers, the construction of nuclear weapons was undertaken as a military project, and the construction of a peaceful atomic energy programme was a secondary benefit believed to accompany the development of a fundamentally military technology. Beginning with India, and to a lesser extent with France, this pattern has been reversed. Future proliferators will most likely go nuclear with materials, facilities, and personnel originally devoted to the generation of nuclear electrical power. Some nations will use a nuclear energy programme to mask international efforts to acquire nuclear weapons. Others will develop nuclear energy with little or no interest in becoming nuclear weapon states. If peaceful nuclear explosions prove to be technically and economically practical, though this is increasingly doubtful, a few nations may even test explosive devices and claim, as India has already done, that the purpose of its nuclear activity is entirely peaceful. Unfortunately, nations that become nuclear or approach that designation for reasons other than national security are likely to generate security problems for their neighbours. India's peaceful nuclear explosion created genuine alarm among the leaders of Pakistan. A Brazilian nuclear test designed to demonstrate technological development or great power status could easily prompt an Argentinian decision to go nuclear and vice versa.

Whether nations are actively seeking access to atomic bombs, or merely energy independence and technological advancement, they will find that their domestic nuclear energy plans are increasingly subject to international scrutiny. The Nuclear Suppliers Group agreed in London to impose uniform guidelines on exports of sensitive nuclear items. American trade restrictions are even more severe, prohibiting the sale of certain equipment and technology and requiring full international inspection of all nuclear activity in countries receiving American nuclear goods.[49] These trade policies may somewhat slow down the development of nuclear energy in the world, and with it the opportunities for proliferation, but they cannot be expected to halt the spread of technology or prevent determined nations from securing information and materials to develop a nuclear option.

The combination of persistent international security problems and expanding nuclear capabilities is likely to result in new decisions to go nuclear.

The literature on the problem of nuclear proliferation contains a variety of policy recommendations but almost admits that an increase in the number of nuclear powers is inevitable. One of the favourite activities of commentators on proliferation is to speculate about which nations will go nuclear in the next five years, the next ten years, or within this century. Scenarios are presented of bad and worse versions of the proliferated world. A careful examination of the history of nuclear decision making, if it demonstrates anything, should make it obvious that this kind of speculation is very problematic. The existing nuclear powers went nuclear for a variety of reasons, having their origins in international realities, domestic politics, bureaucratic interests, and strategic doctrines. In attempting to unravel these reasons, the difficulty of making predictions becomes evident. Several nations could go nuclear in the near future, but perhaps none will. Paradoxically, a dismal future might contribute the most to a serious international effort to solve the problems inherent in nuclear arms. The debates about the utility of nuclear arsenals, small or large, and the dangers of deterrence could be resolved with cruel decisiveness if an accidental or futile nuclear war were ever to occur. But it is precisely these possibilities that advocates of non-proliferation so frequently predict and so fervently attempt to prevent.

NOTES AND REFERENCES

1. Some would contest that India does not belong on this list because the Indian government claims that its 1974 test was a peaceful nuclear explosion not followed by the manufacture of any weapons. Others would argue that Israel and South Africa should be added to the list in light of evidence that they may have secretly developed, as yet untested, nuclear weapons. The ambiguity about which nations have gone nuclear is, of course, part of the current problem with proliferation.
2. The full quote from the NPT defines a nuclear weapon state as any nation that 'has manufactured and exploded a nuclear weapon or other nuclear explosive device prior to January 1, 1967.' This definition technically means that India could not be a nuclear weapon state under the terms of the treaty.
3. It is not known exactly which countries other than the acknowledged six currently possess the material and technological resources necessary to manufacture a nuclear weapon, but Canada, West Germany, Italy, Japan, and Sweden are generally believed to be among them.
4. The best discussion of what it means to go nuclear can be found in Thomas Schelling, 'Who Will Have the Bomb', *International Security*, vol. 1, no. 1 (Summer 1976).
5. Britain had atomic bombs and Vulcan bombers in the mid-1950s. I have elected to date the deployment of a British deterrent in the early 1960s because that was the period when Britain had a stockpile of thermo-nuclear warheads, several squadrons of Vulcan bombers, and plans to build or acquire a more modern delivery system. The fact that it would be debatable when Britain possessed a meaningful deterrent only proves that the exact time of a 'nuclear decision' is hard to pinpoint.
6. According to historian David Holloway, Soviet scientists were making good progress on the construction of an atomic bomb when their research was interrupted by the German invasion. See Walter Pincus, 'German Attack Delayed Soviet Atomic Bomb', *Washington Post*, 27 July, 1979.
7. Lawrence Scheinman, *Atomic Energy Policy in France Under the Fourth Republic* (Princeton University Press, 1965) p. xv.
8. Japan abandoned nuclear research before the war.

9. Morton Grodzins and Eugene Rabinowitch (eds), *The Atomic Age: Scientists in National and World Affairs* (New York: Basic Books, 1963) p. 12.
10. Statement by the President of the United States, Harry S. Truman, 6 August, 1945.
11. The Franck Report quoted in Robert Gilpin, *American Scientists and Nuclear Weapon Policy* (Princeton University Press, 1962) p. 46.
12. A. J. R. Groom, *British Thinking About Nuclear Weapons* (London: Frances Pinter, 1974) p. 2.
13. Sampooran Singh, *India and the Nuclear Bomb* (New Delhi: S. Chand, 1971) p. 98.
14. Don Oberdorfer, 'Arms Sales to Pakistan Urged to Stave Off A-Bomb There', *Washington Post*, 6 August 1979.
15. There is also a drawback to this policy since nations desiring conventional weapons may be given an incentive to develop a nuclear option merely to exert pressure on the suppliers of their conventional arms.
16. Alton Frye, 'How to Ban the Bomb: Sell It', *The New York Times Magazine*, 11 January 1976.
17. Harry S. Truman, *Years of Decision* (Garden City, NY: Doubleday, 1955) pp. 417–18.
18. For the argument that the Hiroshima and Nagasaki bombings were unnecessary, see Gar Alperovitz, *Atomic Diplomacy: Hiroshima and Potsdam* (New York: Simon and Schuster, 1965).
19. Alan Dowty, 'Nuclear Proliferation: The Israeli Case', *International Studies Quarterly*, vol. 22, no. 1 (March 1978) p. 112.
20. Presidential action that overrules trade restrictions is subject to legislative veto.
21. Hansard, *Parliamentary Debates Commons*, vol. 537, col. 1899, 1 March 1955.
22. Secretary of Defense Robert McNamara publicly argued that small independent nuclear forces were 'dangerous, expensive, prone to obsolescence, and lacking in credibility as a deterrent'. Ann Arbor Speech, 16 June 1962.
23. Hansard, *Parliamentary Debates Commons*, vol. 537, col. 1899, 1 March 1955.
24. For a summary and critique of Gallois, see Raymond Aron, *The Great Debate* (Garden City, NY: Doubleday, 1965).
25. Raj Krishna, 'India and the Bomb,' in K. K. Sinka (ed.), *Problems of Defense of South and East Asia* (Bombay: Manaktalas, 1969) p. 148.
26. Col. R. D. Palsokar, *Minimum Deterrence: India's Answer to China* (Bombay: Thacker, 1969) pp. 77-8.
27. Quoted in Wilfrid L. Kohl, *French Nuclear Diplomacy* (Princeton University Press, 1971) p. 96.
28. A similar argument was made by Clement Attlee in his explanation of the 1945 British decision to build an atomic bomb. 'At that time we had to bear in mind that there was always the possibility of their (the United States) withdrawing and becoming isolationist again. The manufacture of a British atom bomb was therefore at that stage essential to our defense.' Quoted in Groom, op. cit., p. 33.

29. Alice Hsieh, *Communist China's Strategy in the Nuclear Age* (Englewood Cliffs, NJ: Prentice Hall, 1962).
30. Quoted in Arthur Huck, *The Security of China* (New York: Columbia University Press, 1970) p. 65.
31. In Great Britain there was an extended public debate on the issue with Sir John Slessor, marshall of the Royal Air Force, arguing for a defence policy based on deterrence and threats of massive retaliation, while Arthur Buzzard, along with others, argued for graduated deterrence. In the United States the same issues separated John Foster Dulles and Robert McNamara.
32. Truman, op. cit., p. 417.
33. William Perry and Sheila Kern, 'The Brazilian Nuclear Program in a Foreign Policy Context', *Comparative Strategy*, vol. 1, no. 1 (1978).
34. Quoted in Kohl, op. cit., pp. 355-6.
35. Chen Yi quoted in Huck, op. cit., p. 66. On the same subject, see B. W. Augenstein, 'The Chinese and French Programs for the Development of National Nuclear Forces', *Orbis*, vol. xi, no. 3 (1967).
36. Shyam Bhatia, 'The Nuclear Weapons Lobby in India After 1964', *The Institute for Defence Studies and Analyses Journal*, vol. vi, no. 1 (July 1973).
37. Hansard, *Parliamentary Debates Commons*, vol. 568, col. 2040, 17 April 1957.
38. Edgar S. Furniss, Jr, *De Gaulle and the French Army* (New York: W. W. Norton, 1977) p. 212.
39. See President Eisenhower's 'Farewell Address'.
40. William D. Leahy, *I Was There* (New York: Whittlesey House, 1950) p. 441.
41. For the influence of the bureaucracy on early French nuclear development, see Scheinment, op. cit., and Kohl, op. cit.
42. Quoted in Lorne Kavic, *India's Quest for Security* (Berkeley: University of California Press, 1967) p. 28.
43. Frank T. J. Bray and Michael L. Moodie, 'Nuclear Politics in India', *Survival*, vol. xx, no. 3 (May/June 1977). See also Bhatia, op. cit., p. 85.
44. Sir Winston Churchill, *Triumph and Tragedy* (Boston: Houghton Mifflin, 1953) p. 639.
45. Groom, op. cit., p. 34.
46. Charles De Gaulle, *The Army of the Future* (London: Hutchinson, 1940) p. 63.
47. Clarence D. Long, 'Nuclear Proliferation: Can Congress Act in Time?', *International Security*, vol. i, no. 4 (Spring 1977).
48. See Richard Betts, 'Paranoids, Pygmies, Pariahs and Nonproliferation', *Foreign Policy*, no. 26 (Spring 1977).
49. In effect, this requires any nation engaged in nuclear trade with the United States to abide by the provisions of the NPT whether they are parties to the treaty or not.

2 Why Nations Go Nuclear: an Alternative History

C. RAJA MOHAN

One of the major problems with the existing literature on nuclear proliferation is the general emphasis on military issues rather than on the political dimension of nuclear weapons. By overemphasizing the factor of military capability and underestimating the political factors involved in a country's exercising the nuclear option, the earlier literature in particular had estimated an absurdly high number of nuclear weapon states. Even in more current analyses, one still finds formulations such as: country A by the year x will have y kilograms of plutonium and hence z nuclear weapons.

This error arises from looking at nuclear options in isolation, outside the complex and intricately interconnected web of international relations. Without understanding the nature of the ruling regime of a particular nation, its internal societal structure, the dominance-dependence relations that bind the given regime to others in the international system, discussions on nuclear weapon options will be incomplete and therefore futile.

Another disturbing, yet sadly amusing, feature of the bulk of the non-proliferation literature, which comes mostly from the United States, is the theme of how to 'control' proliferation and 'manage' the world order. It is disturbing because it reveals the basic framework within which Americans approach the problem; it is amusing because it has a hollow ring at a time of declining American influence all over the world.

Any scientific analysis of nuclear proliferation should be able to explain all the available facts. It should also explain why 'classical' proliferation is limited to the five recognized members of the nuclear club and also why current cases of proliferation are ambiguous, a form of 'quasi-proliferation.' Furthermore, a scientific analysis should explicate the various qualitative levels of proliferation. This

27

analysis cannot limit itself to the discerning of motivational categories such as fear, prestige, utility, or momentum. The abstraction and separation of these categories from the context of the historical evolution of the world system only leads to falsification. What follows is an effort to analyze scientifically the emergence of nuclear weapons in the United States, their spread to Soviet Union, Britain, France and China, the subtle variations involved in each case, and finally the new character nuclear proliferation has acquired in its second phase.

NUCLEAR WEAPONS IN THE US AND THE USSR

The first fundamental advances in nuclear physics took place neither in the United States nor in the Soviet Union but in Europe. Prior to the growth of nuclear weapons research, however, two events of world importance took place which were to influence other developments, including the direction of nuclear research. The first was the Russian revolution and the second was the emergence of fascism in Europe. The first event brought into being a socialist nation in opposition to the capitalist system of nations. Since 1917, there have been, in effect, two contradictory and contending systems. However, with the subsequent growth of fascism in Europe, the two contending systems became locked in an uneasy alliance to defeat fascism. The contradictions between the two were not resolved in this alliance; the moment it was clear that fascism faced defeat, these unresolved differences came to the fore and the alliance was dissolved.

The first step in the American nuclear effort was taken in the fear that Nazi Germany might acquire nuclear weapons, when Albert Einstein wrote his famous letter to President Roosevelt. The first and the most difficult task was to demonstrate the practical feasibility of nuclear weapons. Blessed by the rich talent of the European emigré scientists and its own tremendous industrial might, the United States had the political will and the economic-industrial-technological capacity to take an idea from the laboratory to the battlefield within the short span of half a decade. Though the fear of Nazi Germany was the initial impulse, the final construction and testing of the bomb occurred after the status of German nuclear research had become irrelevant. Indeed, as J. Robert Oppenhemier noted years later, 'I don't think there was a time when we worked harder at the speed up than after the German surrender.'[1] Why did the United States accelerate its effort after the German surrender? To understand this, one should not view the nuclearization of the United States as a single, limited decision. The acquisition of the first nuclear weapons took place in a period of radically shifting alliances in the world system. Therefore, in harnessing a radically new technology to the requirements of war, American policy makers could not be expected to be completely oblivious to the Soviet factor. As Major General Leslie Groves, the chief of the Manhattan Project pointed out:

> I think it important to state – I think it is well known – that there was never from about two weeks from the time I took charge of the project any illusion on my part but that Russia was the enemy and that the project was conducted on that basis.[2]

Nuclear weapons thus influenced US foreign policy even before they were tested. As the work on the Manhattan Project progressed, American policy makers presumably awaited nuclear weapons as their trump card for dealing with the USSR. Although the Soviet Union was an ally in the anti-fascist struggle, the United States, one may speculate, could hardly be unmindful of (a) the long-term differences it had with the USSR and (b) the immediate differences in their approaches to the structure of post-war Europe. Both in meetings in Moscow and at the Yalta Conference, the western allies or, at least, Britain reached understandings with the USSR on the spheres of influence each side would control after the war. In fact, the allies had little choice in any such understandings, as the Red Army was the most heavily engaged in Europe. But, in 1945, the prospect of nuclear weapons seems to have forced a reconsideration of the situation. The United States, or some in its leadership, may have wondered whether the nuclear factor would enable them to renegotiate any agreements already reached and force the Red Army to march back to the Soviet frontiers. The English government, even before the end of the war clearly perceived that 'Soviet Russia has become a mortal danger to the free world.'[3] The outstanding issues dividing the allies towards the end of the war in the European theatre were the nature of the Polish Government, the control of Balkans, the question of the withdrawal of the Red Army to the Soviet frontiers, and the continuing validity of the October 1944 agreements between Prime Minister Churchill and General Secretary Stalin on the post-war European settlement.[4] Stalin contended he had kept his word on Greece. Would the Anglo-

Americans do so on Bulgaria and Romania? Would the West also stand by the guarantee of Yalta that a government favourable to the Soviet Union would be installed in Poland?

The advent of nuclear weapons seems to have had a profound influence on the behaviour of the West not only in regard to the foregoing European issues but also in connection with the Far East. By the time of the Potsdam Conference in July, 1945, nuclear weapons were a reality. The British, who had originally intended to persuade the Americans to join the October, 1944, agreements, now felt that the West could dictate terms to Stalin.[5] At Yalta, the allies had agreed that Russia, which had not been at war with Japan, should open a front against the Japanese. But at Potsdam, Churchill told President Truman that Soviet participation in the Japanese theatre would be unnecessary, that European problems would be faced 'on their own merits' and that the balance of power had been redressed.[6] At Potsdam, it seems evident that the West, in the possession of nuclear weapons, had decided to end its partnership with the USSR in world affairs. Truman bluntly accused Stalin of rigging Bulgarian and Romanian elections, asked him to vacate the Balkans, and strongly opposed Soviet suggestions on reparations and zonal booty systems in defeated countries.[7] Truman knew his hand was much stronger holding the 'royal flush'.

Meanwhile, the Japanese were sending peace feelers through Moscow. Washington was informed. Yet the Americans nevertheless bombed Hiroshima and Nagasaki. Even Eisenhower admitted, '. . . I was against it (the atomic attack) on two counts. First the Japanese were ready to surrender and it wasn't necessary to hit them with that awful thing. . . '[8] One tends, after a close study, to agree with PMS Blackett that the dropping of the bomb was 'not so much the last military act of the Second World War, as the first major act of the cold diplomatic war with Russia now in progress'.[9] Whatever the subjective intentions of the various actors involved in the 'great nuclear decision' might have been, four plausible reasons can be inferred for the United States' use of the bomb in Japan: (1) to back out of the commitments made to the USSR at Yalta and prevent it from entering the war in the Far East;[10] (2) to terminate the war before the Red Army penetrated too deeply into China, if Russia did enter the Far Eastern theatre; (3) to prevent the USSR from staking any claim to occupation zones in Japan;[11] and (4) the possible effect a combat demonstration of the new weapon would have in reinforcing US proposals for peace settlements around the globe.

Thus the process of the United States 'going nuclear' should be seen, not as a response to a single military fear, but as a complex development occurring at a time of a changing correlation of forces in the world. As nuclear weapons came close to reality towards the end of the war, fascism no longer presented any threat. The main thrust of the new weapon was thus against the USSR. Whatever the initial impulses, once the United States produced this new technology of war, pressures to use the new weapon both politically and militarily in the altered world situation would likely prove irresistible. And the history of the proliferation of nuclear weapons to other nations demonstrates that, once a particular nation is in possession of a new military technology, pressures build up not only on its adversary but also on its allies to develop the same weapons.

THE SOVIET INCENTIVE FOR NUCLEAR WEAPONS

There were no spectacular advances in nuclear science in the Soviet Union as there had been in Europe. But nuclear research had had a firm grounding in the Soviet Union since the founding in the 1920s of the Leningrad Radium Institute.[12] Research received a further stimulus in the 1930s when many new laboratories were set up. By 1935, the Soviets had a van de Graaf generator and, by 1940s, a cyclotron. In the same period the Kurchatov group discovered the phenomenon of spontaneous fission, while in 1939-41, Flerov did pioneering work on emission and absorption as research committees on isotopes and uranium were set up. By 1941, the Russians seem to have been aware of the military potential of the atom.[13] Though it is evident that the Soviets were well advanced in nuclear research by 1941, the exigencies of the war had diametrically opposite effects on nuclear developments in the United States and the USSR. While the United States, its territory not directly involved in the war, could mobilize vast resources for nuclear research, the USSR was engaged in a battle for survival, and had to divert all available resources to defeat fascism. Nuclear weapons research was naturally set back.

Conditioned by its Marxist-Leninist world view and its bitter experience of Western intervention in Russia immediately after the October Revolution in 1917, the Soviet Union was aware that it had to arm itself to protect and defend 'socialism in one country' against encirclement by imperialism. The defeat of Hitler uncovered the strains in the alliance between the West and the USSR and finally culminated in hostile behaviour after the bombing of Japan with atomic weapons. In possession of nuclear weapons, the West began to adopt an aggressive posture aimed at containing communism and reneging on its earlier agreements with Stalin.

On 9 August 1945, the same day as the second atomic attack on Japan, President Truman announced that Eastern Europe would not be the sphere of influence of any power.[14] Attlee looked forward with hope to 'the emergence of democratic governments based on free elections in the Balkans'.[15] Thus, moves to exclude the USSR from the Balkans came immediately in the wake of its exclusion from Japan and the East. The Balkan understanding, which Churchill described as 'the best possible',[16] were thrown out in favour of nuclear weapons, which it was assumed had redressed the balance of power. While Stalin had kept his word on Greece, the West was not prepared to do so on the Balkans.

The American desire to achieve a nuclear monopoly and to derive political and economic benefits from it was further evident in the Baruch Plan of 1946, which was transparently one-sided in its proposal for international control of atomic energy activities in all states. Under the plan, American relinquishing of its atomic weapons would be a step-by-step process so that the United States would remain in a favourable position with regard to nuclear strength in case the process of achieving international control broke down at any point. No-one could have expected the Soviet Union to accept a plan so obviously directed toward maintaining the US monopoly on nuclear weapons technology.[17]

The Truman Doctrine of March 1947 and the Marshall Plan of June 1947 were further efforts to 'contain communism' and fight the 'Red menace'.[18] If the Truman Doctrine posed a military threat to the Soviet Union, the Marshall Plan was perceived as the economic means for US consolidation of its position in Europe and as a method for driving communists out of coalition governments. These initiatives were seen as a means of using US military and economic might to force Soviet withdrawals to their own borders and to prevent the spread of communism. It was also suggested that a strategy of containment would weaken or modify presumed communist territorial drives.[19] Thus, for some in the West 'containment' was interpreted to mean 'roll back'. Achieving containment was the major task of US foreign policy in the post-war era. Two major assumptions of this policy were reflected in a faith in the effectiveness of nuclear weapons and a belief in the value of strategic bombing that prevailed in the US Air Force and among some political leaders as well.

The Soviet answer to this strategy was 'to ensure by all means possible that her effective military frontiers are pushed as far away from the homeland as possible...'[20] Stalin achieved this by establishing communist power in Poland, Czechoslavakia, Hungary, Rumania, Bulgaria and Yugoslavia. By 1948, the division of Europe was complete and Soviet conventional military power confronted US forces backed by atomic bombs at the Elbe.

As the ideological and political adversary of the West, convinced of the need to defend Marxism-Leninism against the possible renewal of Western intervention, faced with a capitalist nuclear opponent, and in possession of basic nuclear know-how, the Soviet Union was under tremendous pressure to manufacture nuclear weapons. It had no option but to do so.

INDEPENDENT DETERRENTS: BRITAIN, FRANCE AND CHINA

The nuclear forces of Britain, France and China have to be put in a category separate from those of the United States and the USSR. The concept of independent deterrence arises from the twin conditions of a nuclear threat and political dependence. It reflects different relationships *vis-à-vis* the two superpowers, one against whom a nuclear deterrent threat is directed and the other from whom independence is sought. For Britain and France, deterrence was directed toward the Soviet Union and independence was sought from the United States. For China. it was the other way around.

French nuclear armament had little to do with its military posture toward a political enemy but a good deal to do with the French position *vis-à-vis* her principal allies.[21] The British case is broadly similar and the Chinese to a much lesser extent. The themes of independence and influence are quite easily discerned in the British and French nuclear proliferation, with the former being the means for achieving the latter.

Britain. In Britain, the idea of an independent deterrent was quite well-entrenched as early as 1943.[22] By the end of the war, Britain had become a second-rate power with meagre resources, over-extended forces and excessive commitments. Much as it would have liked to, Britain lacked the capital and the industrial-technological resources to launch a nuclear weapons programme on a scale similar to that of the United States. Moreover, by the end of the war, the role of the

Western or capitalist gendarme had passed from Britain to the United States.

It was clear to Britain that, on its own, it would be unable to 'contain' the Soviet Union in Europe. Yet, once the United States had shouldered this burden, it became imperative both to influence American policy and to retain a certain degree of autonomy from the Americans. These twin objectives could be achieved only by going nuclear. The modest character of the British nuclear force is only one reflection of the reduced circumstances of Britain. It is not difficult to find evidence of the British desire to retain some autonomy *vis-à-vis* the Americans. As Clement Attlee pointed out: 'I do not believe it is right that his country should be absolutely dependent on the USA. This is one good reason for going ahead with our own work on the A-Bomb.' Said Conservative Leader Harold Macmillan: 'The fact that we have it (the A-Bomb) makes the United States pay a greater regard to our point of view'.[23] While the strategic and technological demands of the British nuclear weapons programme were largely determined by the capability of the perceived likely adversary, the Soviet Union, the political requirement for the nuclear force stemmed from Britain's alliance with the United States. In many respects, the British nuclear weapons programme can be considered a function of Washington, rather than of Moscow. While the British government did seek to deter the Soviet Union, its nuclear weapons programme had as its major aim providing a basis for maintaining the 'special relationship' with the United States.[24]

France. If British proliferation reflects primarily the theme of influence, the French proliferation stresses the theme of independence. As in the British case, the military arguments for a national nuclear force were 'couched in terms of resisting an attack from the East, the political arguments dwelt on inter-allied relationships'.[25]

The chief goal of the French nuclear weapons programme was to bolster its position in the Western alliance system. If Britain, as much a second-rate power as France, can at least appear to have the ability to influence American policies, why not France? The apparent politico-diplomatic advantages of nuclear weapons, the general inclination to return to the great power concert of former years, a determined desire to win as much manoeuvrability as possible *vis-à-vis* the Anglo-Saxon powers, and the hope of gaining pre-eminence in Western Europe were the main considerations in the French decision to acquire nuclear weapons. The declaratory French rationale and strategic doctrine, which cast doubt on the American will to defend Western Europe in view of the Soviet ability to devastate the American homeland, was only a military justification for a political nuclear decision.

The two comparatively small nuclear powers of Europe may continue to find utility in their independent deterrents in the 1980s. In the West European context, independent deterrents may constitute part of the answer to the 'dilemma of European defense in a time of increasing pressures for American withdrawal'.[26] If this is true, France and Britain will have to modernize their deterrent forces to retain their usefulness.

China. China, unlike Britain and France, felt a strong need for an independent deterrent against a threatening nuclear adversary. Thrice in eight years she was at the receiving end of nuclear threats from the United States – in 1950, 1953 and 1958.[27] The Taiwan Straits incident of 1958 amply demonstrated to the Chinese that they would not be able to rely for protection on the Soviet nuclear umbrella, driving home the need for independent nuclear forces.[28]

Another important factor was the completely different conceptions of nuclear weapons, and their role in modern warfare, of the Communist Party of China (CPC) and the Communist Party of the Soviet Union (CPSU) after the death of Stalin. The meaning of nuclear weapons was, in fact, one of the central themes of the debate between the CPC and the CPSU during the period of Sino-Soviet rift.

At the Twentieth Congress of the CPSU in 1956, the Soviets formulated the proposition that, because of the tremendous destructiveness of nuclear weapons, wars with the capitalist system would not be desirable. They also asserted later that, not only are wars with imperialism not desirable, they are not inevitable and should be averted at all costs. On the basis of this formulation, the Soviets also declared that it is necessary to 'peacefully coexist' with imperialism, that imperialism can be overcome by 'peaceful competition' and, finally, that there will be a 'peaceful transition' from capitalism to communism.

The Chinese criticized this line of the CPSU as revisionist and un-Marxist-Leninist.[29] They pointed out that treating the character of war in terms of its scope and destructiveness obscures the real root and substance of war and is no substitute for a class analysis of conflict.[30] The Chinese also rejected the Soviet theory that an increase in the number of nuclear weapon states increases the danger from nuclear weapons.[31] The conclusion of the Limited Test Ban Treaty in 1963 was a further confirmation to the Chinese of the compromising attitude of the USSR towards the United States. Commenting on the treaty, the *Peking Review* said: 'The real aim of the Soviet leaders is to compromise with the United States in order to seek momentary ease and to maintain a monopoly of nuclear weapons and lord it over the socialist camp'.[32]

Unlike Britain and France, the Chinese began to acquire nuclear weapons in response to serious nuclear threats from the United States and in the midst of deteriorating relations with its former nuclear protector, the Soviet Union.

PROLIFERATION: THE NEW PHASE

The course of nuclear proliferation today is quite different from the classical model of proliferation, owing to the completely different set of actors involved and the tremendous growth and spread of civil nuclear technology, which is the central concern of anti-proliferation strategists. The ambiguous and ambivalent nuclear weapons status of countries like Israel, South Africa and India typifies the second phase of proliferation. Any theory of proliferation needs to develop a typology for these new cases. Two categories of countries are widely recognized as serious potential proliferators. The first is the so-called 'garrison' or 'pariah' states – Israel, South Africa, Taiwan and South Korea – which may have aggravated security problems. The second is the 'prestige states' – India, Brazil, Argentina – which are the most advanced among the Third World nations.

Pariah states. The term 'pariah' describes only part of the truth. Although, the 'pariah states' have been ostracized by a majority of nations, they have had the consistent support of those who matter – the United States and the West. Israel, South Africa, Taiwan and South Korea can thus be more correctly characterized as the *outpost states* of the West in economically and strategically crucial areas. The significance for the United States of Taiwan and South Korea has plummeted with the recent Sino-American entente. There is speculation that this development might reinforce the motivation for Taiwan and South Korea to exercise their nuclear option.[33] Yet the strategic irrelevance of Taiwan and South Korea to the West after the American recognition of China, and the total dependence of these regimes on American support for their survival, makes it unlikely that these two will go nuclear in defiance of American wishes.

However, the Israeli and the South African cases are quite different. Situated in two areas of crucial political, strategic and economic importance – the Middle East and the Southern Africa – Israel and South Africa are as badly needed by the West as these two need the West for their survival.

It is now generally believed that Israel is already in possession of nuclear weapons, if not fabricated and tested, at least 'in the basement' and ready to be assembled.[34] There also appears to be Western involvement in the diversion of weapons-grade nuclear material to Israel.[35]

South Africa may likewise possess nuclear weapons, with possible aid from the West. An apparent nuclear test by South Africa in August 1977 seems to have been averted by the diplomatic pressure from the United States and the USSR.[36] Yet a recent, revealing study has amassed evidence to demonstrate the role of the West, particularly the United States and West Germany, in the clandestine transfer of nuclear materials and technology to South Africa.[37] The study also suggests that the US Government, at least in some of its agencies, has been pursuing a policy of collaboration with South Africa in both the civil and military nuclear spheres. Assuming it is in the interests – both strategic and corporate – of the United States and the West to maintain a pro-Western, white minority regime in these difficult times for American interventionism, then the argument could be made that South Africa needs nuclear weapons to ensure the survival of political and economic white supremacy amidst a predominantly black population surrounded by other black nations.

Covert transfer of nuclear weapon materials and technology to Israel and South Africa, if true, would make a mockery of the pious pronouncements of the West on nuclear proliferation, creating the appearance that the United States is not opposed to the selective proliferation of nuclear weapons technology to its outpost states. However, for the West to maintain its facade of concern about nuclear proliferation, the transfers have to remain clandestine, so that the nuclear status of Israel and South Africa remains ambiguous, and yet functional.

Prestige states. The so-called 'prestige states' are the more developed among the developing nations. India, Brazil, Argentina and others have had considerable economic progress – however skewed – over the past three decades. These are leading countries in the non-aligned movement, the champions of a new international economic order, and, of course, non-signatories of the Non-proliferation Treaty, as well as its most trenchant critics. Most of the regimes in these countries are authoritarian, politically unstable and economically vulnerable. While striving their best to end all internal pressures for a just social order, they use radical rhetoric against imperialism and clamour for a just world order and a new North-South equation. In essence, they are seeking a redistribution of world power to their own advantage. Against this background, it is not difficult to see that nuclear technology has tremendous value as a symbol of modernity, technological development, and potentially independent growth.

In the Western proliferation literature, however, numerous theories have been advanced which exaggerate the proliferation potential of Third World countries. For example, the 'chain theory' presumes that once India goes nuclear, then Pakistan will do so, then Iran, and then the entire Middle East.[38] Similarly, if Brazil goes nuclear, the whole of Latin America will follow. This kind of theorizing betrays a lack of understanding of the nature of the Third World regimes and their complex relations with the rest of the world. Most Third World governments are caught in strong economic dependency ties with the United States, the West, the World Bank, and the International Monetary Fund. The Soviet Union, normally the first to come to the aid of developing countries when industrial technological aid is denied by the West, is in total agreement with the United States on the issue of controls and safeguards on nuclear technology, which tends to help perpetuate the condition of nuclear and economic dependence.

In these circumstances, it will be very difficult even for the advanced developing nations to create independent nuclear programmes. They neither have the economic-industrial infrastructure to sustain a completely independent nuclear programme nor the political strength to stand up very long against the restrictions of the 'London Club' of nuclear technology suppliers. India could go the farthest along the road of nuclear independence, thanks to an early start and farsighted leadership. Yet, after the 'peaceful nuclear explosion' of 1974 the Indian nuclear programme is today at a crossroads.[39] Long delays have occurred, Canadian nuclear aid has been cut off, enriched uranium supplies from the United States are in jeopardy, and inexplicable accidents in heavy-water plants have pushed back the target date for self-sufficiency in the production of heavy water for its nuclear reactors. India is under strong pressure from both the United

States and the USSR to accept full-scope safeguards and its nuclear programme is in the doldrums through dependence on the USSR for heavy water and the United States for enriched uranium. If this is the position of the leader of the Third World nuclear aspirants, the status of others can be no better. Although Brazil has contracted for a complete nuclear fuel cycle, it will be under the most stringent safeguards. Pakistan's hopes of getting a reprocessing plant may have been dashed. Argentina is only cautiously edging forward along the nuclear road. The fortunes of nuclear power in Iran have plunged along with those of the Shah. And, in general, pursuing the light water reactor nuclear energy cycle, instead of more advanced concepts, will only reinforce the dependent relations of Third World nations through its reliance on enriched uranium produced by Western suppliers.

The Third World regimes will thus, quite justifiably, view the new tactics of the West to limit nuclear proliferation by limiting technology transfer as 'part of an overall strategy to slow down the diffusion of military, political and economic power to the Third World.'[40] The Third World faces a number of obstacles in trying to exploit the full range of potential nuclear options and the attempt to do so is going to be very difficult, risky, and expensive. But these countries may strive to come as close to the nuclear weapons threshold option as possible, if only to demonstrate their ability to overcome a dependent status.

NOTES AND REFERENCES

1. US Atomic Energy Commission, *In the Matter of J. Robert Oppenheimer: Transcript Hearings Before the Personal Security Board* (Washington, DC: GPO, 1954) p. 3223.
2. Quoted in R. Palme Dutt, *Problems of Contemporary History* (London: Lawrence & Wishart, 1963) p. 50.
3. Winston Churchill, *The Second World War*, vol. vi: *Triumph and Tragedy* (London: Cassell, 1954) p. 198.
4. The agreement gave the dominant influence in Romania and Bulgaria to Russia and in Greece to the Anglo-Americans, with equal influence in Yugoslavia and Hungary for the Russians and the Western allies.
5. Arthur Bryant, *Triumph in the West: A History of the War Years Based on the Diaries of Field Marshall Lord Alan Brooke* (London: Collins, 1959)
6. Ibid., p. 363; Churchill, op. cit., p. 638.
7. US Department of State, *Foreign Relations of the United States, Diplomatic Papers: The Conference of Berlin*, vol. II (Washington, DC: GPO, 1961) p. 207.

8. *Newsweek*, 11 November 1963.
9. P.M.S. Blackett, *The Military and Political Consequences of Atomic Energy* (London: Turnstile Press, 1949) p. 139.
10. The commitments included the restoration of Russian rights over Manchuria which ended in 1905. The commitments applied only if USSR entered the war; if the war ended earlier, they were to be annulled automatically.
11. Stalin had made it clear in May 1945 that the USSR would lay claim to Japan in terms of occupational zones, which the United States was determined to deny.
12. For the history of nuclear developments in the Soviet Union see: Arnold Kramish, *Atomic Energy in the Soviet Union* (Stanford University Press, 1959); George Modelski, *Atomic Energy in the Communist Bloc* (Carlton: Melbourne University Press, 1959); and V.S. Emelyanov, 'Nuclear Energy in the Soviet Union', *Bulletin of Atomic Scientists* (Chicago) vol. 27, no. 9 (November 1971) pp. 41-3.
13. A Soviet nuclear physicist, Kapitsa, is reported to have said in 1941 that'. . . an atom bomb, even one of small size, if it can be manufactured could easily destroy a major capital city. . .' Quoted in *Kramish*, op. cit., p. 41.
14. Harry S. Truman, *Public Papers of the President*, vol. I (Washington, DC: GPO, 1961) p. 210.
15. House of Commons, *Parliamentary Debates*, 5th series (London: 1945) p. 102.
16. Churchill, op. cit., p. 288.
17. Blackett relates the episode of a well-known US general who, with Baruch, had been putting 'teeth' into the earlier Lilienthal Plan and said, 'Now we have made it so stiff that even the Russians won't be fool enough to fall for it.' *Atomic Weapons and East-West Relations* (Cambridge University, 1956) pp. 90-1.
18. For a discussion of the implications of the Truman Doctrine and Marshall Plan see chs. XVI and XVII of D.F. Fleming, *The Cold War and Its Origins: 1917-60*, vol. I, 1917-50 (New York: Doubleday, 1961) pp. 433-503.
19. George F. Kennan, 'The Sources of Soviet Conduct', *Foreign Affairs* (July 1947).
20. Blackett, *The Military and Political Consequences of Atomic Energy*, p. 73.
21. Wolf Mendl, *The Deterrence and Persuasion* (London: Faber & Faber, 1970) p. 18.
22. Margaret Gowing, *Britain and Atomic Energy 1939-45* (London: Macmillan, 1964) p. 394.
23. For Attlee's remark, see Hansard, 5 March 1952, col. 437. Macmillan is quoted by R.E. Osgood, *NATO: The Entangling Alliance* (Chicago University Press, 1962) p. 243.
24. A.J.R. Groom, *British Thinking About Nuclear Weapons* (London: Francis Pinter, 1974) p. 556.
25. Mendl, op. cit., p. 204. Lawrence Scheinman also points out the preponderance of political and diplomatic factors in French proliferation

in *Atomic Energy in France Under the Fourth Republic* (Princeton University Press, 1965) pp. 215-20.

26. Graeme P. Auton, 'Nuclear Deterrence and Medium Powers: A Proposal for Doctrinal Change in the British and French Cases', *Orbis* (Summer 1976) p. 399.
27. For the first case, in 1950, see Cabell Phillips, *The Truman Presidency* (London: Penguin, 1969) p. 329.
28. Alice Hsieh, *Communist China's Strategy in the Nuclear Era* (Englewood Cliffs, NJ: Prentice Hall, 1962) pp. 122-4.
29. Classical Marxism-Leninism states that wars are inevitable as long as capitalism exists and that war is only a continuation of politics by other means. See, V.I. Lenin, *Socialism and War* (Moscow: FLPH, 1950).
30. Raymond Garthoff, *Soviet Military Policy: A Historical Analysis* (London: Faber & Faber, 1966) p. 196.
31. Document No. 7, W.E. Griffith, *The Sino-Soviet Rift* (Cambridge, Mass.: MIT Press, 1964) p. 340.
32. *Peking Review*, 15 August 1963, p. 13.
33. *International Herald Tribune*, 26 December 1978, p. 5, and *International Herald Tribune*, 22 December 1978, p. 6.
34. For a discussion of the evidence see, Alan Dowty, 'Nuclear Proliferation: The Israeli Case', *Sage International Studies Quarterly*, vol 22, no. 1 (March 1978) pp. 79-120.
35. *Rolling Stone*, in its December 1977 issue, revealed that about 8000 pounds of uranium and plutonium missing in the United States had found their way to Israel. Investigations by successive US administrations were desultory and gave the appearance of trying to cover up the incidents. Also reported were similar instances involving France, West Germany and Britain in clandestine nuclear transfers to Israel. None have been acknowledged by the respective governments, presumably out of fear of political consequences.
36. *SIPRI Yearbook 1978* (Stockholm: Almquest & Wiksell, 1978) pp. 77-9.
37. Z. Cervanka and B. Rogers, *The Nuclear Axis* (London: Friedmann, 1978).
38. For example see, Lewis Dunn, *India, Pakistan...: A Nuclear Proliferation Chain?* (Croton-on-Hudson, NY: Hudson Institute, March 1976).
39. For the current crisis, see, R.R. Subramanian, 'India's Nuclear Situation: Where to?', *IDSA Journal* (Delhi), vol. x, no. 4 (April-June 1978) pp. 304-21.
40. Richard Falk, 'The Nuclear Teaser,' *Alternatives*, vol. 3, no. 2 (December 1977) p. 177.

3 A Theoretical Approach to Non-proliferation Policy

HARALD MÜLLER

The argument has been made that any attempt to analyze general motivational, situational, and structural factors contributing to nuclear proliferation is useless. This approach has been criticized as neglecting the more important specific situation and the goals of a particular proliferator and, therefore, as adding no applicable knowledge to the fund needed for case-by-case crisis diplomacy.[1] Although the necessity of dealing specifically with actual proliferation cases is not questioned here, there are convincing arguments for developing a general approach as a 'second pillar' for a non-proliferation policy.

First, even in actual cases, policy must be guided by some kind of general concept. Where better to derive it than from principles drawn from a thorough analysis of experience? Second, a case-by-case diplomacy for dealing with proliferation is likely to be developed *ex posteriori* after the events have revealed the imminent candidacy of a proliferator. Neither politicians nor political analysts are able to predict every future international conflict in time that could dramatically increase the incentives for antagonistic countries to go nuclear. Very few people can pretend that they predicted the Cambodia-Vietnam war beforehand. To avoid the dangers of a crisis-like non-proliferation diplomacy, general principles should be developed for application if a conflict becomes a 'nuclear case.' Finally, by creating a proliferation-resistant political climate in the international community, many, if not most, of the conflicts can be prevented from becoming virulent. Indeed, this idea underlies all existing and relatively successful non-proliferation policies including the Nuclear Non-proliferation Treaty (NPT). Non-proliferation policy, therefore, should include general and case-by-case approaches.

42

GAME THEORY AS AN INSTRUMENT FOR NON-PROLIFERATION POLICY

In order to contribute to a general approach to non-proliferation, one has to consider the common characteristics of proliferation situations, as revealed by experience. It seems useful to differentiate between a non-nuclear situation, in which neither conflict partner has yet acquired nuclear weapons but one or both of them will probably do so, and a semi-nuclear situation in which one 'have-not' faces a nuclear-armed adversary. Although different, both situations share some general characteristics:

1. A manifest conflict in which each side has something to lose;
2. An enemy whose technical capacity or political intentions are not precisely known;
3. A certain urgency which compels decision makers to avoid 'being second'.
4. A choice between different decisions: to go nuclear or not, to use one's own nuclear weapons or not.

The situation is thus characterized by conflict, strategic choice, information insecurity, and different outcomes with different values or utility for each actor. Such situations have been well analyzed by game theory[2] because of its unique ability to model the security dilemma, one of the most prevalent patterns in the system of nation states.[3] Due to the lack of reliable information about the capacity and intentions of a potential enemy, no nation knows reliably that it will not be the victim of aggression; its government therefore feels forced to prepare for defence; both sides pursue their defence in a 'conflict dyad' which breeds a self-perpetuating arms race and thus aggravates the security dilemma of both sides.[4]

Game theory analyzes this pattern by formalizing it in a matrix for a game of two independent players, each of which has its own utility (preference) scale and at least two different strategies from which to choose. The strategy a player will most likely choose depends on the outcome this strategy will provide in the 'worst case,' i.e., when the enemy selects its optimum strategy. Therefore, players follow the rule of 'safety first'. They are not likely to opt for a strategy with a big potential profit if the same strategy could bear disastrous costs. Because the enemy's choices are not known in advance, each player tends to minimize the risk of loss and only strives for profit if the danger of catastrophe is safely avoided. Under conditions of information insecurity, he will therefore choose the strategy that maximizes utility with a minimum of risk (minimax strategy).

In cases where the probability of the enemy's good intentions tends toward unity (one is sure the enemy will not attack), the minimax strategy can be replaced by a more cooperative concept. Out of three possible cases – information insecurity, assured information about bad intentions, assured information about good intentions – only the last case is likely to engender disarmament opportunities. The degree of available information and the utility values of each player are therefore the two important parameters of each game.

The game theoretical model does not mirror reality perfectly.[5] Rather, it is a useful discovery device that shows certain traits of the decisional situation in an ideal and, therefore, clearer way than verbal description can do, thereby provoking new perspectives helpful in dealing with this situation.

THE SECURITY DILEMMA AND PROLIFERATION

The non-nuclear situation. In the history of nuclear proliferation, there is a precedent-setting case of a government's deciding to go nuclear in a totally non-nuclear environment. When Franklin Roosevelt started the Manhattan Project, he felt pressed by a conflict situation characterized by the following features:

1. A manifest, violent conflict with considerable probability of threatening the American mainland with destruction, if not invasion;
2. An enemy theoretically able and willing to develop nuclear weapons, as revealed by its peaceful research in nuclear physics;
3. A deep uncertainty about the probable performance of the enemy in the field of nuclear development; i.e., its actual capacity, and, likewise, its plans to use this capacity;
4. A temporal pressure on decision makers due to the dangerous situation and the risk of being second in this new technology;
5. A real choice between two opportunities: to stay non-nuclear and therefore to conduct the conflict in the conventional way; or to concentrate research and development on the production of a nuclear device in the shortest possible time.

Here, then, is a situation characterized by strategic choice, information insecurity, and different outcomes with different pay-offs for each side. This legitimizes the application of the game theoretical model. Though we live in a world commonly called nuclear, the American case could be replicated in other regional conflicts or power balances.

This suggests a preference scheme that can be translated as follows:

1. A non-nuclear conflict environment to be preferred to any nuclearized conflict (since the probability is that the enemy will strive to equalize any nuclear lead);
2. In a nuclear conflict setting, monopoly of nuclear weaponry to be preferred to any other situation;
3. A nuclear balance to be preferred to an enemy's monopoly;
4. An enemy monopoly represents the worst case.

If the enemy is conceived as subject to similar considerations, the situation can be defined as a non-zero sum game: no side wins just what the other one loses; both sides could get their maximum utility or pay-off by staying non-nuclear. However, this strategy exposes both to the risk of disastrous loss: being at a decisive disadvantage in case the enemy goes nuclear. The minimax rule, therefore, forces both sides to go nuclear, because the enemy's strategic decision is not known in advance.

In non-nuclear conflict dyads there exists a high premium on co-operation under optimum information conditions, but an even higher incentive against cooperation exists under circumstances of limited information.[6] From information theory we know that information for communicators can be enlarged: (a) by increasing communication time; (b) by building additional communication channels; and (c) by using the maximum capacity of given channels. These abstract principles have been confirmed by experimental research on non-zero sum games of this type, the so-called prisoners's dilemma game. The studies of Anatol Rapoport, in particular, reveal that cooperative behaviour is more likely to result from enhanced decisional information (i.e., from exploiting existing channels by processing all data given by them), from the length of the game series (i.e., from expanding communication time) and by establishing direct communication networks between players (i.e., from creating new channels).[7]

All these measures, if translated into policy, are likely to reduce the incentives to 'go nuclear', because they lower the probability of the worst case. An additional incentive in this direction revealed by studies of the prisoner's dilemma model is a positive premium on cooperative behaviour. Such a premium if built into the rules of the game, enlarges the utility value of the non-nuclear option independently of the enemy's strategy.

Therefore, the following rules may be derived for non-proliferation policy:

1. Enhancement of adaptation time through avoidance of a rapid growth in nuclear weapons capabilities;
2. Establishing a high premium on staying non-nuclear, not just sanctions for going nuclear;
3. Enlargement of mutual information about real capacities and intentions.

It is worth noting that at least two of these principles are embedded in the NPT. By providing free access to civil nuclear technology, a premium has been established; by giving conflict partners information about the counterpart's intention to stay non-nuclear, information grew considerably; by establishing international safeguards on nuclear power plants to prevent diversion of materials, new communication channels have been built that guarantee timely information about the worst case. Today's non-proliferation regime thus relies on both time and information, even in this worst case. The concept of 'timely warning' – warning through a detected violation of safeguards plus the 90-day notification required for withdrawal from the treaty – will give the potential conflict partner and the international community the opportunity to react in a deliberate, non-crisis way.

However, this regime has now been jeopardized by the technological advances and rapid growth of the nuclear market. The highest risk is the spread of sensitive facilities, particularly nuclear fuel reprocessing plants. By producing stocks of weapons-grade plutonium under national control, reprocessing plants render safeguards useless. They could reduce the time needed to build a bomb to a few days, or, in the best case, a few weeks and, therefore, undermine the concept of timely warning.[8] As a consequence, a potential opponent will lack the guarantee of being informed in advance. That automatically enhances the probability of the opponent facing the worst case and, therefore, offers him incentives to go nuclear, or, at least, to acquire a reprocessing facility, too. This could lead to a civil-military nuclear capacity race up to the weapons threshold, as has been observed already in the last few years in South America between Brazil and Argentina.[9] From this analysis, the US policy of avoiding stocks of plutonium under national control seems to be quite rational. New kinds of incentives are needed, however, since the NPT's incentive – free access to nuclear energy technology – now appears to counteract the NPT principle of enhancing timely warning. The principles developed thus far apply to the non-nuclear cases, which may increase in the future. For the actual semi-nuclear conflicts, India-Pakistan or China-Taiwan, additional emergency diplomacy is needed.

The semi-nuclear situation. In semi-nuclear situations, one conflict partner has chosen to acquire nuclear weapons. The other one understands its worst case has been realized. So a new game begins. The non-nuclear player must still choose between staying non-nuclear or developing a bomb. The choice of the nuclear partner is between using its weapons for threat or aggression or, alternatively, refraining from any political or military use and behaving more or less as a non-nuclear state.[10] This permits the following preference schemes for the non-nuclear state:

1. To achieve parity in a non-threatening environment is the best, because most secure, situation, assuming it persists.
2. To stay non-nuclear but free from threat is preferable to any situation of tension.
3. Nuclear parity in a state of tension is preferable to helplessness.
4. To face a nuclear threat without any opportunity for launching, responding to, or deterring a nuclear attack is the worst case.

For the nuclear weapon state, the situation is quite different:

1. In the absence of any other constraint, using nuclear superiority to attain military or political goals could confer a significant benefit.
2. Showing restraint toward a non-nuclear counterpart and avoiding tensions is preferable to facing a nuclear enemy.
3. The enemy's going nuclear is the worst case, whether this situation arises because of or despite one's own actions.

The non-nuclear country's consideration has its classic parallel in the development of the Soviet nuclear capacity after the Second World

War. The Soviet Union was confronted with a nuclear weapon state as a potential conflict partner in an environment that proved to be more and more hostile. The USSR was not sure about American intentions. It was by no means clear whether the US would use its nuclear monopoly not just militarily but as a political weapon. These doubts were strong enough for the Soviet Union to defy the Baruch Plan with its cooperative schemes for nuclear energy and weapons. The timetable in the Baruch Plan would have exposed the USSR for a while to a situation of absolute inferiority. This was deemed too high a risk by the Soviet leadership, whose extensive security considerations restrained their flexibility to a considerable degree. They therefore decided to achieve nuclear parity as early as possible.

American behaviour sheds some light on the nuclear state's preference scheme. In one case, 1945, nuclear weapons were used against an adversary in a war. In the Quemoy-Matsu crisis of 1958, the US nuclear threat against the People's Republic of China served the political purpose of barring a supposed Chinese attack against Taiwan. In three other cases – Korea, Dien Bien Phu, and the Vietnam war – introduction of nuclear weapons was discussed at the highest political levels and by the attentive public in America. The US leadership decided against the use of nuclear weapons. Its adversaries, however, had to contemplate the possibility of a nuclear attack and, therefore, a subtle yet real threat.[11] Nuclear proliferation has been stimulated through these half-nuclear conflict dyads: US-USSR, China-India, and India-Pakistan. Whether China responded in its nuclear weapons decision to a perceived threat from the USSR, from the US, or from both cannot be judged without further information.

While these examples reveal the value assigned to a threatening posture by the nuclear weapon states, they likewise demonstrate some restraint. This suggests that the values for a nuclear weapon state of peaceful and threatening behaviour may not be too different. They may thus be influenced situationally and environmentally, rather than by some inherent and inevitable dynamic.

The one-sided nuclear game does not yield a pleasant solution. The most probable result is a threatening nuclear nation and a have-not going nuclear. This can be a dangerous and unstable situation, especially in view of the relative weakness and vulnerability of first-generation nuclear weapons. They may well suffer from a lack of reliability, mobility, and target precision, as well as warning systems and launchers. The nuclear enemy thus knows there is a high premium in striking first to disarm the adversary. The nuclear newcomer is forced to a launch-on-warning strategy, with all the risk entailed in this doctrine and so broadly discussed in the early 1960s. With one side induced to strike first, the other to launch-on-warning, the chance of accidental or catalytic war is raised considerably.

However, there are some signs of hope and possible guides for policy: a considerable number of non-nuclear states in one-sided conflict situations have decided to stay non-nuclear. West Germany, for example, is not likely to go nuclear in the foreseeable future, although it is in the centre of the European tension theatre and faces both a conventional and a nuclear threat. The nuclear shelter provided by the US is perhaps the primary but not the only condition ameliorating the German position. Another, more recent, ameliorating factor is the 1970 treaty on the non-use of force between the USSR and the FRG. It expresses their mutual interest in non-violent, non-military conduct, establishes a minimum of trust, and gives a framework for the growth of economic and cultural relationships. A third condition is the twenty-year-old arms control relationship between the superpowers. The establishment of special communications links, such as the Washington-Moscow 'hot-line', and of ongoing communications, such as arms limitation talks, exemplify their common interest in avoiding a holocaust, made explicit in the US-USSR agreement on the prevention of nuclear war.

Germany's status as a non-nuclear country thus involves pledges and communications at several levels. The nuclear guarantee reduced the fear of being threatened. Ties to the Soviet Union supply the information that the potential enemy's intentions are, at least, not the worst ones (at the same time they lessen the United States's fear of being drawn into a nuclear exchange by an irresponsible ally.) Soviet-American détente reduces incentives to go nuclear still further by reducing the overall tension level in a situation that remains potentially conflictual and crisis-prone.

This trilateral relationship is by no means the result of conscious political planning but of the dangerous experience of the Cold War. It can nevertheless be used as a model for semi-nuclear conflicts. It suggests that, since the one-sided nuclear game is without a stable solution, the game needs to be changed by introducing a new player, the nuclear guarantor. Most studies of nuclear guarantees raise fears about the risk of exchanging the instability of a semi-nuclear situation with the instability of a nuclear arms race.[12] In game-theoretical terms, the two-nation game between the nuclear country and the non-nuclear country is replaced by a two-nation game between the nuclear nation and a coalition of the non-nuclear nation and its guarantor. The approach suggested by the German case, however, seeks to dissolve this situation into three games with different dyads or coalitions of interests.

The first coalition is between the non-nuclear state's potential adversary and its nuclear guarantor, because they share an interest in avoiding nuclear war and keeping the non-nuclear country from going nuclear. The second is between the guarantor and its client: both wish to reduce the risk of political threat or military aggression by the nuclear adversary. The third dyad is the usual one between the have and the have-not. But, because of the two other games, this one has clearly changed to a more cooperative structure. The German-American-Soviet triangular relationship serves to illustrate the kinds of treaties and communication channels that must be set up to lessen tensions. By replicating this enlarged semi-nuclear game over time, information critical to decisions may be expanded, minimum necessary confidence levels attained, and the impulse to acquire nuclear weapons lessened for a larger number of partners in the complex relationship.

Morever, the existence of stable, non-proliferative but potentially conflictual relations between nuclear and non-nuclear states not sheltered by a nuclear partner should not be overlooked. An example is the relationship between Finland and the USSR; although this case admittedly owes much to special circumstances, similar relationships may evolve and bear careful scrutiny.

*   *   *   *   *

The security dilemma lies at the centre of the proliferation problem. It determines the formalized matrices of non-nuclear and one-sided nuclear games. There are, however, additional factors based on international or national structure, which, without changing the basic pattern, influence considerably the value of the pay-offs: namely prestige, the drive for independence, and bureaucratic-industrial dynamics.

PRESTIGE AND INDEPENDENCE

In the history of nuclear proliferation, at least two states decided to develop a nuclear capacity without an immediate security problem.

Although the strategic aspects of East-West tensions contributed partly to the nuclear decisions of France and Great Britain, the desire to demonstrate Great Power status and independence of decision was a more important motive than these considerations.[13]

Prestige is an index for national self-identification. It reflects a nation's recognition by the international community. It is thus an important factor in the process of nation building and supports the stability of social and political systems. For the potential proliferators in the Third World, this motive is therefore of crucial importance.

That nuclear armament tends to enhance a nation's prestige can be demonstrated primarily by the behaviour of the nuclear countries themselves. They share the privileged permanent seats in the UN Security Council and have not been willing until today to open the door for any non-nuclear member. Moreover, the number one nuclear nation, the United States, did not feel any necessity to accept the People's Republic of China before its nuclear detonation of 1964. Henry Kissinger concedes that it was the nuclear bomb that served China as a ticket to the theatre of Great Power politics.[14]

There is, however, a group of states whose prestige has grown without the aid of nuclear weapons. Saudi Arabia is a recent example. Mexico, Algeria, Egypt, and India (until 1974) in the Third World; Sweden, Japan, and West Germany in the First World; and Yugoslavia and Rumania among the socialist countries belong to this group. Whether these countries gained prestige by natural resource endowment, economic strength, political model, or ideological leadership is not decisive. What is evident is that prestige can be acquired by instruments other than armaments.

On the other hand, nuclear armaments did not confer a first-class power status on Great Britain and France. Great Britain's power status has been undermined badly by its low economic performance over the years. France's political independence allegedly caused by its nuclear power status faced a serious test in 1973. Then the results of its independently developed special relations to the Arab world were at stake. But the international energy system and different domestic policies left France worse off during the oil embargo than non-nuclear West Germany. Both nuclear powers, moreover, experienced a growing gap in the capability and quality of their nuclear weapons compared to the two superpowers. The never-ending pressure to modernize warheads and launchers left only two choices: letting their own nuclear armament become obsolete or enhancing their forces by adding to the burdens on their economies. Thus, besides being dubious as instruments of prestige, nuclear weapons diminish the changes of developing a healthy economy as an alternative source of prestige.

The nuclear bomb did little, too, to enhance India's status. After arousing some attention in 1974 and causing, unwittingly, the third generation of non-proliferation efforts, India found itself forced under a new government to renounce Mrs Ghandi's promise of more nuclear explosions. And India gained no benefit in terms of economic development or internal stability.

This leads to the issue of decisional independence. This assumes that an independent nuclear shelter is the basic condition for avoiding over-reliance on, or political intervention by, a powerful nuclear ally or adversary. Based on a dubious division between the functional areas of security and economy, this assumption reveals a profound misconception of present realities by political élites. In the cases of Great Britain, India, and France, nuclear arms did not stem the erosion of economic independence through the growing inter-dependence of the world economy.

International linkages of trade, raw material dependency, and currency flows limit the autonomy of every government. Even the US was relatively helpless against the Arab oil embargo of 1973. Military means, and specifically nuclear arms, are totally unsuitable for coping with the problem of economic warfare based on resource dependence. Studies show that no realistic military option could secure access to Arab oil fields.[15] Britain's dependence on US nuclear arms research and development resembles a caricature of the concept of independence through the atomic bomb. It makes Great Britain a victim of American unilateralism as can be seen quite early in the decision on the *Skybolt* missile in the early 1960s.

Although France's 'independent' performance looks a bit better, its ambiguous relationship to the International Energy Agency reveals that its official distance from this organization – justified by France's independent posture – is a rather symbolic, insubstantial display. Abstaining formally from membership, France pledged to behave as if it were a member because it is too heavily involved in the energy system of the industrialized world to risk an outsider's position, especially in an emergency. Indeed, in the most relevant world energy dialogue, in the CIEC, France did not separate itself from the European Group and Western positions.

Otherwise, no nuclear state other than the superpowers and China has ever reached so independent a standing, not only from the nuclear 'senior partners' but from traditional security thinking, as has non-nuclear Rumania: Its government resisted enlarging its defence budget because, in its view, the international situation did not require greater expenditure.

Although independence and prestige may not be very realistic expectations for a nuclear pretender, both incentives must be taken seriously. Their symbolic value cannot be underestimated. The British, French, and Indian examples seem to transfer to the world scene Ted Gurr's finding in social group behaviour, that the use of force gains momentum whenever the gap between aspiration and achievement tends to widen.[16] If the prestige and independence of an ambitious power are not equal to its wishes, a motivation to go nuclear would be created, for declining as well as for emerging powers. This applies particularly to the economic 'take-off' states widely assumed to be potential proliferators.

In game-theoretical terms, while not changing the matrix structure, the difference between pay-offs of the various strategies can be enlarged or diminished considerably by prestige and independence. For a potential proliferator, they put an additional premium on the nuclear way. For its rival, knowledge of this premium makes its worst case more probable and thus provides it with additional incentives to go nuclear. Cases of non-proliferation where it might have occurred suggest the need to switch from armaments criteria for prestige and independence to non-military substitutes.

INSTITUTIONAL DYNAMICS AND NUCLEAR INCREMENTALISM

In the nuclear weapon states, the nuclear community is a social sub-system of its own, with its own interests, belief systems, thinking style, communication links, and sources of influence. Every large organizational network develops an institutional pattern of economic and bureaucratic interests, shared images, and decisional momentum; strives to enhance the scope and amount of its power; and defends itself against any threat. Structures comparable to the military-industrial complex exist in the nuclear field and include research centres, the nuclear industry and its labour force, nuclear-oriented parts of the bureaucracy, and the military. Of special importance is the strong identity of civil and military interests. A review of the Indian case reveals that civil scientists and military personnal joined in a successful attempt to enlarge nuclear programmes. This coalition produced such pressure that top politicians had little choice but to confirm step-by-step decisions already prepared and advanced by the civil-military nuclear coalition. Similar developments are reported in Argentina and Brazil.[17]

The danger created by this kind of nuclear complex does not lie in its direct influence on political decisions. Its main characteristic is a dynamic combination of subtle civil and military pressures. Challenged by international efforts on behalf of non-proliferation, as well as by internal criticism, the nuclear complex tends to dissolve the big step to a nuclear weapon into a series of little steps, each of which narrows the distance to the weapons threshold. Starting with a small nuclear research programme, the first basis of technical know-how, trained manpower is created. In the next phase, a commercial reactor produces plutonium. The acquisition of a reprocessing plant, then, opens the door to weapons-grade material. The blueprint for an explosive device, presumably declared to be for peaceful purposes, follows. The construction of non-nuclear parts for such a device can be justified as preparing for an emergency and short of actually building the bomb. Detailed emergency plans for assembling nuclear and non-nuclear parts shorten the time necessary for deploying actual weapons. Where, then, is the nuclear weapons threshold? As Thomas Schelling points out, in such incremental development, the threshold is defined by the observer, not by the nature of affairs.[18]

This tendency to avoid a clear nuclear weapon decision through incremental steps avoids psychological thresholds. The spread of civil nuclear power makes the pattern a prevalent one. In the civil-military nuclear coalition, each step will find avid supporters and can be justified as not amounting to the one decisive step.

From the game-theoretical view, domestic structure and nuclear incrementalism influence both parameters of the choice situation: utility and information. Nuclear incrementalism avoids highly risky steps. Because potential disincentives from sanctions (i.e., negative utility) are minimized by incrementalism, while the positive utility of each step remains equal (to retain optimum security, to sustain technological progress), the utility of going nuclear appears to rise.

The emergence of a nuclear community as a part of the political élite changes the value preferences of this élite as a whole. The nuclear-industrial complex has a stake in going nuclear since this would enhance its prestige, power, and size inside the élite. Although it is only part of this élite, its high utility plus its near monopoly of information in nuclear decisions tends to change the overall perspective of the political élite, at least slightly. This can be observed in the US and in India. In America, it is the nuclear establishment in the weapons laboratories, in the Energy Department and in the military that resists the comprehensive nuclear test ban because such a treaty would reduce its importance.[19] In India, the civil-military coalition pressed a hesitating government toward the 1974 detonation.

Developments of this kind influence the other parameter: information. The existence of a nuclear establishment and a growing nuclear capacity cannot be concealed. The presumptive adversary thus observes an incremental growth of the probability of its enemy going nuclear. This development necessitates its own preparations for the worst case.

The nuclear weapon states and countries with a large nuclear industry now face the problem of checking the influence of their nuclear communities. It seems illogical to foster such complexes in other countries. A more reasonable approach is to place as much nuclear responsibility as possible in international bodies, although the development of such international regimes takes time.

THE NEED FOR A COMPREHENSIVE NON-PROLIFERATION POLICY

The foregoing analysis shows that nations go nuclear for several inter-related reasons, including:

The striving for security, reinforced by worst-case analysis under conditons of information insecurity.

The attempt to assure great power status, on the assumption that this purpose can be achieved through nuclear armaments.

Attaining independence of decision and of capacity at a time when interdependence is a clear trend in world affairs and autarky appears obsolete.

A dynamic nuclear community with a stake in widening the scope of its own power.

A step-by-step approach toward the nuclear weapons threshold.

Any external proposal to prevent other countries from following these imperatives may be resented as hegemonic or imperialistic, while the great powers at the same time often serve, ironically, as models for aspiring nuclear nations. Thus, conscious or unconscious intervention in nuclear decisions by the nuclear weapon and nuclear supplier states may tend to promote proliferation. The advanced nuclear nations, however, may be rather poor models. The right to development is not a licence to lead in the wrong direction, counter to the long-range, essential economic and security interests of the people. Any reasonable non-proliferation policy should thus encompass the following elements:

1. Slowing the growth of civil nuclear energy. This growth should not be faster than the capacity of international institutions and nation states to adapt to it. Restraint in export policy and checks against international and internal nuclear establishments are also needed.

2. Increasing the mutual information flow among potential adversaries. This means strengthened safeguards covering all nuclear facilities, even non-nuclear facilities able to produce needed parts for reprocessing or enrichment plants. Moreover, the nuclear suppliers' 'trigger list' of potentially dangerous exports should include parts for sensitive facilities in research laboratories.[20] If such parts are sold in international trade, the destination should be announced to the International Atomic Energy Agency (IAEA). The agency should reserve the right to prove the alleged destination by inspection. Other confidence-building measures could include exchange of personnel between adversary nuclear facilities and common nuclear programmes on the part of potential enemies, directed by the IAEA. Bilateral treaties not to develop nuclear weapons against each other, worked out on the initiative and under the leadership of IAEA could supplement the NPT. By extending this new type of treaty over a region, a gradual process leading to regional nuclear-weapon-free zones, which are so hard to achieve by multilateral diplomacy, could be started.

3. Reducing the status of the nuclear power. This could involve altering the veto power in the UN Security council, the permanent seats in this council, while providing an opportunity for the admission of non-nuclear countries as permanent members (e.g. Sweden or Yugoslavia) and the dissolution of the permanent co-chairmanship of the US and the USSR in the IAEA.

4. Providing a higher premium for states to remain non-nuclear by enlarging development aid, special trade preferences, and assistance in non-nuclear energy planning.

5. Internationalizing the entire nuclear fuel cycle to avoid the development of national nuclear complexes and to safeguard proliferation-prone elements of the fuel cycle for civil energy.
6. Initiating crash programmes in non-nuclear energy research, development and commercialization, including establishment of a well-funded international non-nuclear energy agency to offset the one-sided promotion of nuclear energy by the IAEA.

NOTES AND REFERENCES

1. Richard K. Betts, 'Paranoids, Pygmies, Pariahs and Nonproliferation', *Foreign Policy*, no. 26 (Spring 1977) pp. 178-9.
2. The author relies heavily on the best German introduction to game theory: Gert Junne, *Spieltheorie in der internationalen Politik: die beschränkte Rationalität strategischen Denkens* (Düsseldorf: Bertelsmann Universitäts Verlag, 1972).
3. John Herz, *International Politics in the Atomic Age* (New York: Columbia University Press, 1959); Gert Krell, 'Zur Theorie der Rüstungsdynamik', in Klaus-Dieter Schwarz (ed.), *Sicherheitspolitik: Analysen zur militärischen and politischen Sicherheit*, 3rd edn (Bad Honnef: Osang, 1978).
4. Gert Krell, 'Military Doctrines, New Weapons Systems, and Arms Control', *Bulletin of Peace Proposals*, no. 1 (1979); Dieter Senghaas, *Abschreckung und Frieden: Studien zur Kritik organisierter Friedlosigkeit* (Frankfurt: Europaische Verlagsanst, 1972), pp. 106-230; and Carl-Friedrich V. Weizsäcker, *Kriegsfolgen und Kriegsverhütung* (München: Hanser, 1971), particularly the studies by Horst Afheldt, Afheldt and Roth and Afheldt and Sonntag.
5. Junne, note 2, pp. 145ff.
6. The non-nuclear constellation can be translated in the game-theoretical matrix in Matrix 1.

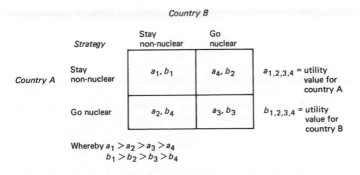

Whereby $a_1 > a_2 > a_3 > a_4$
$b_1 > b_2 > b_3 > b_4$

MATRIX 1

7. Anatol Rapoport, *Two-Person Game Theory: The Essential Ideas* (Ann Arbor: The University of Michigan Press, 1966).
8. Richard Wilson, 'How to Have Nuclear Power Without Weapons Proliferation', *Bulletin of Atomic Scientist* (November 1977), says one week is the critical time-span needed to build the bomb, if weapons-grade plutonium and non-nuclear parts are already available.
9. As described by Norman Gall, 'Atoms for Brazil, Dangers for All', *Foreign Policy* (Summer 1976) pp. 155-202.
10. The semi-nuclear or one-sided situation can be translated into Matrix 2

Nuclear have (b)

Strategy	Behave peacefully	Threat
Nuclear have-not (a) Stay non-nuclear	a_1, b_1	a_4, b_2
Go nuclear	a_2, b_4	a_3, b_3

Whereby $a_2 < a_1 < a_3 < a_4$
$b_2 < b_1 < b_3 < b_4$

MATRIX 2

11. George Quester, *Nuclear Diplomacy*, 2nd edn. (New York: Dunellen, 1973) pp. 9-44. The relationship between the security dilemma, government perceptions, and nuclear armament in the Soviet case is noted by Robert Jervis, 'Minimizing Misperception', in G. Mathew Bonham and Michael J. Shapiro (eds), *Though and Action in Foreign Policy* (Basel and Stuttgart: Birkhauser, 1977) pp. 181ff.
12. The renunciation of the defence agreement with Taiwan by the US Government, if accomplished without secret guarantees, runs some risk that the Taiwanese élites now will try to acquire a nuclear weapons capability.
13. For the English and French positions, see George Quester, *The Politics of Nuclear Proliferation* (Baltimore: Johns Hopkins University Press, 1973).
14. Henry A. Kissinger, *American Foreign Policy,* 3rd edn (New York: Norton, 1977) p. 60, writes: 'China gained more in real military power through the acquisition of nuclear weapons than if it had conquered all of Southeast Asia. If the Soviet Union had occupied Western Europe but had remained without nuclear weapons, it would be less powerful than it is now with its existing nuclear arsenal within its present borders'.
15. *Oil Fields as Military Objectives: A Feasibility Study,* prepared for the Special Subcommittee on Investigations of the House Committee on International Relations by the Congressional Research Service (Washington, DC, 1975).
16. Ted Robert Gurr, *Why Men Rebel* (Princeton University Press, 1971).

17. See the excellent study by Ashok Kapur, *India's Nuclear Option: Atomic Diplomacy and Decision Making* (New York: Praeger, 1976).
18. Thomas C. Schelling, 'Who will have the Bomb?', *International Security* (Summer 1976) pp. 77-91.
19. William H. Kincade, 'Banning Nuclear Tests: Cold Feet in the Carter Administration', *Bulletin of the Atomic Scientists* (November, 1978) pp. 8-10.
20. John R. Lamarsh, *On the Extraction of Plutonium from Reactor Fuel by Small and/or Developing Nations,* report prepared for the Congressional Research Service of the Library of Congress, 19 July 1976.

Part II
New Candidates for the Nuclear Club

4 The Garrison States

PIERRE LELLOUCHE

The study of the proliferation incentives and disincentives of those internationally isolated countries known as the 'garrison' or 'pariah' states opens a new but difficult avenue in non-proliferation research. The approach is new in so far as it runs counter to the 'classic' trends of strategic thinking about the spread of nuclear weapons. While nuclear proliferation has traditionally been envisaged either as a purely national problem which needs to be solved on a case-by-case basis or as a global phenomenon requiring a global solution, the garrison states approach develops a 'group theory of proliferation'.[1] The aim will be to identify a group of states that share a similar set of politico-military characteristics, which in turn may be the crucial links to the nuclear option.

Further, while much of the recent non-proliferation literature resulting from the 1974 Indian nuclear test has given priority to technico-economic barriers as the most effective anti-proliferation tools, the garrison states approach emphasizes the fundamental importance of proliferation motives over technical capabilities. Also underlined is the crucial role of politico-military disincentives as the basis for an effective non-proliferation policy.[2] In short, this approach is meant to focus on those states which are the 'hard cases' in terms of elaborating and implementing a non-proliferation strategy.

In so doing, our purpose is not to perform yet another exercise of academic curiosity or to propose a new typology in the theory of international relations, in addition to the numerous classifications already introduced, such as 'pariah states', 'outlaw states', 'crazy states', or 'paranoids' and 'pygmies'.[3]

The analysis of the garrison states' proliferation incentives and disincentives is warranted for two important reasons. First, this analysis is needed because of the importance of these states to the success or failure of global non-proliferation efforts; failure to control

63

proliferation decisions by desperate garrison states could indeed trigger the long-dreaded 'nuclear domino effect', or legitimize the nuclear ambitions of other potential proliferators, ending in the total breakdown of the existing international nuclear regime.[4]

Second, this approach is also meant to redress some crucial 'fallacies of emphasis' which pervade much of traditional western thinking about the entire non-proliferation issue, and in particular, about 'what causes the threat, who the candidates for proliferation are, and what strategies are applicable to such candidates'.[5] Too often is the past, eager proliferation opponents in the West have tended to propose non-proliferation strategies which, by relying upon global compromises and a series of 'technical fixes', have carefully avoided addressing the key issues raised by those 'hard cases'. This reluctance to face up to the full issue of non-proliferation is easily understood, for it is much easier to concentrate on weapons-related capabilities than on political, psychological and security incentives. Had the latter issues been squarely addressed, the self-contradictory aspects and the present-day limits of these traditional western non-proliferation 'strategies' would have clearly revealed themselves.

By focusing on the difficult issues raised by the garrison states' incentives to acquire nuclear weapons, this paper therefore attempts to clarify the current international controversy about non-proliferation while showing the limits to what can be done by way of managing these hard cases.[6]

THE GARRISON STATES

Defining 'garrison status' involves analysing the phenomenon of isolation in international relations. Rather than attempting to search for a scientifically 'tight' definition of garrison states, the purpose here is to present a set of minimum criteria which provide a common denominator for garrison status. Though imperfect and empirical, these criteria relate to both the physical characteristics of the state itself (size, power) and to the process of international isolation which it is subjected to. First, garrison states are generally small and relatively weak nations, outnumbered by their surrounding adversaries. Unlike the USSR or the Peoples' Republic of China (PRC), which for a long period had also been subjected to exclusion from the international community but still succeeded in regaining their place in the community of nations by the sheer weight of their human and physical resources, garrison states are particularly vulnerable to international isolation because of their limited size and resources. The 'modern' garrison state cannot hope to reverse, by itself alone, the process of international ostracism to which it is subjected. Indeed, its dependence on outside sources of support and protection can only be expected to increase as the process of isolation deepens.

The reasons for international isolation vary widely according to particular cases as well as periods in history. The common denominator is that these reasons relate to the very legitimacy of the state, by involving the origins of that nation, its policies or both. International isolation may result from moral considerations related to the nature of the state's political system (South Africa's apartheid); the ethnic structure of the state (Israel, South Africa); repeated violations of international behavioural norms (Israel's occupation of Arab territories); as well as the threat of security isolation, (i.e. Taiwan, and to a lesser degree South Africa and the Republic of Korea (ROK).

Garrison status is the end result of a *process* in which a majority of nations progressively rejects certain members of the community by denying their legitimacy as states.[7] The process of international isolation cannot, however, be fully explained by external factors alone. Of particular importance is the psychological or perceptual dimension of isolation which manifests itself within certain states and which may, in some cases, lead to a phenomenon of self-isolation. In the case of Pakistan, for example, where no severe diplomatic isolation exists, the persistence of a potential (and sometimes actual) threat by superior adversaries (India, USSR) had led to the development of a siege mentality of great influence in the country's perception of the outside world. This 'paranoid mood' led successive Pakistani Governments to alienate their main sources of outside support, such as the United States (for military aid) and France (for nuclear cooperation).[8]

A further criterion involves the *scope* of international isolation. By contrast to a great number of states which have been subjected to regional isolation (Chile, Cambodia, and Uganda, among others), garrison states are subjected to global isolation. Over time, an isolation which was originally limited to a regional situation (i.e., the creation of Israel, South Africa, South Korea, Taiwan and Pakistan) turns into a global phenomenon in which rejection and hostility are progressively supported by a growing number of states external to the region.

This phenomenon is aggravated by the fact that all of the states mentioned above are not only smaller but also, in reality or subjectively, isolated in comparison to the powers or combination of powers that they face. This unfavourable geostrategic setting serves to worsen the security implications of isolation by rendering more fragile the lines of potential outside support in case of emergency.[9]

The *nature* of international isolation is another defining factor. Cumulative political and military isolation is typical. Already in a precarious security position in terms of political or territorial integrity, garrison states suffer further from the lack of reliable security assurances from foreign powers. Where such assistance does exist, the guarantor's commitment appears to shrink and unravel over time as the garrison state's international isolation deepens.[10]

Military isolation differs in degree. Pakistan, while a party to several security pacts, enjoys no protection from a foreign guarantor as against its Indian adversary; however, it still receives military hardware from several suppliers.[11] The Republic of China (ROC) and the ROK, which have long benefited from a US security guarantee, have seen in recent years a gradual loss in the credibility and effectiveness of such protection. One step further in military isolation is Israel, which is not protected by a formal US commitment, while its crucial weapons imports have been reduced to this unique supplier. Finally, South Africa may be the symbol of complete military isolation with no security guarantees in force and the recent imposition of a UN arms embargo.

Also important is the time factor. Garrison status arises from the *persistence* of a conflictual relationship and international isolation over a long period of time, which in turns gives rise to certain special characteristics. Among these is the development of the psychological syndrome of a besieged state (i.e. the 'Masada complex') which dominates all aspects of the nation's cultural and political life.[12] Similarly, the continuous war effort imposes a permanent and overwhelming strain on the garrison state's economic life.[13]

Five countries appear now to share these minimum criteria and can presently be identified as garrison states, namely: Israel, South Africa, South Korea, Taiwan, and Pakistan.[14]

THE TEMPTATION OF NUCLEAR WEAPONS

Analysis of garrison state proliferation incentives raises several complex questions:

Are garrison states more likely than others to go nuclear?

What particular motivations are at work in a garrison state's decision to acquire nuclear weapons?

Are security incentives alone sufficient to lead to the nuclear option?

Would the acquisition of nuclear weapons effectively enhance the security of garrison states?

Would such acquisition improve the political status of these states or, on the contrary, aggravate their political isolation?

A preliminary answer to these questions may already be available to the extent that some of the existing nuclear weapon states were in a garrison situation when they decided to go nuclear.

Of the six current nuclear weapon states, at least three can be considered to have been in certain respects in a garrison situation at the time of their 'proliferation' – the USSR, the Peoples Republic of China (PRC) and India.[15] In the immediate post war period, the USSR was both politically isolated in a community of western-aligned nations and militarily vulnerable to the US nuclear monopoly.[16] Similarly, the PRC, excluded from the rest of the world after the 1949 revolution, was also subjected to direct atomic threats from the United States both during the Korea War and the Quemoy and Matsu crisis.[17] Moreover, for ideological reasons, both states chose to insulate themselves from the rest of the world, deepening the international ostracism. India, though a leading nation in the Third World, had directly experienced the military threat of its numerically superior neighbour, China. After 1964, India perceived the Chinese nuclear capability as a direct threat which could not be counterbalanced by Nerhu's philosophy of non-alignment.[18] The fact that no effective security guarantees could be obtained from the Great Powers was in itself a form of international isolation comparable to that of Pakistan today.[19]

Yet the USSR, China, and India are physically large states. The USSR and China in particular, possess significant territorial space, important military capabilities, manpower, and other key resources which successfully deterred adventures by superior adversaries or neighbours even before their accession to the Nuclear Club. Moreover, despite their political and military isolation and their paranoid mood, all three states also had ambitious ideological and political goals, which went beyond that of mere survival. Prestige considerations thus played a considerable role in their nuclear decisions, together with strong security incentives. Both the USSR and the PRC had to show to the rest of the world that the vanguard states of communism were in no way inferior to the capitalists, even in the sophisticated technology of nuclear weapons.[20] Similarly, India, aiming at the leadership of the emerging Third World, had to prove that a poor 'developing nation' could also take part in the nuclear race.[21] Though the USSR, China, and India clearly shared several characteristics of garrison status, their situation was in no way as extreme or desperate as that of current garrison states.

In looking at the situation of today's garrison states, it is necessary to examine whether a mixture of political and security incentives is still at work, or whether in a 'perfect' garrison situation, proliferation presures derive from survival considerations alone. Another crucial question is whether garrison status alone is conducive to nuclear proliferation or whether the opponent's actual or possible resort to nuclear weapons is a necessary condition of exercising the nuclear option. While directly relevant to three garrison states which do not directly face a nuclear opponent, i.e. Israel, the ROK and South Africa, this question cannot easily be answered. Two observations are pertinent, however:

> Where there is no garrison status, the existence of some nuclear threat (however remote or indirect) provides a 'security ablibi' for those states which desire nuclear weapons for political purposes (i.e. France and the United Kingdom (UK).[22]
> Where garrison status does exist, the occurence of a nuclear threat serves to exacerbate pressures to nuclear proliferation. In such a case, the emergence of a nuclear rival can act as a *trigger* for all previous and perhaps latent motivations and pressures leading to the exercise of the nuclear option.[23]

In assessing the benefits derived by the USSR, the PRC, and India from their decisions to acquire nuclear weapons, the interpretation of the complex balance-sheet of political and military advantages is entirely dominated by *perceptions*, rather than by facts. Politically, nuclear weapons seem to have helped a great deal in ending the isolation of the two communist nations, while allowing all three states to register important prestige gains in the international arena and to speed up the process of their re-integration at no political cost to them.[24] The lesson that proliferation so far has been, not only politically advantageous, but also a cost-free decision, may have been learned in many capitals of the world.

Security benefits offer an even clearer case of the divergence between reality and perception. Looking at military facts alone, it appears that one nuclear test is far from enough to guarantee one's security. The USSR China, and India all had to face the problem of establishing a credible nuclear force and strategy. The Soviets achieved credibility after enormous effort was committed for a long period to the strategic arms race. China also remained for a very long time extremely vulnerable to a preemptive attack from the US or the USSR and is only beginning now to attain credibility.[25] India still has to solve its own strategic dilemma: should a nuclear weapons programme be launched, New Delhi would have to decide how much is enough to deter a Chinese attack effectively. Nevertheless, once a minimum nuclear capability achieves credibility, as in the case of China, the overall security posture may be perceived as having been improved by the introduction of nuclear weapons. The costs of conflict are raised in the eyes of actual or potential opponents and this is recognized in the garrison state perceptions of their security.

Perhaps the most important lesson to be learned from past experiences, is thus that political and military incentives for atomic weapons are primarily dominated by perceptions, not by reality. This may be all the more the case when one is dealing with desperate garrison nations.

NUCLEAR PROLIFERATION INCENTIVES TODAY

Security incentives. Distinguishing between those garrison states confronted with a direct nuclear threat (whether real of perceived) such as Taiwan and Pakistan, and those facing a purely conventional menace, such as Israel, South Africa, and South Korea, is necessary in addressing the question of whether garrison status alone is conducive to nuclear weapons, or whether an opponent's nuclear capability is a necessary condition of going nuclear.

Though the security position of Taiwan was demonstrably altered by the normalization of relations between the United States and the PRC in December 1978 and the consequent abrogation of the Washington-Taipei mutual security treaty, US protection for its offshore ally had been deteriorating in an ambiguous way at least since 1971, when the Sino-American rapprochment began.[26] The effect of developments since the end of 1978 has been to exacerbate, not initiate, the dilemma of Taiwanese security. The progressive American disengagement from South East Asia after the Vietnamese War had considerably reduced the geostrategic importance of Taiwan in American policy. The Carter Administration, though not endorsing direct weapon sales to the PRC had openly supported European arms sales to Peking, including presumably the British sale of Harrier fighter aircraft.[27] These developments are part of a profound shift in the Soviet-American-Chinese triangle which has significant consequences for Taiwan.

While the defunct US-Taiwan security agreement, reinforced by American actions over Quemoy and Matsu in 1958, had the effect of providing a nuclear umbrella for Taiwan, the nuclear force developed by mainland China after 1964 has never been directed toward Taiwan. Were Peking to decide to reunify its island 'province' with the mainland it would certainly not do so by means of a destructive nuclear strike. China's accession to the nuclear club did not therefore alter Taiwan's basic security problem, which was and remains fighting off a conventional invasion with inferior forces.

The security incentives for Taiwanese nuclear weapons cannot be explained, then, by a simple 'domino effect' whereby China's acquiring nuclear weapons elicits the same behaviour from Taiwan. It has been the gradual erosion of American protection which is triggering proliferation pressures in Taipei. Indeed, even if Peking had no nuclear weapons, Taiwan would have incentives to go nuclear, given the disparity in conventional forces between the mainland and the island and the withdrawal of American support from Taiwan. To the Taiwanese, nuclear weapons may seem the only possible means of compensating for the American defection and Taiwan's increasing isolation in the international community. It would be no coincidence if, as reported, Taiwan sought to develop a clandestine plutonium reprocessing plant in the early 1970s, following President Nixon's 1971 visit to China and the gradual withdrawal of US troops from Taiwan beginning in 1972.[28] The atomic force of the PRC may nevertheless represent a plausible security alibi for Taiwan, should it decide to acquire its own nuclear weapons.

While nuclear proliferation incentives thus seem understandable, it is by no means clear that nuclear weapons would automatically solve Taiwan's security problem. The nuclear forces of small powers face a basic credibility problem when confronted with large scale nuclear arsenals.[29] Taiwan, unlike France or Britain, does not enjoy the luxury of a superpower's nuclear umbrella in addition to and above its own. Moreover, in order to halt or deter an invasion from the mainland, the Taiwanese planner, even supplied with nuclear weapons, would have to solve basic strategic problems. Taiwan could choose to rely on a massive retaliation strategy, although penetration and delivery vehicles would be a major hurdle, despite repeated efforts to acquire modern nuclear-capable aircraft and to develop national ground-to-ground missile systems.[30] On the other hand, although a PRC amphibious invasion fleet headed for Taiwan 'would represent a very inviting target', Taiwan's geographic size offers even less room than the German territory for a tactical nuclear war.[31] Finally, Taiwan remains extremely vulnerable both to nuclear attack and to conventional strike, should the PRC decide to preempt Taiwan's nuclear ambitions.

From a security standpoint, then, nuclear weapons have simultaneously a very high value and a very high cost for Taiwan. The value derives from the inevitable erosion of the US security commitment which only a national nuclear arsenal could be expected to replace. The security costs are two-fold: by choosing nuclear weapons, Taiwan would directly invite a retaliatory strike by its adversary and it would also invite retaliatory steps on the part of its American protector. In view of the historical United States commitment to the cause of non-proliferation, a Taiwanese nuclear decision could, among other responses, trigger the sanctions provided for in the Non-proliferation Act of 1978.

Since 1974, *Pakistan* has faced an Indian nuclear threat in addition to India's already superior conventional forces. Despite a 1955 mutual security treaty with the United States, Pakistan did not enjoy US protection against India; neither did it possess a Chinese umbrella, nor a British one within the Central Treaty Organization (CENTO).[32]

Pakistan had strong proliferation incentives before 1974. The nuclear weapons option was perceived as the only effective means of arresting or reversing the chronic deterioration of the conventional balance of forces between Isalamabad and New Delhi, which probably caused Pakistan's rejection of the NPT.[33]

The 1974 Indian nuclear test has thus had an immediate and direct impact on Pakistan's attitude towards nuclear weapons. In contrast to China and Taiwan, the Indian proliferation immediately prompted new nuclear decisions in Pakistan. It is no coincidence that the Indian explosion was followed in a few months by the signature of a French-

Pakistani contract for the sale of a plutonium reprocessing plant to Islamabad.[34]

What deserves emphasis here is the remarkable importance of psychological factors in Pakistan's reaction, or over-reaction, to the Indian test. Islamabad reacted as if the Indians had suddenly deployed a whole arsenal of nuclear medium-range ballistic missiles (MRBMs) aimed at Pakistani cities instead of carrying out a nuclear explosion. So great is the gap between reality and perception, between actuality and anticipation, that the nuclear option has now become a national and somewhat religious crusade in Pakistan.[35] The fact that India has not constructed or deployed atomic weapons and the fact that the government of Morarji Desai pledged to stop nuclear testing appeared totally irrelevant to the Pakistani determination to acquire nuclear weapons at all costs.[36] Similarly, the fact that Indian nuclear weapons – assuming they will be built – constitute an anti-Chinese guarantee, not an anti-Pakistani force, does not seem to enter into the calculations of the Pakistani leadership. At the same time, India's proliferation provides a perfect alibi for Pakistan's own nuclear ambitions, which might explain part of the apparent Pakistani paranoia.

Again, however, the security advantages which could be derived by Pakistan from nuclear weapons are far from clear. Certainly, the 'equalizing' effect of nuclear weapons is a tempting objective for the Pakistani planner, who may well think that Pakistan could finally succeed in obtaining some credible deterrent against India's 660 million people. For the non-European, the image of the small and valiant French '*force de frappe*' which keeps the Russians at home may still remain a tempting example. With nuclear weapons at its disposal, Palistan might compensate for an inferior conventional balance of forces and attain an equal voice in the Indian sub-continent.

Yet the road to such objectives is filled with serious hurdles. In the first place, penalties could be imposed by Pakistan's adversary. A Pakistani nuclear weapons programme might immediately trigger an Indian response, either in the form of a preemptive strike (conventional or even nuclear) or in the form of a nuclear arms race. Given India's very large advantage in nuclear as well as conventional weapons technology, such a race might well condemn Pakistan to permanent nuclear inequality instead of the present conventional inequality.[37]

In addition to the risk of an Indian response, Pakistan may also have to pay an important security price as a result of retaliatory steps taken by allies and friends. US and French reactions to Pakistan's somewhat too obvious determination to acquire a French reprocessing plant have included US withdrawal of its offer to provide A-7 fighter-bombers and a cut-off economic assistance and French demands for plutonium co-processing followed by a rethinking of the contract altogether.[38]

Despite these drawbacks to pursuit of a nuclear weapons programme, the perception may yet persist in Islamabad and Taipei that, while the benefits of nuclear forces are speculative and militarily questionable and the price quite steep, the costs are manageable and the situation will not improve without the political-perceptual impact of a nuclear weapons programme. Such a belief has its precedents in the motivations of the current nuclear-weapon states.

Israel, South Africa and South Korea, on the other hand, are not confronted by nuclear rivals. They are, however, facing opponents superior either numerically or in conventional military strength. The basic security problem facing each of these states is to compensate for such inferiority by the introduction of technologically superior weapons or by relying on foreign security guarantors. At the same time, because of their political and military isolation, these states are in the worst possible position for coping with the constant deterioration of the balance of forces between themselves and their rivals. While their vital lines of weapons supplies grow more and more tenuous, the garrison states cannot count on great nations' security commitments to protect them. Indeed, where such guarantees do exist, they seem to slowly unravel while the isolaton of each garrison state grows deeper.

South Korea is perhaps the most striking example of this condition. Having already suffered a North Korean invasion, the ROK armies, while numerically superior, remain inferior to the North's in such crucial dimensions as air and armoured forces.[39]

Until recently, this unfavourable military balance was largely compensated for by constant injection of large quantities of US military aid and by a clear US commitment to the protection of the ROK.[40] Symbolized by the massive intervention of US troops during the Korean War, the American guarantee was later written into a formal defence treaty and maintained by the presence of 40,000 American soliders and 1000 US tactical nuclear weapons on South Korean soil.

This did not reassure the Seoul regime completely, however, The ROK did sign the NPT in 1968, as most faithful US allies did. Yet security considerations not only delayed Seoul's ratification until 23 April 1975, (when pressure was applied by the Ford Administration) but they also led during that same period to the launching of a secret nuclear weapons programme, which was apparently cancelled in 1975 under the same US pressure.[41] The signature of a Franco-Korean contract for the sale of a plutonium reprocessing plant to Seoul brought forth US pressure which forced cancellation of the deal in 1976.[42]

The nuclear issue became even more prominent with the announcement of US force withdrawal plan by the Carter Administration.[43] The potential threat of a nuclear South Korea became a major bargaining chip in the negotiations over the implementation of the plan.[44] In skillfully playing nuclear diplomacy, the South Korean leaders have allowed more and more vocal demands for an indigenous nuclear force in the Natonal Assembly and also announced in 1978 an enormous nuclear programme providing for 46 nuclear power plants by the year 2000.[45]

Such threats did not go unnoticed in the United States. In spite of a generally hostile attitude both in the Congress, in the American press, and in public opinion, as a result of several public scandals involving South Korean officials, the Carter Administration took a number of steps to reassure the Park government. US decisions to provide the ROK with a $2 billion military aid compensation grant, to leave a strong USAF presence, and delay some of the withdrawals originally planned illustrate the effectiveness of South Korean new nuclear diplomacy and occurred before more recent US assertions of support in the wake of President Park's death.[46]

The subtle relations between South Korea's rapid progress in nuclear technology and the implementation (or rather the delayed implementation) of the US withdrawal plan clearly show the dual-dependence relationship that now exists between a garrison state and its protector. If the Ford Administration did obtain some success in the non-proliferation sphere by delaying South Korean acquisition of sensitive nuclear technology, subsequent administrations, by contrast, had to pay for this victory in the form of an increased military commitment.

Complicating this bilateral nuclear bargaining relationship is the constant shadow of a third, but even more important, actor: Japan. In a sense, perhaps the most effective card at the disposal of the South

Korean leadership is not so much the threat of the South Korean proliferation, though it is of considerable importance, but the very real risk of Japanese proliferation resulting from it.[47] Implicitly, the US decision to withdraw from South Korea is linked not only to proliferation risks in South Korea itself, but also in Japan. The South-Korean survival problem, in spite of the ROK's isolation, is linked to an international issue of far greater geostrategic importance. The result is that American checks on Korean proliferation will likely remain effective only as long as US military personnel are physically present in South Korea.

Whether nuclear weapons would enhance South Korean security is another matter. Once again, the problem of establishing a credible nuclear force and strategy without the United States will be very hard to solve, although Seoul, unlike Taiwan, does have delivery vehicles.[48] As an equalizer of superior North Korean armies, a South Korean nuclear force could be useful to Seoul both in a tactical and a strategic mode, provided that Pyongyang does not decide to nip any such nuclear ambition by a preemptive strike on the South. As with America and Europe, and with the other cases analyzed, nuclear weapons appear to overcome disparities in conventional forces or manpower, while the fear of preemption justifies an early start on a nuclear weapons program before the presumed adversary can mobilize conventionally or undertake a nuclear weapons programme of its own. Considerations of timing could thus be crucial to South Korean or other garrison state nuclear decisions. An inhibiting factor, however, is the possible reaction of nuclear powers such as the PRC and the USSR.

These problems may, however, have very little influence on Seoul's proliferation decision, should certain triggering events occur, such as a US decision in favour of total withdrawal, followed by a period of tension along the Demilitarized Zone. In this case, the fear of invasion (Vietnam type) could overcome fear of a risky nuclear deterrent. Moreover, such a situation would provide the new leadership in Seoul with the perfect nuclear alibi set forth in Article X of the NPT.[49]

Israel's security problem has become more acute in recent years.[50] While its access to weapons has narrowed to a unique source, the United States, its opponents have become a prime market for all major weapons suppliers, including the USSR, France, the UK and the United States. With abundant oil funds, the Arab countries have been able to buy large quantities of the most modern weapons and are now in the process of acquiring the weapons technologies themselves.[51] At the same time, Israel's small economy is less and less able to sustain a comparable effort.[52] It must rely more and more on US military grants, with three consequences:

> Though, in the short term, most analysts believe that Israel enjoys a qualitative superiority over its adversaries, such superiority is mainly due to Arab deficiencies which could be corrected in the future.[53]

> With the enormous escalation of the conventional arms race in the entire Middle East since the 1973 war, there is now a possibility that Israel will not be able to sustain its effort accomplished so far and that it will be incapable of stopping or reversing the long-term deterioration of the balance of forces.

> Despite considerable effort by Israel to decrease its dependence on US weapons through the development of a strong national armaments industry, the monitoring of the conventional balance of forces is out of Israeli hands. It is the US government which now decides which weapons are needed, how many of such weapons are necessary, when they are needed, and in what form they will be paid for.[54]

The danger of an asymmetrical development of the conventional arms race not only increases for Israel the temptation of a quick preemptive strike aimed at gaining time but also reinforces the need for a long-term nuclear deterrent. From an Israel perspective, such logic is all the more confirmed by the recent evolution of US diplomacy in the region. While the United States has not been willing to give more than a de facto commitment to the security of Israel, recent years have seen the United States become a major ally and arms supplier of Saudi Arabia, Sudan and, more recently, Egypt.[55]

One can therefore scarcely talk of proliferation 'incentives' in the Israeli case, since the atomic option is the only way Jerusalem can preserve a national decision-making power over its own security. Indeed, Israel already has an atomic diplomacy, although purposely veiled in a 'maybe we do, maybe we don't' posture with the repeated statement that 'Israel will not be the first to introduce atomic weapons in the Middle East'.[56]

Though not officially acknowledged by either of the two superpowers, the Middle East situation has already nuclearized, at least partially. All of the parties involved feel that Israel has the bomb and that it will use it under certain conditions.[57] If, as noted earlier, the United States is now the sole referee of the balance of forces in the region, each of its decisions in the weapons transfer area, as well as in the diplomatic game, must take into account Israel's atomic capability.

Moreover, the nuclear race has already started in the Arab world but at a much slower pace than might have been expected, perhaps because of the world wide non-proliferation efforts undertaken in recent years.[58]

In this context, it is difficult to assess the long-term effect of the Israeli nuclear capability on the country's security.[59] One scenario is that the present situation will continue, with Washington acting as the moderator of the balance of conventional forces through more and more sophisticated arms deliveries to Israel and the Arab world. In the long run, this situation will only bring a further deterioration of the balance of forces, thereby forcing Israel to clearly announce its '*force de frappe*' and its determination to use it.

Another scenario depends on the USSR. The Soviet Union is believed to have given secret nuclear security guarantees to several Arab countries in the event of overt Israeli proliferation.[60] Should Russia decide to publicize these guarantees, it could force on the United States basic and drastic choices with respect to Israel's diplomatic and security posture.[61]

Finally, the ability of the Arab states to reach the nuclear threshold, particularly Iraq and Libya, two potential garrison states which may be tempted to intervene directly in the conflict with nuclear weapons, should not be underestimated.[62]

Once again, while the indispensibility of nuclear weapons to Israel might be conceded on the grounds of its military and diplomatic isolation, there is still room for doubting that an Israeli nuclear arsenal (whether official or not) would safeguard the security of the country in the long run.

Prior to *South Africa's* aborted Kalahari nuclear test affair in 1977, most observers, while considering Pretoria a serious nuclear aspirant, thought that proliferation incentives could be checked from within by the simple argument that South African nuclear weapons would serve no military purpose, in view of the country's overwhelming conventional superiority over its adversaries.[63] While partially correct, this assessment misses two basic points: (1) nuclear proliferation incentives have, in the South African case, a profound psychological and symbolic nature which has to be distinguished from the existing military balance and (2) Pretoria's strategic posture has considerably worsened in recent years as a result of external factors, thereby increasing the purely military value of nuclear weapons.

Indeed, Pretoria's incentives for nuclear weapons have long had a psychological element distinct from the existing military balance. South Africa's early interest in nuclear technology (1946) reveals a permanent concern to keep all options open, no matter how strong the country was in conventional military forces. An interesting coincidence exists between each phase of the South African nuclear programme and the politico-military evolution of Black Africa.[64] South Africa's breakthrough in uranium enrichment technology coincided with the fall of Portugal's colonial empire.[65] Similarly, the Kalahari test affair occurred when the UN arms embargo against Pretoria was being prepared. It thus appears that South African nuclear capacity is primarily aimed at intimidation of non-nuclear Black Africa and making the West pay attention to Pretoria.[66] A further aim is to reassure a beleaguered white population by guaranteeing the permanent character of the South African state in its present form.

New nuclear incentives have recently arisen as a result of the deterioration of Pretoria's security posture due to: (1) the fall of the last white bastions in Portugal's colonies and Rhodesia; (2) the UN arms embargo; and (3) the military penetration of the USSR and Cuba in the African continent, and, in particular, in areas neighbouring Namibia and South Africa's territory. These external events have transformed latent proliferation pressures into immediate military choices. At the same time, however, the strategic equation to be solved with nuclear weapons has also become more complex.

In the present situation, the main threat still remains that of protracted guerrilla warfare within South Africa's borders. Though the utility of nuclear weapons remains low, such weapons could be an effective means of intimidation with respect to those African nations which assist the guerrillas. If the ambiguous radiation phenomenon in the waters south of Capetown in 1979 proved to be a South African test of a low-yield weapon in the two-kiloton range, then it is possible Pretoria is considering tactical nuclear weapons for use against guerrilla concentrations and bases.[67] With a further growth in Soviet and Cuban involvement in the region, the likelihood of heavy conventional warfare between Pretoria and African nations massively supported by communist hardware and personnel might become a reality. South Africa's conventional forces would face for the first time the risk of qualitative inferiority, in addition to their chronic numerical weakness. Nuclear weapons may well become a tempting and even an effective military answer for targets such as the concentrations of communist-supplied armour used by Ethiopia against Somalia. Perhaps the most immediate result of Soviet-Cuban military intervention in Africa has been to enhance the justification of South African nuclear weapons. While various worst case scenarios can be imagined to rationalize Pretoria's steady progress toward a nuclear weapons capability, none of them seem especially plausible and the actual military effectiveness of nuclear weapons in this region – as distinguished from their deterrent or intimidation value – is likely to remain dubious.

Table 4.1 summarizes the preceding discussion, from which several tentative lessons may be drawn.

First, in each of the five garrison states there has been a general increase in the perceived security value of national nuclear weapons, a phenomenon which seems directly related to deterioration of these states' security posture. Such a deterioration is due to a variety of factors, including the reduced protection, real or perceived, afforded by a foreign protector, direct actions by a hostile superpower, and the enhanced military capability of local opponents. As the perception of threat grows and neither military manpower nor conventional weaponry appear capable of meeting it, nuclear weapons are likely to seem attractive equalizers, much as they did in the West in the 1940s and 1950s when numerical communist superiority in manpower and conventional arms provided a powerful impetus or rationale for going nuclear.

Second, despite the increase in perceived value, nuclear weapons pose troublesome questions in terms of their actual military effectiveness. In addition to unresolved technical issues, such as the number and quality of available nuclear weapons and delivery systems, the existence of secure command and control arrangements, and the penetration and survival capacity of these nuclar forces, other problems are the tactical or strategic rationale for nuclear weapons, the potential reactions of hostile nuclear power, and the risks of adverse reactions by foreign protectors. However, if, as the experience of the current nuclear weapon states seems to demonstrate, the politico-military value of nuclear weapons is not closely tied to their actual military 'usability' or to technically credible forces and doctrines, then these issues of adverse reaction and military utility may pale in comparison to the appeal of having a nuclear equalizer, however crude.

Third, keeping the nuclear option open – or introducing the weapons in a clandestine or quasi-clandestine manner – is generally beneficial to the garrison states' security posture. Maintaining and reinforcing this option has proved to be an effective bargaining tool for extracting conventional arms supplies and continued security or other commitments from foreign protectors and in complicating the calculations of adversaries.

TABLE 4.1   Nuclear weapons and the security of garrison states

Country	NPT status	Type of security threat	State of military balance	Security guarantees in force	Opponent's security guarantees	Expected type of nuclear strategy
Israel	No	Conventional	Not favourable (long term)	No	Conventional (possibly nuclear?)	Defence against invasion Weapon of last resort
S. Africa	No	Conventional	Not favourable (long term)	No	Conventional (US and USSR security agreements with several Black African states)	Intimidation of non-nuclear rivals Weapon of last resort
S. Korea	Yes	Conventional	Not favourable (without US)	Nuclear (US troops and tactical nuclear weapons)	Conventional (possibly nuclear?)	Defence against invasion Weapon of last resort
Taiwan	Yes	Conventional and nuclear	Not favourable	(US weapons supplies)	(PRC)	Defence against invasion Deterrence Weapon of last resort
Pakistan	No	Conventional and nuclear	Not favourable	No	(India) (conventional – USSR)	Deterrence

POLITICAL INCENTIVES

Political prestige and international influence are conventionally considered to be among the major incentives for nuclear weapons proliferation. While such motives *per se* are largely irrelevent for the garrison states, it is worthwhile examining whether nuclear weapons may be a useful tool to force upon the international community some sort of recognition and re-integration. The experiences of the USSR and the PRC which were long isolated from the world community, may not be without meaning to the leaders of today's garrison states. The Soviet Union clearly perceives that nuclear weaponry has played a major role in its present international status. Chinese nuclear strength forced the recognition of the PRC by the West after 1964, a first step towards Peking's full membership in the UN. Thus, commanding respect and fear, if not attracting friendship, may provide a powerful political motivation for acquiring nuclear weapons. The possible political incentives for the garrison states are portrayed in Table 4.2.

South Africa, whose isolation is near-total (just short of outright exclusion from the UN), might deem an overt nuclear capability the only way to exist in a hostile environment. Nations such as Taiwan or South Korea may find nuclear weapons attractive as a means to demonstrate their 'national viability', independence, and military and technological power.[68] India is another case in point. The attitudes of the major powers underwent a sudden change after the nuclear test on 18 May 1974. The 'benign neglect' policy of the United States and others gave way to a more equal relationship.[69] Israel's *de facto* nuclear diplomacy has shown results, in terms of separate peace negotiations with Egypt, continued supplies of weapons, and the continued US commitment to non-recognition of the Palestine Liberation Organization (PLO).

A 'proliferated world' consisting of nuclear garrison states may thus confront the superpowers with a host of new diplomatic problems. Atomic blackmail is not reserved to subnational groups alone.[70] A beleaguered garrison state could use a nuclear threat as a means of extracting a favourable diplomatic settlement from the superpowers, a settlement which would otherwise have been impossible.

One possible drawback to these political benefits could be a backlash of international public opinion which would aggravate a garrison state's political isolation. Yet, when a state has reached a stage of total or near-total isolation in the world community, such a

TABLE 4.2   Nuclear weapons and the political isolation of garrison states

Country	Degree of political isolation	Political benefits from nuclear weapons	Political costs of nuclear weapons	Expected type of proliferation	NPT status
Israel	High	Bargaining tool with US Intimidation	Risk of break-down in US support Aggravation of isolation	Quasi-clandestine	No
S. Africa	Very high	Intimidation Domestic political gains Bargaining tool with superpowers		Open or quasi-clandestine	No
S. Korea	High	Bargaining tool with US Intimidation Domestic political gains	Risk of break-down in US support	Clandestine or or quasi-clandestine	Yes
Taiwan	Very high	Bargaining tool with US Domestic political gains	Risk of break-down in US support	Clandestine or quasi-clandestine	Yes
Pakistan	Increasing	Influence on subcontinent Domestic political gains		Open	No

state is likely to ignore the reaction of the rest of the world. Indeed, a state is most vulnerable to political constraints when it is an integral part of the international arena. South Africa, already considered an 'outlaw state', would not submit to the same political protests which eventually halted the French atmospheric nuclear testing in the Pacific.[71] An outlaw state can, and is even expected to, violate international behavioural norms.

Hence, the most effective political restraint arises from the relationship between the garrison state and its ally, guarantor or foreign source of support, not from international public opinion. This restraint, however, does not affect the nuclear option itself, but rather the way in which such an option is played. In the cases of Taiwan, South Korea and Israel, the need to preserve vital weapons supplies will likely inhibit any announcement of the acquisition or intent to acquire nuclear weapons. None of these states would take the risk of losing whatever is left of the US commitment for the possible political benefits of demonstrating their capabilities either in a nuclear weapon test or by a decision to launch an overt military nuclear programme. Thus, these three countries would be forced to follow a clandestine or quasi-clandestine proliferation route, at least as long as the US commitment continues to be valid. This appears to be confirmed by periodic reports of these countries clandestine nuclear weapons programmes.[72]

The isolated status of a garrison state may allow it to exploit the concerns of the international community in other, more subtle ways. Though it was widely claimed at the time that joint US-Soviet political pressure in August 1977 prevented South Africa from conducting an atmospheric nuclear explosion in the Kalahari Desert, superpower action may have had the effect of publicly acknowledging South Africa's nuclear weapons potential, without Pretoria having to pay any significant political price for the deterrent value of this recognition.

Pakistan is in a somewhat intermediate position between dependence on a single supplier or guarantor and the total absence of foreign support. Islamabad receives conventional weapons from various sources and thus enjoys some flexibility.[73] Pakistan was able to reject US non-proliferation pressures, including the 'carrot' offered by the Ford Administration in the form of 100 A-7 fighter-bombers. On the other hand, in the nuclear field, Pakistan is totally dependent on France for the delivery of nuclear fuel reprocessing technology. Pakistan appeared to be in a very vulnerable position when France decided in 1978 to modify its original contract to include 'co-processing.' The French reversal was largely due to the evolution of the international community's perception of the nuclear proliferation issue and shows that garrison states, even when they are free from bilateral alliance relationships, can be vulnerable indirectly to changes in international behavioural norms. Such a vulnerability requires, however, a common front by all suppliers of arms and nuclear technology, a condition which is not easily fulfilled.

In terms of garrison states' proliferation incentives, then, political considerations appear to be of far less importance than security incentives. In particular, 'classic' political motives, such as prestige, which are commonly found to influence some nuclear aspirants, do not seem to affect the behaviour of garrison states, except perhaps as a secondary, reinforcing, or residual motivation. Moreover, such prestige as might accrue from possession of nuclear weapons or the capacity to make them seems directed more toward intimidation and deterring security threats than toward re-integration in the international community. Finally, the greatest political value of nuclear weapons or the nuclear option seems to lie in their utility as bargaining chips for influencing foreign protectors or the attitudes of the larger global community.

By contrast, the potential political costs of nuclear weapons, though probably insufficient to reverse the drive to acquire nuclear weapons, do affect the way in which this drive is managed, as well as the timing of nuclear decisions. The political costs of going nuclear can lead to covert or unacknowledged military nuclear programmes or to delaying such initiatives. The political price of acquiring nuclear weapons is highest where garrison states remain dependent on a superpower. When no such relationship exists, the costs of going nuclear are less and hence external political sanctions are much less effective and considerably more difficult to achieve.

The proliferation incentives of the garrison states may prove so strong in each case that classic methods advocated to stop the spread of nuclear weaponry, particularly technical-economic barriers, seem to be ineffective. The first task, then, is to determine in what area and in what form, if any, successful non-proliferation constraints could be applied. In order to establish what type of non-proliferation efforts might be undertaken, the following vulnerability chart (Table 4.3) displays the effects of three categories of possible non-proliferation constraints on each garrison state:

> *Classic non-proliferation strategies* are usually applied to the entire world community. These methods are technical-economic barriers, such as the London Suppliers' Group export regulations and IAEA or bilateral nuclear safeguards, as well as arms control measures. The latter are either global (i.e., SALT, which is aimed in part at reducing the discrimination between nuclear-weapon states and non-nuclear weapon states in the NPT framwork) or regional (i.e., regional nuclear weapons-free zones and curbs on weapons sales).
>
> *Internal constraints* derive from the particular situation of the

garrison state itself and relate to the technological and economic level achieved by the state and to its particular security situation. Internal constraints could be accentuated by external actors, in particular, an ally or guarantor.

Sanctions have never been explicitly used in a non-proliferation context, nor are they provided for in the Non-proliferation Treaty. More recently, however, sanctions were introduced in the multilateral London Suppliers Group guidelines and in the US Nuclear Non-proliferation Act of 1978 (NNPA).[74]

TABLE 4.3   Vulnerability of garrison states to non-proliferation constraints

Disincentives and constraints upon proliferation	Vulnerability to non-proliferation constraints					Possible adverse effects
	Israel	South Africa	South Korea	Taiwan	Pakistan	
1. *Classic non-proliferation strategies*						
A. Technical and economic barriers						
Suppliers' restrictive export policies on sensitive equipment	No	No	High	No	High	Risk of creation of 'nuclear black market' among garrison states.
Safeguards	No	No	No	No	No	
Multilateral nuclear arrangements	No	No	No	No	No	
B. Moral Suasion	No	No	No	No	No	
C. Arms Control						
Global arms control	No	No	No	No	No	
Regional arms control:						
Nuclear free zones	No	No	No	No	No	Risk of accelerated deterioration of
Limitation of arms transfers	High	No	High	High	High	balance of forces – increase of security incentives to proliferation
No first use pledges	No	No	No	No	No	
2. *Internal constraints*						
A. Technical and economic constraints						
Cost	No	No	No	No	No	
Limited technological base	No	No	No	No	High	
Dependence on foreign nuclear inputs	No	No	High	No	High	
B. Security constraints						
Risk of opponent's proliferation	High	No	High	–	–	
Risk of involvement of hostile nuclear power	High	High	High	–	–	Risk of clandestine or quasi-clandestine types
Risk of breakdown of alliance relationship	High	No	High	High	No	of proliferation with the resulting
Problems of developing a credible nuclear strategy	High	High	High	High	High	complication for overall non-proliferation efforts.

continued overleaf

TABLE 4.3 – *continued*

Disincentives and constraints upon proliferation	Vulnerability to non-proliferation constraints					Possible adverse effects
	Israel	South Africa	South Korea	Taiwan	Pakistan	
3. *Sanctions*						
A. Multilateral (UN sanctions)						
Economic sanctions	High	High	High	High	High	If not applied, could
Arms embargo	High	No	High	High	High	accelerate breakdown
Cut-off nuclear material and						of NPT system and
assistance	No	No	High	No	High	international
						safeguards. Would
						reinforce proliferation
						incentives in other
						near-nuclear countries.
Military intervention	High	High	High	High	High	Unlikely. Could
						precipitate use of
						nuclear weapons by
						garrison states.
B. Bilateral sanctions (from ally or guarantor)						
Breakdown security guarantees	High	No	High	High	No	Could, if applied, in-
Arms embargo	High	No	High	High	No	crease desperation in
Cut-off nuclear materials and						garrison state involved.
Assistance	No	No	High	No	High	May precipitate use of
Cut-off economic and						nuclear weapons as
diplomatic support	High	No	High	High	No	warning.

Classic non-proliferation strategies. Table 4.3 shows that classic non-proliferation strategies are not very helpful in deterring garrison states from going nuclear. Moreover the implementation of such strategies may also have disruptive or adverse effects. External constraints on the garrison states' technical capabilities in the 'sensitive' parts of the fuel cycle (i.e., enrichment and reprocessing) appear to be only partially effective. Three of the five garrison states are already beyond the reach of such restraints. Israel, South Africa and Taiwan have achieved the indigenous technological capability necessary for the production of weapons-grade nuclear materials in the form of enrichment facilities in South Africa and Israel and small spent fuel reprocessing facilities in Taiwan and Israel, as shown in Table 4.4. Only South Korea and Pakistan are vulnerable to the London Suppliers Group guidelines on nuclear exports, which require the suppliers to 'exercise restraint in the transfer' of plutonium reprocessing plants and other 'sensitive facilities.'[75]

The guidelines, however, do not apply to the French-Pakistani reprocessing agreement because it was signed before the guidelines were adopted. Yet France's decision to modify the plant promised to

TABLE 4.4 Nuclear capabilities of garrison states

Country	NPT Status	Uranium deposits	Research reactors		Power reactors		Enrichment facilities		Reprocessing facilities		Bomb potential[a] (years)
			In operation	Planned operation	In operation	Planned operation	In operation	Planned operation	In operation	Planned operation	
Israel	No	Yes	2	2	1	–	1[b]	1[b]	1[c]	1[c]	0
S. Africa	No	Yes	2	2	2	–	2	1[d]	–	–	0
S. Korea	Yes	Yes	1	1	46	1	–	–	1	–	4-6
Taiwan	Yes	No	2	2	6	2	–	–	2[e]	1[e]	0-3
Pakistan	No	Yes	1	1	26[f]	1	–	–	1	–	4-6

[a] Based on ERDA estimates (April 1977), in *Nuclear Proliferation Factbook*, US Congress, September 1977, p. 334.
[b] Laboratory scale facility, possibly using laser enrichment technology. See Todd Friedman, 'Israel's Nuclear Option', *Bulletin of the Atomic Scientists* (September 1974) pp. 31-2.
[c] Laboratory scale facility. See Harkavy, 'The Pariah State Syndrome', op. cit., p. 647.
[d] This pilot facility located at Valindaba has been operating since 1976. It will be turned into an industrial plant (size unknown) according to a recent decision of the South African Government. See *The Financial Times*, 23 December 1977; *Le Monde*, 15 February 1978.
[e] These installations are laboratory scale facilities. See *Nuclear Proliferation Factbook*, op. cit., p. 198. They were apparently dismantled on US request. See *SIPRI Yearbook 1977*, p. 48.
[f] See 'Industry Report 1976-1977', *Nuclear News* (February 1977).

Islamabad to include 'co-processing' does create a new set of political problems for Pakistan. Technically, however, it would be erroneous to overestimate the value of 'co-processing' as a proliferation-resistant 'technical fix.' Co-processing does not eliminate plutonium but simply mixes it with various highly radioactive elements to render the separation of the resulting mixture more difficult. Yet the mixture obtained from a co-processing unit can be chemically separated to obtain pure plutonium.[76] Should Pakistan accept the co-processing plant now offered by France, it would be able to obtain substantial quantities of a plutonium mixture which could be chemically separated at a later stage. What co-processing thus does is to delay acquisition of fissile material without affecting the bomb potential of the recipient state. Were France to decide to cancel the entire contract, Pakistan would find itself considerably slowed down in its plutonium programme, despite the fact that all the blueprints for the reprocessing plant have already been provided by the French and that, presumably, Pakistan could build the plant on its own at a slower place.[77] Thus, of the five garrison states, South Korea is the only one which is really hurt by the suppliers' restraint policy with regard to the transfer of reprocessing technology. However, in view of South Korea's large technological base and its earlier secret efforts in this field, it is quite possible that South Korea possesses the means to develop an indigenous reprocessing technology.

Similarly, the effectiveness of IAEA safeguards in checking the garrison states' proliferation potential is also open to question. The effect of safeguards is lowest in the Israeli and South African cases since their sensitive facilities are not safeguarded.[78] It is unlikely that either government would accept in the future the concept of full-scope safeguards (covering all nuclear facilities) advocated by the United States. On the other hand, both Taiwan and South Korea, whose nuclear programmes are heavily dependent on US nuclear cooperation, would have to submit to the full-scope safeguards condition provided for in the US nuclear Non-Proliferation Act of 1978. Failure to accept this condition requires a cut-off of all US nuclear aid, including the supply of nuclear fuel, which would have substantial consequences for the entire spectrum of political and security relations between the United States and these Asian natons.

It is understood that Pakistan's plutonium reprocessing plant would be subjected to a trilateral safeguard agreement involving the IAEA, Pakistan, and France.[79] This amounts to a full-scope safeguard situation, since Pakistan's Candu reactor is already subject to international safeguards. As in the other cases, technical checks may help to buy time; they fail, however, to address the garrison states' security and political motives for acquiring nuclear weapons.[80]

Moral suasion has also been advocated as a non-proliferation instrument but in the garrison states' desperate security situation, moral arguments are likely to have very little effect.[81]

Arms control efforts are a different and more complex matter. Global arms control efforts among nuclear-weapon states and particularly between the superpowers, have, at best, a very limited influence on a garrison state's decision to go nuclear; SALT, Mutual and Balanced Force Reduction (MBFR) 'ceilings,' and a ban on 'killer' satellites do not have any direct impact on the security problems of these states. Furthermore, the argument advanced by Alva Myrdal and others that superpower arms control will affect beneficially the nuclear propensity of other nations is irrelevant to the security concerns of garrison states.[82] Indeed, for them the opposition between 'vertical' and 'horizontal' nuclear proliferation, though useful for propaganda purposes, is largely cosmetic. The central worry of the garrison states is horizontal nuclear proliferation in their respective regions, not the vertical, superpower accumulation of nuclear weapons.

Should a Comprehensive Test Ban Treaty (CTBT) be concluded, it is also unlikely this agreement would have any influence on a garrison state decision to go nuclear. At best, a CTBT might induce these states to maintain a covert nuclear capability, which in the long run could have adverse effects on the entire range of non-proliferation efforts. Four out of five garrison states have ratified the Limited Test Ban Treaty or Moscow Treaty of 1963, while Pakistan has signed but not ratified. The Limited Test Ban Treaty does not affect incentives for going nuclear, as the cases of France, China and India reveal. It may only have delayed in certain respects the nuclear programmes of the garrison states. A CTBT cannot reasonably be expected to do more.

Should all global arms control efforts with global implications succeed in the next few years (conclusion of SALT II, positive follow-up to the International Fuel Cycle Evaluation (INFCE), conclusion of a CTBT, a productive NPT Review Conference with lasting results, and other progress through the new UN disarmament machinery), it might be argued that a new anti-proliferation consensus would constitute an important limitation on garrison state nuclear decisions. Setting aside the improbable assumptions on which this argument is based, it is unlikely that such a situation would have much impact on the garrison states other than leading them to choose a clandestine or quasi-clandestine route to nuclear weapons, if their perceived security imperatives remain compelling.

With respect to regional arms control efforts, nuclear-weapons-free-zones have long been advocated as a means to check proliferation.[83] This solution was proposed by the black African countries in 1963 as a means to check Pretoria's nuclear ambitions.[84] If revived, the project could hardly have any influence on Pretoria. Similarly, a nuclear-weapons-free zone proposed by Pakistan after the 1974 Indian nuclear explosion was implicitly rejected by India.[85] In the Middle East, such a regime would only have a chance of being implemented in the context of a general peace agreement going well beyond the Egyptian-Israeli peace treaty.[86] The PRC proposal for a Pacific nuclear-weapons-free zone has been ignored since 1963.[87]

Nuclear no-first-use pledges by either the major or regional nuclear powers would not have much meaning for garrison states – unless mutually exchanged on the basis of equal nuclear forces or nuclear weapons capability – since they might entail political solutions distasteful to the garrison states and lack credibility in circumstances where the vital national interests of the pledge-giver are perceived to be at stake. As yet, no-first-use of nuclear weapons pledges have never been exchanged among potential adversaries without significant qualifications that undermine whatever slight impact they might have on incentives to acquire nuclear weapons.

In contrast, agreements among major arms suppliers for the regional limitation of conventional weapons transfers would have an immediate impact on all garrison states except South Africa, which is already subject to a UN embargo. Agreements of this kind could provide a potent non-proliferation lever – forcing states to forgo the nuclear option in return for assured supplies of conventional arms – if all major suppliers are bound and all states in a given region are subject to such limitations. Yet this scheme presupposes the creation of an arms suppliers group along the lines of the London Nuclear Group. The prospects for such an arrangement are remote because of the continuous rivalry between the superpowers (as reflected in competitive arms sales to volatile regions) and the negative attitude of major European suppliers who seek political influence and a larger share of the arms market. Moreover, several garrison states already possess impressive national arms industries, especially Israel and South Africa and, to a lesser degree, Taiwan and South Korea.[88] The key issue for the garrison states would be the level at which such a regional arms limitation agreement would freeze the conventional balance of forces. If an agreement merely perpetuates an unfavourable balance of forces, whether real or perceived, which cannot be compensated by weapons produced by a garrison state's national industry, then it can only be expected to stimulate new proliferation incentives.

The strategies briefly outlined are thus likely to be only partially effective but may also have adverse effects. First, were more stringent safeguards and other technical-economic barriers to be applied to the nuclear programmes of garrison states, these states might be tempted to develop among themselves a kind of nuclear 'black' or 'gray' market.[89] Signs of this have already appeared. South Africa is providing uranium to Taiwan and Israel, perhaps in exchange for technology in the plutonium area.[90] There have also been rumours of South Korean-Taiwanese cooperation in the plutonium field.[91] More importantly, these garrison states along with other nuclear weapons aspirants (Yugoslavia, Brazil, and Iran, among others) have taken the lead in forming a group to counter the London Suppliers 'cartel'. This 'Persepolis Group' emerged during an Iranian-sponsored conference on nuclear energy in April 1977 and has deliberately aggravated the North-South confrontation in international nuclear relations, by threatening the leaders of the London 'cartel' – the United States and the USSR – with creation of a 'free' nuclear market and the collapse of the NPT system.[92] France, and, to a lesser extent, Germany have shown some sympathy toward the Persepolis Group.[93]

Meanwhile, in the field of conventional weapons, arms deals have been completed between Taiwan and Israel and between South Africa and Israel.[94] Although the five garrison states make 'incongruous bedfellows', an intensificiation of such military cooperation cannot be ruled out, especially if arms limitation measures and/or embargoes are implemented by the major suppliers.[95]

Constraints. Garrison states are also subject to certain internal constraints on acquiring nuclear weapons. These constraints result from technological or economic considerations involved in any nuclear programme and from their precarious security situation. Among economic constraints, the issue of *cost* is certainly the least restraining.[96] In light of the top priority given to scurity expenditures in garrison state budgets, the cost of a military nuclear programme will be no obstacle even if the nationals of these countries have to 'eat grass', as the late Mr Bhutto of Pakistan once said.

With perhaps the present exception of Pakistan (and, to a much lesser degree, South Korea), all garrison states possess an advanced if narrow technological base which may allow them to overcome purely technical constraints on nuclear programmes. All possess research or power reactors and are familiar with nuclear technology. At least three of them – Israel, South Africa and Taiwan – have mastered 'sensitive' technologies such as reprocessing or enrichment. Moreover, Israel, South Africa, Taiwan and South Korea also have missile programmes, while Pakistan has access to modern fighter-bombers. Thus, the technical means do exist in each case for the indigenous development of modest, though by no means negligible national nuclear forces. Internal technical limitations may, in the absence of outside support or cooperation, in certain cases delay the progress of national nuclear programmes, especially in Pakistan and South Korea, but it is unlikely that such barriers alone could force the cancellation of military nuclear programmes.

Yet the garrison states are vulnerable to internal non-proliferation considerations deriving from their very security difficulties. The risk of having one's opponent 'go nuclear' is the major proliferation barrier, particularly in the case of Israel and South Korea. Taiwan and Pakistan already face nuclear threats, while South Africa does not have to worry about proliferation in Black Africa for many more years to come.

The risk of drawing a hostile superpower into the regional conflict also plays a significant – though hard to assess – role in Israeli, South African, and South Korean decisions to go nuclear openly. Furthermore, the danger of a breakdown in a *de facto* alliance relationship could also be a major concern for the two garrison states which depend on US support: Israel and South Korea. Finally, as noted earlier, all five garrison states share the same problem with regard to the development of a credible nuclear force and strategy.

Each of these limiting factors might usefully be exploited as part of a non-proliferation strategy especially adapted to each garrison state. But in no case could such efforts be free of risk themselves in terms of promoting proliferation. One of these risks is the possibility of forcing these states into clandestine or quasi-clandestine proliferation. The existence of 4 or 5 unacknowledged or ambiguous nuclear powers alongside the official atomic club could change the rules of the strategic game among the nuclear powers and accelerate the breakdown of the NPT system. Widespread or individual clandestine nuclear forces could force NPT states to reconsider their commitment and provoke a domino effect among NPT signatories and non-signatories alike.

Non-proliferation sanctions. Sanctions against proliferative behaviour must be viewed from multilateral and bilateral perspectives. While the NPT does not provide for sanctions in the case of a violation of a safeguard agreement, limited sanctions have been introduced in the London Suppliers Group guidelines of 1977.[97] So far, multilateral non-proliferation sanctions have been limited to nuclear-related measures, such as a cut-off of nuclear assistance and cooperation.[98] Measures going beyond international nuclear cooperation, such as economic sanctions, arms embargoes or even retaliation by a UN military force, have not been publicly discussed at the international level. Although most of these measures could definitely deter the garrison states from going nuclear, at least in an open way, the enormous political difficulties involved in the organization and implementation of such sanctions make their introduction very unlikely.

The most likely form of multilateral sanctions which could be applied to the garrison states to deter or retard proliferation remains penalties relating to international nuclear trade and nuclear cooperation. The effectiveness of such measures is directly related to the degree of dependence of each garrison state's nuclear programme on foreign sources of support. Israel and South Africa are already beyond the reach of nuclear sanctions. Israel's Dimona reactor does not require enriched uranium and natural uranium is produced from local phosphates imported from South Africa. South Africa itself will soon be able to enrich uranium locally. On the other hand, multilateral nuclear sanctions would be more effective against Pakistan, although its small Candu reactor requires only natural uranium. They would be especially effective if invoked against Taiwan and South Korea which are heavily committed to the light water reactor technology and therefore dependent on American supplies of enriched fuel. The threat or the implementation of multilateral nuclear sanctions could thus be expected to deter at least three garrison states from overt proliferation. It seems unlikely, however, that the threat of a nuclear cut-off could lead any one of these states to renounce its nuclear option entirely. The most probable course would be to comply during an initial phase with all international requirements in order to build up an indigenous technological base, which would then be sufficient to ensure at a later stage the viability of a national weapons programme, even if a nuclear embargo is imposed. In the final analysis, sanctions would at best buy time to permit development of more lasting solutions to the problem of proliferation.

Yet sanctions are a two-edged sword: if applied, they may force a garrison state into desperate action; yet, if sanctions are brandished and then not applied or loosely implemented, the resulting failure would accelerate the breakdown of the NPT system by the demonstration that going nuclear is a punishment-free decision. This could reinforce proliferation incentives in many other near-nuclear countries.

Though always implicit in the pressures applied by the nuclear weapon and technology-supplying states on potential proliferators, explicit bilateral non-proliferation sanctions have now been legislated in Section 307 of the NNPA. In addition to references to international sanctions in Section 104, the NNPA also provides for 'termination of (US) nuclear exports' under several conditions, including the detonation of a nuclear explosive device, the termination of IAEA safeguards, the violation of IAEA safeguards, or the violaton of an agreemnt for cooperation with the United States. Also in the law is a provision going far beyond the London guidelines and directly relevant to garrison state nuclear programmes:

No nuclear materials and equipment or sensitive nuclear technology shall be exported to
(1) any non-nuclear weapon state that is found by the President to have at any time after the effective date of this section,
(D) engaged in activities involving source or special nuclear material and having direct significance for the manufacture or acquisition of nuclear explosive devices, and has failed to take steps which, in the President's judgment, represent sufficient progress toward terminating such activities...[99]

This language considerably extends the scope of explicit US sanctions but they would be effective only against those garrison states which depend heavily on American support for their nuclear programmes. This provision, and the requirement for full-scope safeguards, explains Israel's reluctance to acquire an American light-water power reactor.

Sanctions must be handled with the greatest caution: not enough pressure could be interpreted by a garrison state as proof of the effectiveness of its nascent nuclear diplomacy; too strong a sanction could accelerate the desperation of the garrison state. Most important, however, the use of 'cut-off' provisions, as provided for in the NNPA, does lead to a basic policy dilemma: resorting to such a sanction may be the right thing to do in terms of showing US determination in the non-proliferation area but the termination of all American nuclear exports may also deprive the United States of any serious leverage (as through the supply of nuclear fuel) on the potential violator. South Africa is a case in point. In spite of repeated actions by South Africa which can be characterized 'as having direct significance for the manufacture or acquisition of nuclear explosive devices', Washington chose in 1977, after the Kalahari test affair, not to vote in favour of a UN nuclear embargo against Pretoria. Instead, the US chose to apply a *de facto* embargo, by withholding the supply of highly enriched uranium required for the Safari-1 research reactor.[100] Withholding rather than mandated denial thus seems a more effective sanction and, in a qualified way, the NNPA permits this flexibility by allowing the American president to exercise his discretion, subject to Congressional veto. Later the US sold fuel to India despite NNPA.

A NON-PROLIFERATION STRATEGY FOR THE GARRISON STATES

The foregoing analysis of the garrison state syndrome suggests the following conclusions and certain policy prescriptions:

First, there appears to be a direct link between garrison status and the development in each case of a national nuclear programme, as well as a national arms industry. The level of indigenous nuclear development achieved in each garrison state is directly related to (a) the degree of international isolation and vulnerability, and (b) the duration of the garrison situation. Thus, the greater and the older the isolation, the more sophisticated and weapon oriented the nuclear programmes, as in South Africa, Taiwan, and Israel. Where the garrison status is not as extreme and is also more recent, as in Pakistan and South Korea, the nuclear programmes still remain at an early stage with a greater dependence on foreign technological assistance.

The second conclusion concerns the link between all five garrison states and the West. Two states are directly tied to the United States while Pakistan, Taiwan, and South Africa were close to the United States in the past and still regard themselves as part of the western or anti-communist camp. This observation is not meant to imply that the garrison status is a plight solely reserved to US allies. Nevertheless, this observation does imply that at present the United States bears a special responsibility for controlling the nuclear impulses of its past or current protégés, even if this turns out to be a very heavy burden and creates constant policy dilemmas, such as maintaining a continuous military presence in South Korea or reassuring Taiwan despite the formal break in diplomatic relations.

Unpleasant as it may be, this burden will have to be borne if the United States wants to avoid a failure of the non-proliferation policy to which the Ford and Carter Administrations and the US Congress have given priority. Should Washington fail to control proliferation decisions on the part of its protégés, the spread of nuclear weapons would be denounced as part of a 'US plot' by the rest of the world and would also undermine the entire non-proliferation effort new being undertaken by the international community, precisely because of American efforts.

The third conclusion involves the very low effectiveness of 'classic' non-proliferation tools such as safeguards and technical-economic barriers in checking the nuclear progress of the garrison states. At best, such policies will lead the garrison states to delay their military programmes; it is unlikely, however, that these tools could *convince* these states to give up their nuclear option. The most likely result of the continuation of classic non-proliferation strategies will be to turn these nations into clandestine or ambiguous members of the nuclear club. The fact that, so far, none of the garrison states has openly gone nuclear cannot be taken as a positive sign. This means rather that the shape of proliferation is simply changing in accordance with the requirements of the international system.

This review of the garrison states has attempted to show the *fundamental* importance of incentives, in contrast with the temporary character of technical capability consideration. In the future, with more and more nations acquiring nuclear knowledge and equipment, the problem of proliferation will only be solved if a reasonable answer to security and political problems is provided by the international community. Economically, the world can probably adjust to several hundred nuclear power plants and may even benefit from them. From a security standpoint, however, the international system may not be able to adjust if the number of garrison states continues to grow and if such states are still determined to turn these facilities into bomb factories due to the chronic insecurity and political discrimination in which they are forced to live. In short, it may not be enough to concentrate on technical capabilities and fuel cycle issues if nothing is done to prevent other nations from swelling the ranks of garrison states.

The solution of the non-proliferation problem of the garrison states should be given the highest priority in view of:

The risk of a breakdown of the existing non-proliferation regime and new efforts now being undertaken at the international level, which would result from a proliferation decision on the part of any one of the garrison states.

The potential nuclear domino effect these states could trigger in their respective regions.

The potential disruption of global strategic relationships which could result therefrom.

Assessment of garrison state susceptibility to various non-proliferation strategies (Table 4.3) suggests the following programme as the most feasible:

Technico-economic barriers and sanctions should be employed with the greatest care to avoid reinforcing the determination of garrison states to achieve a nuclear capability and the related risk of provoking the emergence of a nuclear 'gray' market.

Priority should be given to political instruments, particularly when an alliance or similar tie exists. The overwhelming objective should be the resolution of regional conflicts in which these garrison states are involved, for these conflicts are the roots of the proliferation incentives at work in all of the garrison states. This in turn means that the superpowers, if they are serious about proliferation, must seek to end or ameliorate these aggravated conflicts and limit their traditional tendency to pursue their rivalry outside Europe in the volatile areas of the Third World. More than ever, successful non-proliferation efforts pre-suppose a fundamental change in the behaviour of both superpowers in Third World regions. Perhaps the most effective contribution of the Carter Administration to its own controversial non-proliferation policy was thus the US role in achieving the Israeli-Egyptian peace treaty.

Short of solving the political roots of the problem, some useful time may be gained by combining bilateral political pressures with the threat of a cut-off of arms supplies. However, this approach must also be used delicately, since it could provoke desperate responses in certain situations.

Positive efforts to gain time should aim at maintaining the stability of the balance of forces in each case by the continuous supply of conventional arms and preserving and increasing US security commitment, where necessary. Ultimately, these policies will achieve little if basic regional antagonisms are not dampened. In the meantime, they will produce unpleasant policy conflicts between non-proliferation and other interests.

NOTES AND REFERENCES

1. George Quester, *The Politics of Nuclear Proliferation* (Baltimore: the Johns Hopkins University Press, (1973); Stanley Hoffman, 'Nuclear Proliferation and World Politics' in A. Buchan (ed.), *A World of Nuclear Powers?* (Englewood Cliffs, N.J.: Prentice Hall, 1966); and Richard Falk, 'A World Order Problem', *International Security*, vol. 1, No. 3 Winter 1977 pp. 79-93.

2. Among many other non-proliferation studies, see: Ford Mitre Report of the Nuclear Energy Study Group, *Nuclear Power, Issues and Choices* (Cambridge, Mass.: Ballinger, 1977); US Congress, *Nuclear Proliferation Factbook* (Washington, DC: GPO, September 1977); Harold A. Feiveson and Theodore B. Taylor, 'Alternative Strategies for International Control of Nuclear Power' in Ted Greenwood, Harold A. Feiveson and Theodore B. Taylor (eds), *Nuclear Proliferation, Motivations, Capabilities and Strategies for Control* (New York: McGraw Hill, 1977); Abram Chayes and W. Bennet Lewis (eds), *International Arrangements for Nuclear Fuel Reprocessing* (Cambridge, Mass.: Ballinger, 1977); Steven J. Baker, 'Commercial Nuclear Power and Nuclear Proliferation', *Peace Studies Program Occasional Paper,* no. 5 (Cornell University, May 1975); Abraham A. Ribicoff, 'A Market Sharing Approach to the World Nuclear Sales Problem', *Foreign Affairs* (July 1976) pp. 763-87.

   In practice, the technical-economic theories have found a direct application in the creation of the London Suppliers Group in 1975 [US Congress, Office of Technology Assessment (OTA), *Nuclear Proliferation and Safeguards* (New York: Praeger Special Studies, 1977) pp. 220-3.]; the launching of INFCE in 1977 [US Department of State, Documents on the Organizing Conference of the International Nuclear Fuel Cycle Evaluation (Washington, 19-21 October 1977)], and in the vote on the US Nuclear Non-proliferation Act of 1978. [For an analysis of the Act, see Marcus A. Rowden, 'The Impact of the Nuclear Non-proliferation Act on US Exports,' paper presented to the Atomic Industrial Forum Conference on 'Nuclear Proliferation and Safeguards,' (New York, 23 October 1978).]

3. For these categories, see Robert E. Harkavy, 'The Pariah State Syndrome,' *Orbis*, vol. 21, no. 23 (Fall 1977) pp. 623-49; George H. Quester, 'What's New on Nuclear Non-Proliferation' (Aspen Colorado: Aspen Institute for Humanistic Studies, 1975), Yehezkel Dror, *Crazy States* (Lexington, Mass: DC Heath-Lexington Books, 1971); and see Richard K. Betts, 'Paranoids, Pygmies, Pariahs, and Non-proliferation', *Foreign Policy*, no. 26 (Spring 1977) pp. 157-83.
4. Harkavy, op. cit., p. 624.
5. Betts, op. cit., p. 157.
6. For German and French critiques of the excessive American reliance on 'technnical fixes' in the current international non-proliferation debate, see Karl Kaiser, 'The Great Nuclear Debate: American-German Disagreements', *Foreign Policy* (Spring 1978) and Pierre Lellouche, 'France in the International Nuclear Controversy; Giscard's New Foreign Nuclear Policy', *Orbis*, vol. 22, No. 4, (Winter 1979).
7. For a brief survey of earlier precedents, see Harkavy, op. cit., pp. 625-6. Israel may be the most striking example: whereas Zionism is today considered as 'a form of racism' by a majority of the community of nations, one must remember that Israel's legitimacy as a Jewish state was precisely founded by the said 'community' only thirty years ago. The difference, of course, is that the community itself has grown from 50 odd states to more than 150 in that same period of time, while the political and ideological balance of power within the community has profoundly been altered.
8. The insistence of the Bhutto government on acquiring a plutonium reprocessing plant led to the cancellation by the Ford Administration in 1976 of the US offer to deliver 100 A-7 fighter-bombers. The similar insistence of the Zia government in rejecting France's proposal to modify the Chasma reprocessing unit to include a 'co-processing' feature gave France an opportunity to back out of this controversial deal in August 1979. See: *International Herald Tribune*, 24 August 1978, and *Le Monde*, 25 August 1979.
9. The fragility of these lines of supply appeared clearly in the case of Israel during the Yom Kippur War, when the United States was prevented from using NATO bases for its airlift to Tel Aviv.
10. The military situation of garrison states is characterized by the following factors:
    1) existence of a military threat (conventional or nuclear) on their territorial and/or political integrity.
    2) the persistence of such threat over a long period of time.
    3) the perception of such threat on the part of the garrison states and the will to resist it by all military means at their disposal.
11. Pakistan is not generally considered as a 'pariah state' (see Harkavy, op. cit.) though other authors have analyzed it as a 'pygmy state' (see Betts, op. cit. p. 165). However, Islamabad's political and military isolation militates in favour of its inclusion in our list of garrison states. Typical of Pakistan's isolation is the fact that the country lost its eastern province as a result of military warfare and that no-one (particularly in the Third World) has objected to this blatant breach of the sacrosanct principle of

national sovereignty, and territorial integrity. Furthermore, despite Pakistan's various 'alliances' (US, PRC, CENTO), no serious security guarantee has been implemented against India. Finally, Islamabad's firm decision to go ahead with a reprocessing plant has led Pakistan to appear increasingly as a 'dangerous state' at least in the eyes of the United States and other developed nations.

12. Harkavy, op. cit., p. 644.

13. In order to measure the economic importance of military expenditures in each garrison state, the following table describes the per capita ranking of these five states (as compared to the 138 states surveyed) in three areas: military, health, and education.

Country	GNP Per capita		Military Public expenditures per capita		Education Public expenditures per capita		Health Public expenditures per capita	
	Rank	US $	Rank	US $	Rank	US $	Rank	US $
Israel	23	3.869	1	1.214	24	159	25	68
Pakistan	122	131	75	10	125	2	116	1
S. Korea	79	478	60	22	80	13	116	1
Taiwan	56	864	42	48	61	31	45	20
S. Africa	48	1.272	44	46	69	21	74	6

Source: Ruth Leger Sivard, *World Military and Social Expenditures 1977* (Leesburg, Va.: WMSE Publications, 1977).

14. Once again, it is important to emphasize that this list of garrison states is valid for the present time only: it represents a 'snapshot' of today's international community. This, in turn, means that the number of garrison states may be decreased if international efforts are undertaken, as part of a non-proliferation strategy in order to achieve a progressive re-integration of such states in the community. Conversely, should no improvement occur with respect to international security, the number of garrison states could increase by the addition of those nations which are potentially in a garrison situation (i.e., Yugoslavia, Libya, Iraq, Cuba and Argentina).

15. India is generally considered a nuclear weapon state, in spite of the fact that New Delhi has apparently not yet decided to launch a weapons programme. See OTA, Nuclear Proliferation and Safeguards, op. cit., p. 102.

16. For an analysis of the Soviet vulnerability during this period, see Edgar M. Bottom, *The Balance of Terror* (Boston, Mass.: Beacon Press, 1971) pp. 1-6; See also Louis J. Halle, *The Cold War as History* (New York: Harper & Row, 1967) p. 170.

17. On US nuclear threats to the PRC: Alice Hsieh, *Communist China's Strategy in the Nuclear Era* (Englewood Cliffs, NJ: Prentice Hall, 1962) pp. 1-18; Morton H. Halperin and Dwight H. Perkins, *Communist China and Arms Control* (Harvard: East Asian Research Centre, 1965)

pp. 50-1; Alexander L. George and Richard Smoke, *Deterrence in American Foreign Policy, Theory and Practice* (New York: Columbia University Press, 1974) p. 59; Winberg Chai (ed.), *The Foreign Relations of the People's Republic of China* (New York: Capricorn Books, 1972) pp. 56-87.

18. Expecting a first Chinese atomic bomb between 1963 and 1965 [See Leonard Beaton and John Maddox, *The Spread of Nuclear Weapons* (London: Chatto & Windus, 1962) p. 140]. Indian leaders developed their technical capabilities in order to have access to plutonium as early as 1963. At the same time, India endeavoured to find credible security guarantees from the United States and the USSR. See George Quester, *The Politics of Nuclear Proliferation,* pp. 64-5. However, even if such guarantees could have been obtained (in particular from the USSR), this would have resulted in sacrificing India's position on non-alignment. See K. Subramanyan, 'India: Keeping the Option Open', in Robert M. Lawrence and Joel Larus (ed.), *Nuclear Proliferation Phase II* (Lawrence, Kans.: University Press of Kansas, 1974) p. 133.

19. Quester, *The Politics of Nuclear Proliferation,* op. cit. India was also particularly active during the NPT negotiations (1965-8) in trying to achieve an effective UN security guarantee system in favour of non-nuclear weapon states. See Disarmament Commission, Official Records, 75th meeting, p. 4, and, generally Enid Schoettle, *Long Term Arms Limitations and Security Requirements for Minimizing the Proliferation of Nuclear Weapons: Implications for the Review Conference of NPT* (Harvard: Program for Science in International Affairs, 1975) unpublished.

20. In the Soviet case both elements are hardly distinguishable in so far as the USSR's military doctrine and practice have always stressed the necessary connection between the possession of superior military power and the successful achievement of political objectives (*Nuclear Proliferation and Safeguards*, op. cit., p. 99).

21. Proponents of nuclear weapons in India have long defended the idea that it is natural and legitimate that a nation of the size and potential of India should aspire to remain outside the sphere of influence of another power. '... in a multipolar world, India will either become a center of power herself or become a weak and nondescript nation under the power penumbra of another nation' (Sisir Gupta, 'The Indian Dilemma' *A World of Nuclear Powers?*, op. cit., p. 59-60).

22. Both nuclear decisions have been thoroughly discussed. With respect to France, see in particular Wilfrid L. Kohl, *French Nuclear Diplomacy* (Princeton University Press, 1971), as well as Lawrence Scheinman, *Atomic Energy Policy in France under the Fourth Republic* (Princeton University Press, 1965). With regard to Britain's nuclear programme, see Margaret Gowing, *Britain and Atomic Energy* (London: Macmillan, 1964) and Elizabeth Young, op. cit., chapter 2.
What is worrisome for the future of proliferation is that the security alibi has been used successfully (both domestically and in foreign policy) by these two countries which belong to the one credible existing alliance, NATO. Considering the fact that every single nation in the world is

directly or indirectly threatened by either superpower (at least in theory) and that most states are not members of either NATO or the Warsaw Pact, possible uses of nuclear alibis seem absolutely endless.

23. The consequences of the 1964 Chinese nuclear test for India's proliferation incentives are described in Sisir Gupta, 'The Indian Dilemma', op. cit., pp. 68-81. On the notion of the opponent's nuclearization as a 'triggering event' of proliferation incentives, see Lewis A. Dunn, and Herman Kahn, *Trends in Nuclear Proliferation, 1975-1995* (Croton-on-Hudson, NY: Hudson Institute, 15 May 1976) pp. 6-7.

24. In the case of India, however, some 'price' may have to be paid as a result of the cut-off provisions set forth in the American Non-proliferation Act of 1978. Although India continued to reject full-scope safeguards on all her nuclear facilities, 24 months after the entry into force of the Act, it was able to avoid the risk of a cut-off of all US nuclear aid, including the supply of fuel for the Tarapur power station.

25. Such a pre-emptive strike was apparently contemplated by the Soviets during 1969, according to H. R. Haldeman's memoirs, *The Ends of Power*. (See Victor Zorza, 'Haldeman's Chinese Puzzle', *International Herald Tribune,* 22 February 1978.) The Soviet Tass Agency immediately denied the claim as a 'lie' (*International Herald Tribune,* 20 February 1978).

    According to General George S. Brown's estimates (1977 *US Military Posture Statement*), 'The Chinese now have a capability for nuclear strikes by missiles and bombers all around the periphery of the PRC at distances up to 5900 km. The Chinese have no present capability to attack the continental United States and are unlikely to obtain one for at least several years'.

    However, in addition to various types of IRBMs and MRBMs [see Harry Gelber, 'Nuclear Weapons and Chinese Policy', *Adelphi Paper*, London: International Institute for Strategic Studies, no. 99, Summer 1973], the Chinese apparently tested a limited range ICBM in November 1976 and are working on a long-range missile (12,000 km). See *Daily Telegraph,* 1 February 1977; *Le Nouveau Journal,* 10 February 1977; and *The Military Balance 1978-79* (London: IISS, 1978).

26. Signed on 2 December 1954, by Secretary of State Dulles, the US-Taiwan mutual security treaty was ratified on 9 February 1955. It required the United States and the ROC to (1) maintain and develop 'jointly by self-help and mutual aid' their individual and collective capacity to resist armed attack and Communist subversion directed against the two countries 'from without', (2) cooperate in economic development, (3) consult on implementation of the treaty, and (4) act to meet an armed attack. Foreign Minister Chou-En-Lai called the Treaty a US attempt to 'legalize its armed seizure of Chinese Territory of Taiwan'. (See Chou-En-Lai speech, 'Oppose US Occupation of Taiwan and "Two-China Plot" ', 8 December 1954, published by Foreign Languages Press. Peking, 1958.)

    For a detailed account of the US response to the Quemoy crisis, see A. George and R. Smoke, *Deterrence and American Foreign Policy,* op. cit., chapter 12; and Kenneth T. Young, *Negotiating with the Chinese*

Communists, the US Experience 1953-1967 (New York: McGraw Hill, 1968) pp. 143-62.

27. Richard Burt, 'US Neutral on West Europe's Arms to Peking', *New York Times,* 8 November 1978; 'Arms for China – In the Open', editorial, *Los Angeles Times,* 13 November 1978; and 'Britain Tells Hua It is Willing to Sell Harrier Jets', *Washington Post,* 2 November 1979.

28. Various reports circulated since 1975, concerning secret reprocessing plants in Taiwan as well as the diversion of radioactive material. See *Revue Générale Nucléaire,* no. 4 (Summer 1976); Edward Schumacher, 'US Gets Report that Taiwan is Reprocessing Nuclear Fuel', *International Herald Tribune,* 30 August 1976; and *Le Monde,* 31 August 1976. Taiwan later denied the charge and pledged to abstain from reprocessing. (See *International Herald Tribune,* 25-6 September 1976.) These installations were apparently dismantled under strong US pressure (See *Nuclear Proliferation Factbook,* op. cit., p. 198, and *SIPRI Yearbook 1977,* p. 48.) During the same period the number of US military personnel stationed in Taiwan was reduced from about 10,000 in 1972 to 1600 in 1977. In 1978, only 750 US military personnel were left in the ROC. (See Jay Mathews, 'US Military in Taiwan Reduced by Half', *International Herald Tribune,* 4-5 November 1978.)

29. See Geoffrey Kemp 'Nuclear Forces for Medium Powers', *Adelphi Papers,* London: International Institute for Strategic Studies, nos. 106 and 107 (Autumn 1974). For a general discussion of the strategic problems faced by small powers and new nuclear nations, see Lewis A. Dunn and Herman Kahn, *Trends in Nuclear Proliferation,* op. cit., pp. 95-113.

30. Taiwan's Air Force is composed of light short-range and somewhat outmoded fighters (F-100s, F-104s, F-5s) which could hardly be used as nuclear delivery vehicles to reach major mainland cities such as Shanghai or Canton. The recent decision by the Carter Administration not to authorize the sale of advanced aircraft to Taiwan (F-16s and F-18s) or even longer-range F-4s or F-5Gs, and to supply only 40 short-range F-5Es does nothing to improve the delivery vehicle capability of the Taiwanese Air Force (*Washington Post,* 7 November 1978). However, the new F-5Es will be equipped with *Maverick* missiles which could be used against an attacking fleet. Recent press reports have mentioned the existence of a missile project in Taipei's top secret Chung-Shan military Research Institute in conjunction with the Institute of Nuclear Energy Research. The latter is reportedly equipped with a plutonium reprocessing facility. See Melinda Liu 'East, West Anxiously Watch Taiwan's Nuclear Progress', *International Herald Tribune,* 2 March 1978. Also worth noting is the fact that the 1978 National Day military parade included for the first time rocket launchers and missiles made in Taiwan (*Washington Post,* 11 October 1978).

31. Harkavy, 'The Pariah State Syndrome', op. cit. p. 643.

32. Alan Dowty, 'The Role of Great Power Guarantees in International Peace Agreements', *Jerusalem Papers on Peace Problems,* the Hebrew University of Jerusalem, no. 3, (1974) p. 17, and W. Norman Brown, *The United States and India, Pakistan, Bangladesh* (Cambridge Mass.:

Harvard University Press, 1972) p. 400.

Despite China's friendship with Pakistan in the period following the Chinese-Indian War of 1962, the PRC carefully stayed out of the Bangladesh War in 1971-2. The PRC's attitude can be explained by two factors: (1) China has always considered itself as a non-superpower so that the Chinese have refused to offer clear nuclear protection to their allies and (2) India was linked with the USSR by a 20-year Pact of Friendship signed on 9 August 1971 which mentioned a joint action in the event of third party attack against the two countries. (See Brown, op. cit. pp. 206-26.)

CENTO is a rather loose alliance which has grown weaker over time. [See *The Military Balance 1977-1978* (London: International Institute for Strategic Studies, 1977).]

33. See SIPRI, *The Near-Nuclear Countries and the NPT* (Stockholm: Almqvist & Wiksell, 1972) pp. 25-7.

34. Commercial negotiations relating to a pilot reprocessing plant (worth around $20 million) were initiated with Saint-Gobain Techniques Nouvelles in 1975. Government-level negotiations were held in Paris in October 1975 during the visit of Premier Bhutto and ended on 17 March 1976, with the signature of an agreement of cooperation 'relating to the construction of a reprocessing plant' between France and Pakistan. (See *Journal Official de la République Française*, 8 July 1976, p. 4112.) At the same time, Pakistan announced plans for the acquisition of 24 nuclear power plants before the year 2000. (See *Enerpresse*, 23 March 1976, no. 1536.)

35. Former Premier Ali Bhutto has stated that he was overthrown (during the July 1977 military coup) because he stood up to American disapproval of the deal. (See *Financial Times*, 24 January 1978.) In a lengthy defence against his death sentence, which he wrote while in jail, Bhutto claimed, 'We were on the threshold of full nuclear capability when I left the Government to come to this death cell. . . . We know that Israel and South Africa have full nuclear capability. The Christian, Jewish and Hindu civilizations have this capability. The Communist powers also possess it. Only the Islamic civilization was without it but that position was about to change'. Mr Bhutto claims that the United States helped finance the opposition to him during the 1977 election and afterwards in a bid to thwart Pakistan's nuclear ambitions. (See *Financial Times*, 5 October 1978.)

36. Frank T. J. Bray and Michael L. Moodie, 'Nuclear Politics in India', *Survival*, vol. xx, no. 3 (May/June 1977) pp. 115-16. Lewis A. Dunn, 'India, Pakistan, Iran. . . . A Nuclear Proliferation Chain?', (Croton-on-Hudson, NY: Hudson Institute, 1976) pp. 13-14.

37. India has achieved a complete mastery of the heavy-water fuel cycle (from heavy water production plants to plutonium reprocessing). It is also the only nation in the Third World capable of building indigenously an entire nuclear power station. The Narora 1 and 2 plants will be totally built with Indian technology and equipment. (See *Défense et Diplomatie*, 15 September 1977; see also Onkar Marwah, 'India's Nuclear and Space Programs, Intent and Policies', *International Security*, vol. 2, no. 2 (Fall

1977) pp. 96-121.) India has recently acquired from British Aerospace a total of 150 Franco-British SEPECAT *Jaguar* fighter-bombers. Of this total, only 40 will be produced in Europe, while India's Hindustan Aeronautics will produce the remaining planes in India. (See *Le Monde*, 15-16 October 1978.) India already produces MiG-21 fighters under licence. (See *Défense et Diplomatie*, 11 November 1976.) Missile work is also being performed in India under the Sarabhai Nuclear Energy and Space Programme initiated in 1971. (See Bray and Moodie, 'Nuclear Politics in India', op. cit., p. 111.)

38. In December 1978 the position of the French government (as expressed to the author in a series of interviews with French officials) was as follows: (1) the contract was not 'cancelled' (as was announced in the US press), although there is clearly little enthusiasm for selling the plant, even if modified by 'co-processing'; (2) negotiations were continuing with Pakistan on the co-processing issue (see *Le Monde*, 5-6 November 1978); (3) France was also ready to sell *Mirage* fighter-bombers to Pakistan, as a result of India's recent acquisition of 150 *Jaguars*; and (4) the link between the two deals was unclear, although the French government would apparently prefer to sell the *Mirages* without having to build the plant, even with co-processing.

39. The North Korean superiority is most striking in artillery (2 to 1), tanks (2.5 to 1), combat aircraft (2 to 1), and naval combatants (4 to 1). See General Richard G. Stilwell, 'The US, Japan and the Security of Korea', *International Security,* vol. 2, no. 2 (Fall 1977). (For a contrary assessment, see Franklin B. Weinstein, 'The United States, Japan, and the Security of Korea', ibid., pp. 68-89.)

40. US military and economic aid to the ROK since 1950 amounts to $38 billion while Seoul has received 2 billion dollars in military aid since 1971. ('Korea and US Policy in Asia', *The Defense Monitor* (Washington: Center for Defense Information January 1976 p. 1.) In recent years, however, the ROK has ceased being a recipient of grant military assistance to become a cash purchaser of military hardware. (See Joseph M. Ha, 'US Withdrawal from Korea: A Means not an End', *Orbis,* vol. 21, no. 3 (Fall 1977) p. 617.)

41. The United States obtained ratification by South Korea barely two weeks before the 5 May 1975 NPT Review Conference.
    A recent report by the International Relations Committee of the US House of Representatives indicates that South Korea had started a secret nuclear weapons programme in 1970, after the Nixon Administration withdrew 20,000 US troops from Korea. The programme was stopped in 1975 after the Ford Administration apparently threatened to terminate all nuclear cooperation. (See 'US Kept S. Korea from Making A-Arms', *International Herald Tribune,* 6 November 1978.)

42. The deal was signed in February 1975 by Saint-Gobain Techniques Nouvelles for a total amount of 170 million francs (*Le Monde,* 21-2 December 1975). The French government has always stated that 'the contract was cancelled by a purely French decision' (Communiqué of the Elysée Palace dated 16 December 1976, *Le Monde,* 18 December 1976). The result of the cancellation was that Framatome lost a further contract

for two 900 megawatt light water reactor plants which was implicitly tied to the earlier reprocessing agreement. The power plant contracts recently went to Westinghouse (*Le Monde,* 8 February 1978).

43. The original Carter plan provided for the withdrawal of 30,000 US ground troops by 1982. The fate of US tactical nuclear weapons deployed in South Korea remains, however, unclear. (See Weinstein, op. cit., and 'Risks of Korean Withdrawal', editorial, *Washington Post,* reprinted in the *International Herald Tribune,* 31 May 1977.)

44. As early as June 1975, President Park had warned that 'If the US nuclear umbrella were removed, we would have to start developing our own nuclear weapons capability' (*Washington Post,* 4 November 1978.)

45. See *Evening Post,* New Zealand, Wellington, 'South Koreans Demand Own Nuclear Weapons' 27 June 1977. President Park told two American columnists that if US support falters, South Korea will build its own bomb. (See Betts, op. cit., p. 180.) For the power plans, see *Financial Times,* 21 January 1978; *Le Monde,* 22 November 1978.

46. The Carter plan was openly criticized in May 1977 by Major General John Singlaub, who was recalled in Washington, reassigned from his position as Chief of Staff of US forces in the ROK and, later, retired. CIA Director, Admiral Stansfield Turner, also warned that the US withdrawal could lead to the ROK's going nuclear covertly, and that the United States could not be assured of discovering such activity. (See William Beecher, 'CIA Chief Sees Risk in Troop Cut in Korea', *International Herald Tribune,* 18 July 1977. See also Bernard Weinraub, 'US Decides to Send 12 F-4s to Bolster Seoul's Air Force', *International Herald Tribune,* 20 February 1978, and William Chapman, 'Brown in Seoul to Reassert Strong Commitment', *Washington Post,* 7 November 1978. For another critical appraisal of the Carter withdrawal plan, see Sen. Sam Nunn, 'What Forces for Asia?, What Forces for Europe?', *The Washington Review,* vol. 1, no. 1, (January 1978) pp. 11-17.)

47. Weinstein, op. cit., p. 73.

48. The ROK already has nuclear-capable F-4 fighter-bombers; moreover, a two-stage ground-to-ground missile, capable of reaching Pyongyang, was recently tested successfully. [See *Defense and Foreign Affairs Daily,* vol. 7, no. 189 (4 October 1978).] Also worth noting in this respect, are recent Korean press reports announcing new programmes for the production of national jet fighters (*Washington Star,* 28 August 1978).

49. Article X, 1 reads: 'Each Party shall in exercising its national sovereignty have the right to withdraw from the Treaty if it decides that extraordinary events, related to the subject matter of this Treaty, have jeopardized the supreme interests of its country...'

50. See, among many other studies: Beaton and Maddox, *The Spread of Nuclear Weapons,* op. cit., chapter 11; Avigdor Haselkorn, 'Israel from an Option to a Bomb in the Basement' in Lawrence and Larus (eds), *Nuclear Proliferation, Phase II,* op. cit., pp. 149-82; Quester, *The Politics of Nuclear Proliferation,* op. cit., chapter 5; Fuad Jabber, 'Israel and Nuclear Weapons' (London: Chatto & Windus, 1971); Robert J. Pranger and Dale R. Tahtinen, 'Nuclear Threat in the Middle East', *American Enterprise Institute Foreign Affairs Study,* Washington, no.

23 (1975). (For a detailed account of US intelligence reports relating to Israel's 'bomb', see Haselkorn, op. cit., pp. 158-9; see also David Burnham, '74 Report Concluded that Israelis had A-Bombs', *International Herald Tribune,* 28-9, January 1977.)

51. For a recent account of the arms build-up in the Middle East, see the *Financial Times,* 'Survey of World Defence Industries', 2 March 1978; see also 'La Course aux Armements au Proche-Orient', [*Problèmes Economiques et Sociaux,* la Documentation Française, Paris, no. 318 (2 September 1977)]. For an account of the weapons projects currently being considered by the multinational 'Arab Industrial Organization', see 'Défense et Diplomatie', 17 March, 7 April and 26 May 1977; see also 'The Transfer of Arms'. *Strategic Survey* (London: International Institute for Strategic Studies, 1976) pp. 18-25, and *Le Monde,* 16 March and 18 November 1978.

52. See W. Seth Carus, 'The Military Balance of Power in the Middle East', *Current History,* vol. 74, no. 433 (1978) p. 30; Andrew Pierre, 'Beyond the "Plane Package": Arms and Politics in the Middle East', *International Security,* vol. 3, no. 1, (Summer 1978) pp. 157-8.

53. Carus, op. cit., p. 36.

54. For an analysis of the limits of the Israeli effort, see Pierre, op. cit., p. 159-61. The US supplied Israel with ground-to-ground *Lance* missiles in 1976 while refusing to supply *Pershing* missiles. Both types can be fitted with nuclear warheads. The *Lance* has a 112 km range, while the *Pershing* has a 724 km range. One example of US control involves its decision to supply Israel with 15 F-15s *Eagle* and 75 F-16s, while Jerusalem had requested 25 F-15s and 150 F-16s. In the same 'package deal' the Carter Administration has included 50 F-5Es (to Egypt) and 60 F-15s (to Saudi Arabia). (See Robert Siner, 'US Plans First Sale of Fighters to Egypt', *International Herald Tribune,* 15 February 1978.)

55. See Michla Pomerance, 'American Guarantees to Israel and the Law of American Foreign Relations', *Jerusalem Papers on Peace Problems,* no. 9, The Hebrew University of Jerusalem (December 1974) pp. 8-18. On US relations with Israeli adversaries, see Pierre, op. cit., and Dale R. Tahtinen, *National Security Challenges to Saudi Arabia* (Washington DC: American Enterprise Institute, 1978).

56. SIPRI, *The Near Nuclear Countries and the NPT,* op. cit., pp. 29-30.

57. '"We are not afraid of Israel A-bomb": Sadat', *Kayan International,* Tehran, 14 April 1976. (See also 'Defusing Israeli Nuclear Power', *Events,* London, 11 February 1977.)

58. While nuclear programmes are being discussed in Morocco, Saudi Arabia, Kuwait and Egypt, nuclear installations are being built only in Iraq and Libya. (See Pierre LeClair, 'L'atome-français intéresse les Arabes', *Le Matin,* 18 July 1977; 'L'Atome et le Monde Arabe', *An-Nahar Arabe International,* Paris, 14 May 1977; and 'Le Potentiel Nucléaire Arabe', FMA, Beirut, no. 156, 17 December 1974). So far seven Arab states have ratified NPT (Iraq, Jordan, Lebanon, Libya, Morocco, Syria and Tunisia), while Egypt, Kuwait and the Arab Republic of Yemen have signed but not ratified the Treaty. Other reasons for the very slow Arab development in nuclear technology are

the lack of funds in the one country which possesses the human resources necessary (Egypt) and the general lack of skilled personnel in all other countries (particularly in the Gulf).

59. For an analysis of possible Israeli strategic options, see Haselkorn, op. cit., pp. 158-73; see also Steven J. Rosen, 'A Stable System of Mutual Nuclear Deterrence in the Arab-Israeli Conflict'. *American Political Science Review* (December 1977) pp. 1367-83.

60. According to one source, the USSR gave such a commitment to Nasser in May 1966 in response to an Egyptian request for Soviet nuclear weapons. (See FMA, Beirut, note 58.)

61. For an interesting scenario, see Robert J. Pranger, 'Nuclear War comes to the Mideast', *Worldview* (July/August 1977) pp. 41-7.

62. Iraq has acquired from France in 1976 a 70 MW 'Osiris' research reactor, renamed 'Osirak'. This reactor uses 93% enriched uranium. According to various sources, several dozens of kilograms of such uranium are to be delivered. Apparently, France has been unable to obtain Iraq's agreement to a modification of the reactor, in order to use 18-20% enriched uranium instead of weapons-grade material. The reactor is being built by a publicly-owned company, TECHNICATOME, which is a subsidiary of the CEA (Commissariat à l'Energie Atomique). Libya has acquired a 440 MW LWR as well as a 10 MW research reactor from the Soviet Union. (See *Défense et Diplomatie,* 22 December 1977.)

63. On the Kalahari nuclear test affair, see P. LeClair and P. Thibau, 'Cette Bombe qui nous menace', *Demain L'Afrique,* no. 2 (October 1977); *SIPRI Yearbook 1978,* pp. 70-8. (See also George Quester, *The Politics of Nuclear Proliferation,* op. cit., pp. 201-2; Edward Bustin, 'South Africa's Foreign Policy Alternatives and Deterrence Needs' in Onkar Marwah and Ann Schulz (eds), *Nuclear Proliferation and the Near Nuclear Countries* (Cambridge, Mass.: Ballinger, 1975) pp. 221-3.)

64. For details of the South African nuclear programme, see US Senate (Sub-committees on African Affairs and Arms Control), 'Proposed Nuclear Reactor Sales to South Africa', *Hearings,* 26 May 1976; African National Congress, 'Conspiracy to Arm Apartheid Continues', Bonn 1977; J. R. Colley, 'South Africa's Nuclear Programme', *The South African Mechanical Engineer,* vol. 25 (August 1975) pp. 203-24; and Barbara Rogers and Zdenek Cervenka, *The Nuclear Axis* (New York: Times Books, 1978).

65. On the similarlity between the Becker enrichment process of West Germany and the South African 'Jet Nozzle' process, see African National Congress, op. cit., as well as A.J.A. Roux and W.L. Grant (respectively, chairman of the Atomic Energy Board of South Africa and Director of Uranium Enrichment Corp. of South Africa Ltd-UCOR), 'Uranium Enrichment in South Africa', presentation to European Nuclear Conference, Paris, April 1975; see also Rogers and Cervenka, op. cit., pp. 175-94.

66. See Frank Barnaby, 'Africa and Nuclear Energy', *Africa,* no. 69 (May 1977) pp. 92-3.

67. Don Oberdorfer, Thomas O'Toole, and Caryle Murphy, 'Two Flashes Near South Africa: Just What Happened That Night', *Washington Post,* 27 October, 1979.

68. *Washington Post,* 27 October 1979. Lewis A. Dunn and Herman Kahn, *Trends in Nuclear Proliferation,* op. cit., p. 4.
69. For an account of Secretary Kissinger's visit to India in November 1974, see Bernard Weinraub, 'Visit by Kissinger buoys New Delhi', *New York Times,* 3 November 1974.
70. See David M. Rosenbaum, 'Nuclear Terror', *International Security,* vol. 1, no. 3 (Winter 1977) pp. 140-61.
71. See Pierre Lellouche, 'The Nuclear Test Cases before the ICJ', *Harvard International Law Journal* (Summer 1975) pp. 614-37.
72. See notes 28 and 41.
73. In particular, France and Britain supply arms to Pakistan; see *World Armaments and Disarmament, SIPRI Yearbook 1976,* pp. 264.
74. See Lewis A. Dunn, 'The Role of Sanctions in Non-Proliferation Strategy', Croton-on-Hudson, New York: Hudson Institute, 2 February 1977. The guidelines are reprinted in *SIPRI Yearbook 1978,* pp. 35-42, and *Nucleonics Week,* 3 November, 1977. The NNPA is Public Law 95-242 of 10 March 1978.
75. See Paragraph 7 of the guidelines, cited in note 74.
76. Lecture by Harold Agnew (Los Alamos Laboratory), Salzburg Seminar in American Studies, Salzburg, Austria, September 1978.
77. *Nucleonics Week,* 9 June, 1977.
78. *SIPRI Yearbook 1977,* p. 51.
79. The full safeguard agreement is published in the *Journal Officiel de la République Française,* 8 July 1976, pp. 4112-13.
80. Mason Willrich, a leading expert on nuclear safeguards writes: 'There is nothing that safeguards alone can do to prevent diversion from occurring once a non-nuclear weapon state decides to embark on a nuclear weapons program', ['The Non-proliferation Treaty: Nuclear Technology Confronts World Politics', *Yale Law Journal,* vol. 77, no. 8 (July 1968) p. 1518]. Also worthwhile quoting is the following excerpt from a study of international safeguards by Douglas E. George and Ralph F. Lumb: 'It has been recognized generally, if not universally, that no safeguards system, however independent, can provide assurance that no diversion has taken place. Nor can any safeguards system provide complete assurance that, should diversion occur it will be detected. *Nevertheless, it has been generally accepted* that there must be a system of international safeguards', (emphasis added), in Mason Willrich (ed.) *Civil Nuclear Power and International Security* (New York: Praeger, 1971).
81. Ted Greenwood, 'The Proliferation of Nuclear Weapons', op. cit., pp. 28-9.
82. For an ardent defence of this argument, see Alva Myrdal, 'The Game of Disarmament', *Impact,* vol. xxii no. 3 (July-September 1972) pp. 217-33, and William Epstein, 'The Proliferation of Nuclear Weapons', *Scientific American,* vol. 232, no. 4 (April 1971).
83. See, for example, Urs Schwarz, 'Inhibition through Policy: the Role of the Non-Nuclear Powers' in *A World of Nuclear Powers?,* op. cit., p. 154-6; see also article vii of the NPT.
84. F. Barnaby, 'Africa and Nuclear Energy', op. cit., pp. 92-3.
85. New York Times, 13 November 1974; UN Document A/10221; see also Betts, op. cit., p. 171. Also worthwhile noting is the continuation of a

major international controversy (since the Tlatelolco Treaty) as to whether nuclear-weapons-free zones prohibit the signatories from conducting peaceful nuclear weapons tests.

86. It is interesting to note that Israel has rejected Egypt's proposal for a reciprocal pledge to renounce atomic weapons as part of the projected peace treaty between the two nations. (See *International Herald Tribune,* 9 November 1978.) In rejecting the proposal, Israel argued that the Treaty did not include other Arab states still at war with Jerusalem.

87. See Statement of the Chinese government, 31 July 1963, reprinted in Jerome A. Cohen and Hungdan Chiu, *People's China and International Law* (Princeton University Press, 1974) vol. 2, pp. 1622-7.

88. Harkavy, op. cit., pp. 634-9.

89. Lewis A. Dunn, 'Nuclear Gray Marketeering', *International Security* vol. 1, no. 3 (Winter 1977) pp. 107-18.

90. Harkavy, op. cit., pp. 647-8; *Défense et Diplomatie,* vol. ii, no. 38, 20 October 1977.

91. Harkavy, loc. cit.

92. Munir Khan, Chairman of Pakistan's Atomic Energy Commission, in 'Nuclear Power and the Developing Countries', *Nuclear News* Special Report, Salzburg IAEA Conference, 2-13 May 1977, pp. 79-82, reviews the position of the Persepolis Group. For the threats against the London Club and NPT, see *Financial Times,* 16 April 1977 and *Nuclear News,* May 1977.

93. For the official French attitude toward the London Suppliers Group, INFCE, and US-led international safeguard efforts, see Bertrand Goldschmidt, 'Le Contrôle de l'Energie Atomique et la Non-proliferation', *Politique Etrangère,* 42, nos 3-4 (1977) pp. 413-30; see also Pierre Lellouche, 'France in the International Nuclear Controversy', op. cit.

94. Several contracts reached between Israel and Taiwan provide for sale of *Shafir* missiles and electronic components (Tadiran), while negotiations have been started on the delivery of 50 *Kfir* C-2 fighters (*Financial Times,* 9 March 1978). South Africa has received several types of equipment ranging from Galil and Uzi light weapons to *Shafir, Reshef* and other types of patrol boats. There are also agreements concerning the *Kfir,* supplies of spare parts for *Mirage* aircraft, the building in South Africa of 'turnkey' electronic factories as well as common production of heavy armour for the Israeli-designed *Markava* tank.

95. *International Herald Tribune,* 23 May 1977.

96. Betts, op. cit., p. 161.

97. The NPT contains one type of sanction, namely the use of the withdrawal clause. This type of sanction is purely political, not legal. (See G. Rathjens, A. Chayes and J. Ruina, *Nuclear Arms Control Agreements: Process and Impact* (Washington DC: Carnegie Endowment for International Peace, 1974) pp. 55-6.)

98. See Article XII of IAEA Statute, paragraph A-7. However, paragraph C of Article XII does set up a procedure for reporting violations to the UN Security Council, a step which is intended to trigger a UN action if necessary (and if possible). See The Atlantic Council, *Nuclear Power and*

Nuclear Weapons Proliferation (Boulder, Colo.: Western Press, 1977) vol. II, p. 24.

99. Section 129 (1) (D) of the Atomic Energy Act of 1954, as amended.
100. *Le Monde,* 7 November 1978.

5 The Prestige States

JO L. HUSBANDS

Depending upon the authority consulted, somewhere between a hand and a bushel full of nations will acquire nuclear weapons in the 1980s.[1] Among the countries that routinely appear on lists of near-nuclear nations, one group appears motivated more by the status and influence that nuclear weapons might bring than additions to national security. Prestige figures somewhere in the calculations of most candidates for nuclear weapons, but it predominates for only a limited number.[2] Decision-makers charged with formulating non-proliferation strategies for the coming decade nonetheless need to consider a number of questions about these 'prestige states': Do particular status drives distinguish these countries? How much and what kind of a threat does proliferation by these countries pose compared with other states? Could special 'prestige' non-proliferation policies be developed and what would be their impact on broader non-proliferation strategies?

The conviction shared by many analysts of nuclear proliferation that prestige is not a legitimate reason to seek nuclear capabilities hampers such analysis. Revulsion explains much of this reaction: Given the dangers nuclear weapons pose for mankind's survival, how could a nation contemplate developing them unless threatened with obliteration?[3] Studies that lump together any and all possible near-nuclear (Nth) countries reinforce this attitude by making non-security motivations appear trivial. Lists based simply on raw technical capacity, such as the Committee for Economic Development's projection of 100 nuclear-capable countries by the year 2000, inevitably include nations whose interest in nuclear weapons appears ludicrous to even the most sympathetic observers.[4] To ensure that non-proliferation strategy addresses the problem's full range, such judgments must be suspended and prestige motivation treated as seriously as security pressures.

Historically, prestige figured heavily in the decisions of several

112

present members of the nuclear club. With the advent of the nuclear age, the prerequisities for great power status changed and nuclear weapons appeared necessary for traditional powers seeking to preserve or restore their international standing. For the third and fourth nuclear powers, Great Britain and France, the desire to close the gap between themselves and the new nuclear superpowers provided the driving force behind their nuclear programmes. Security sparked the first British interest in an independent nuclear capability, but this soon faded and status emerged as the primary motive.[5] In the French case, status spurred their nuclear programme from the beginning.[6] That nuclear weapons did not restore France and Britain to their full pre-war status and that they remain 'great' not 'super' powers does not affect the fact that prestige served as sufficient motivation for their choice.

As a motivation for acquiring nuclear weapons, fears of fading glory offer only a limited explanation for present national aspirations. After 30 years, the international system has more or less adjusted to the initial disruption of the power structure wrought by nuclear weapons. The great powers from the pre-nuclear era have either already gone nuclear – the United States, the USSR, Britain, and France – or appear to be pursuing influence along alternative, non-nuclear paths – West Germany and Japan – albeit not initially through choice. If either Japan or West Germany now chose to 'go nuclear,' the explanation would lie more with a perceived collapse of the American security commitment than with a conviction that nuclear weapons had become essential to maintaining their international standing.[7]

For today's potential nuclear nations, the Argentinas and Brazils, nuclear weapons offer a means for gaining, not retaining, international standing. While it is misleading to lump these aspiring nations together, a few generalizations apply. Most are Third World countries, and most already have considerable status within their region or among the developing nations. But, by almost any standard measure of power, the gap between their prestige and the prestige of the major powers still yawns.[8] For these countries, nuclear capabilities offer the ticket for admission to the ranks of the powerful.

Nuclear weapons may hold a special allure given the bitter resentments that colour the relations between North and South today. The openly discriminatory character of the Non-proliferation Treaty (NPT) with its attempt to freeze the world into nuclear 'haves' and 'have nots' endows the acquisition of nuclear weapons with the extra glamour of a gesture of defiance.[9] Status and independence from the second class citizenship they perceive the developed countries imposing upon them are inextricably linked in the nuclear ambitions of the prestige states. Indian defences of its 1974 'peaceful' nuclear test express this link clearly:

It is the nuclear Brahmins that advocate the maintenance of purity of their caste at the expense of the lesser breed. It is they who preach that the other states should be required to place all their nuclear facilities and reactors under strict international safeguards, and should not be allowed to conduct PNEs [peaceful nuclear explosions], while they themselves remain free to manufacture nuclear weapons, conduct tests, and develop reactor technologies. Such a concept implies a grave abridgement of the sovereignty of developing countries and is tantamount to a sort of nuclear colonialism.[10]

Fortunately, nations will not go nuclear in fits of pique; however despised, the non-proliferation regime embodied by the NPT and the London Suppliers Group guidelines still provides a deterrent. Nuclear weapons, or at minimum the capacity to develop them readily, nevertheless offer an aspiring nation an attractive means to force the traditional powers to acknowledge its claims to a seat at the high table.

Nuclear weapons may provide a shortcut to status for nations frustrated in their attempts to acquire the traditional accoutrements of prestige. Economic development, the prescribed route for most, is a slow, painful, and unsettling process with uncertain rewards. International recognition for its achievement or for other attributes may then be slow in coming, further increasing a nation's initial frustration. Brazil's 'economic miracle' has brought it nothing approaching the prestige of Japan or West Germany, even though its GNP now ranks tenth in the world.[11] Their control over precious oil resources bought the OPEC countries immense importance to the world economy, but their influence generally remains within a circumscribed political and economic sphere, and those subject to it expend considerable, if not coordinated, efforts to diminish that clout.[12] For nations denied the prestige they believe they deserve, nuclear weapons promise instant international recognition, a surefire way to bridge the gulf between themselves and the major powers.

OPEN OPTIONS

The non-nuclear powers have long recognized and railed against the contradiction inherent in the non-proliferation policy of the nuclear powers.[13] In this sense, the link between horizontal proliferation (nuclear weapons in more countries) and vertical proliferation (more weapons in the same countries) remains strong.[14] While the nuclear nations, particularly the US and the Soviet Union, insist on their exclusive right to set the nature and pace of arms control and disarmament, it will be that much more difficult to convince would-be great powers that nuclear weapons hold no potential payoff for them. Successful conclusion of the Strategic Arms Limitation Talks Treaty (SALT II) and the Comprehensive Test Ban, unlikely in the current climate of US-Soviet relations, nonetheless represent important steps to advance the non-proliferation cause.

One response to the apparent temptations nuclear weapons present to ambitious nations would be to accord them the status they seek through other, less potentially dangerous status symbols. This presumes a certain degree of interchangeability among symbols, so that memberships in international organizations, leadership positions, invitations to important conferences, and the like could somehow sum to the prestige equivalent of a nuclear weapon capability. There are, after all, alternative routes to international prestige and different scales upon which to weigh status. Japan and West Germany have translated economic success into wider influence and standing. Mexico, Yugoslavia, and Egypt have pursued status through leadership of the non-aligned bloc; prestige among one's peers sometimes translates into international standing. Closer attention by the major powers to issues dear to the aspiring nations would accord them indirect status by recognizing their particular interests. The Carter Administration came into office facing demands for a New International Economic Order and promising greater concern for North-South issues. Performance did not match promise, but, should these issues ever move toward the centre of the policy stage, they may, as a side benefit, slow proliferation.

Yet nuclear weapons are not the simple equivalent of other symbols of international prestige, and non-proliferation advocates have good reason for not wishing to diminish them to the equal of steel mills, conference chairmanships, or national airlines. Preserving the special character of nuclear weapons forms an essential part of the non-proliferation regime, as does the threat that new nuclear powers will find themselves beyond the pale.[15] Nevertheless, for the last 30 years nuclear weapons have been the standard for defining a superpower. The continuing calls for an America with a nuclear arsenal 'second to none' during the US debate on strategic arms limitaton and the USSR's propaganda about the advantages of Soviet nuclear parity for world socialism retard efforts to de-emphasize the military potential of nuclear weapons and to diminish their value as symbols of power.

An alternative to satisfying the general status drives of would-be proliferators would be to accept a country's desire to acquire the capabilities for nuclear weapons but to try to make it very costly actually to go nuclear. This approach rests on the assumption that for many, perhaps most, threshold nuclear countries, maintaining the option to acquire nuclear weapons is as important, if not more so, than having the weapons themselves. Independence in nuclear and energy matters provides the status in such cases, while the acknowledged capacity to develop weapons creates a potential deterrent without the disadvantages of actual deployment. The prescription, then, is to accord these nations the status they seek by accepting their 'open option', an intermediate position between being a nuclear and a non-nuclear weapons state.

In practice, such a non-proliferation strategy would accept the diffusion of nuclear technology, specifically of the full nuclear fuel cycle. At the same time, to raise the penalties for going beyond the capability to actual production of nuclear weapons, the strategy would concentrate on: (1) improving and universalizing the international nuclear safeguards system; (2) pushing forward with research on alternative energy sources and 'proliferation resistant' nuclear fuel cycles; and (3) promoting further adherence to the NPT. The international non-proliferation regime already encompasses most of these three elements, but tolerating the spread of the full fuel cycle would be a radical break from US practice since the 1974 Indian test.[16] Present US policy has moved far from that regime, with its acceptance of national desires for the entire range of nuclear technology in return for foreswearing nuclear weapons, as enshrined in the NPT. Article IV reads in part:

> Nothing in this Treaty shall be interpreted as affecting the inalienable right of all the Parties to the Treaty to develop research, production, and use of nuclear energy for peaceful purposes without discrimination. . . . All the parties to the Treaty undertake to facilitate, and have the right to participate in, the fullest possible

exchange of equipment, materials and scientific and technological information for the peaceful uses of nuclear energy.[17]

From the earliest days of the US Atoms for Peace programme, non-proliferation policy distinguished between the military and civilian applications of nuclear energy; under appropriate safeguards, development of the latter should be free and unrestricted. India's 'peaceful' nuclear test destroyed that barrier, for if a nation like India could produce nuclear explosives through its civilian energy programme, this route was, or soon would be, readily available to others.[18] By 1976 a consensus emerged among the nuclear suppliers – institutionalized in the London Suppliers Group – that tighter controls should be imposed on the export of sensitive nuclear technology and materials. The Suppliers supported the principle of free technological access, but agreed that the most proliferation-prone technology – enrichment and reprocessing capabilities – should be denied to any nation refusing to accept stringent safeguards on its major nuclear facilities. US policy, set forth in the Nuclear Non-proliferation Act of 1978, goes beyond this to demand full-scope safeguards on a nation's entire nuclear programme, and furthermore, to advocate abstention from sensitive technology and the full fuel cycle for the near future.[19]

The US policy rests on simple, straightforward logic about the nature and risks of the proliferation process: nations go nuclear when they combine the desire or perceived need for nuclear weapons with the capabilities to produce them. Of the components of proliferation, motivation is both most subject to sudden change and most resistant to outside pressure. That leaves capabilities, which US policy-makers believe can be affected more readily and have, therefore, become the focus of US non-proliferation efforts.[20] Under present US policy, a nation's pursuit of nuclear capabilities signals, if not the intent to develop nuclear weapons, then at least the refusal to genuinely foreswear that option.

This policy directly contradicts the prescription for an 'open options' strategy, which would take a nation at its word that it has no intentions to acquire nuclear weapons. The arguments in favour of open options include:

The conviction that the spread of nuclear technology is already beyond the control of the primary suppliers so continued restrictions will only exacerbate the bitterness already apparent among the importing countries and further diminish the suppliers' limited influence.

That the option will be enough and the prestige states are unlikely
to go nuclear.

That non-proliferation efforts should concentrate on nations more
likely actually to develop nuclear weapons, and whose nuclear
status would pose a greater threat to regional or international
stability.[21]

Open options need not force the US or others to embrace the
diffusion of nuclear technology through declaratory policy; acceptance does not require promotion. It does demand an altered view of
the risks posed by nuclear capabilities in the hands of the prestige
states, and an altered diplomatic style for dealing with them. In short,
all near-nuclear nations are not equal; a wise non-proliferation
strategy would acknowledge and capitalize on that.

The other side of the open options strategy requires insuring that
the penalties for violating the trust and going nuclear be severe and
automatic. The United States and others committed to non-
proliferation already possess the capability to make the price of
possessing nuclear weapons very high indeed, but this approach
demands a willingness to exact it.[22] That willingness, however, is
necessarily constrained by fears for other foreign policy and economic
aims that sanctions for deploying nuclear weapons would frustrate.
Moreover, withdrawal of military and economic assistance, trade
embargoes, diplomatic isolation, withholding of nuclear fuel, and
other penalties, in addition to thwarting unrelated objectives, could
split an emerging anti-proliferation coalition, end any access to the
proliferator's decision making and, finally, ultimately encourage
rather than discourage nuclear weapons deployment. While preventing nuclear proliferation clearly will be a major goal in the 1980s for
many in the international community, and although some countries
have shown an increasing willingness to sacrifice other interests to this
objective, it remains far from certain that the sacrifices will be enough
or that strong medicine will cure rather than aggravate the problem.

With an open options policy, the persistent non-proliferation
problem of discrimination would continue or worsen, for the policy
implicitly tolerates a latent nuclear weapons capacity not expected to
lead to bomb production and deployment but penalizes the same
capacity if production and deployment can be foreseen. With
sensitivity to discrimination already at a high pitch in the internationl
community more discriminatory policies could further aggravate the
situation.

Such an approach also requires establishing a consensus among suppliers of nuclear technology about which are prestige states and which are garrison states, as well as agreement on what constitutes a nuclear weapons capability. Is the line of demarcation to be drawn at possession of a full fuel cycle, detonation of a 'peaceful' nuclear device, attaining the resources for quantity production, or acquisition of plausible delivery systems? The current international standard – actual explosion of a nuclear device – while it has the merit of comparative visibility, may not prove to be adequate or realistic for an open options policy.

In view of the many conceivable routes to a nuclear weapons capability, developing an acceptable new definition may be extremely difficult. The 'trigger list' of sensitive technologies developed by the London Nuclear Suppliers Group is implicity a definition of capability. It may represent the most that suppliers can agree on and still be inadequate as a basis for an open options policy. Complicating the picture are the growing nuclear technology assistance agreements between the potential proliferators and other nations looking to nuclear power for relief from energy bills. As indigenous nuclear technology improves among the hitherto major importers, the traditional exporters are finding their near-monopoly of this commodity a less and less potent lever. Their agreement on definitions and measures may not suffice to reduce proliferation potential. Finally, verification requirements for a new capability standard may prove so intrusive as to be intolerable even to the most zealous advocate of proliferation prevention.

If, on the other hand, the exploration of a more tolerant and differentiated non-proliferation policy exposes many hazards, it should also illuminate the pitfalls of an indiscriminate and insensitive approach. The assumption that prestige motivations are frivolous or illegitimate is an obstacle to a realistic policy that recognizes the difference between being able to develop a significant nuclear weapons inventory and actually doing so. Years of trying to prevent the spread of nuclear weapons should have made clear that prestige drives are strong and resistant to both persuasion and coercion, even if generally less urgent than those arising from direct security concerns. The resentment created by lumping potential bomb-makers together with potential bomb-throwers is, moreover, a barrier to effective implementation of a non-proliferation policy of any kind. An examination of the nuclear programmes of the foremost prestige states, Argentina and Brazil, illustrate both the conceptual appeal and the practical pitfalls of the open options strategy.

ILLUSTRATIONS

The potential for nuclear proliferation in Latin America offers a good site for the analysis of prestige motivations, since most observers regard the region as, objectively, devoid of security incentives.

Armed forces are needed in Latin America principally to maintain law and order, and to deter and eliminate subversion. There is little objective military need for any Latin American country to acquire a military capability to defend itself against other states in the region or to defend the region as a whole against attack.[23]

Suspicions and rivalries are plentiful among Latin American nations, but there has been a remarkable absence of the bloodshed that plagues regions such as the Middle East. The violence Latin American governments and their citizens inflict upon one another is not the sort for which nuclear weapons are appropriate. Moreover, aside from the intrusion of the Cuban missile crisis and its recent, pale imitation, Latin America has never figured as a major theatre in the Cold War, so nuclear weapons are unlikely to be introduced in an extension of the East-West conflict. Under present conditions, if nuclear weapons appear in Argentina or Brazil – the most likely candidates – it will be because the prestige of possessing them presented a temptation those nations could not resist.

Six Latin American nations have active national nuclear energy programmes: Mexico, Argentina, Brazil, Chile, Colombia, Cuba, and Venezuela. In addition, Bolivia, Ecuador, Peru, and Uruguay all plan to acquire research reactors in the near future.[24] Of these, only the Brazilian, Argentine, and Mexican programmes are advanced enough to be significant to non-proliferation policy in the 1980s. The other programmes are either embryonic or confined to research reactors and cooperative projects with the International Atomic Energy Agency (IAEA) in such fields as desalinization and food production.[25] Mexico, however, unilaterally declared itself a one-nation, nuclear weapon-free zone in March 1962 and has been a consistent and zealous advocate of such zones in Latin America. Brazil and Argentina, on the other hand, appear frequently on 'most likely Nth country' lists. Each has ambitions for regional dominance and international status. Neither is a party to the Non-proliferation Treaty (NPT), although both have signed the Treaty for the Prohibition of Nuclear Weapons in Latin America (the Treaty of Tlatelolco).[26] They have declared publicly that they do not intend to develop nuclear weapons but are nonetheless acquiring capabilities that would make it relatively easy for them to do so. Brazil and Argentina thus represent nearly perfect specimens of prestige states.

Argentina. Argentina was the first Latin American nation to launch a nuclear energy programme, in part with the help of refuge scientists from Hitler's Germany.[27] President Juan Peron issued a decree creating the National Commission for Nuclear Energy (CNEA) in 1950. Five years later the CNEA signed an Atoms for Peace agreement with the United States, allowing Argentina to benefit from US financial and technical assistance, as well as supplies of American enriched uranium. While the turmoil in Argentina's political and economic life has kept the nuclear energy programme from developing at the anticipated rate – causing continual delays in funding, administrative frustrations, and the consequent loss of trained personnel – there has been remarkably little direct political interference in the CNEA's operations over the years.[28]

Argentina's six research reactors include the first active nuclear facility on the continent, RA-1, commissioned in 1958.[29] The first facility was built with US assistance, but the CNEA designed and constructed the other five entirely on its own. As early as 1957, Argentine leaders had decided to develop an independent nuclear programme, designing and building its own research reactors and training a pool of qualified nuclear scientists and technicians. Argentina's nuclear programme today ranks with India's as among the most advanced in the Third World across almost the full range of atomic technology, clearly leading the field of nuclear technology in Latin America. Its nuclear energy programme is well established, relatively uncontroversial domestically, and likely to maintain its technological edge through at least the mid-1980s.

The desire for independence and indigenous development also influenced the 1968 decision to rely on heavy-water power reactors, using natural uranium, of which Argentina has an adequate supply for its currently projected needs, rather than the less expensive light-water variety that depends on enriched uranium – whose supply the US nearly monopolizes.[30] The first power plant, Atucha I, purchased from West Germany, began operating ('went critical') in 1974 and currently produces 319 megawatts of electricity (MWE).[31] A second plant, Cordoba (Embalse), which will generate over 600 MWE, is being built by a Canadian firm but has suffered from serious cost overruns and production delays.[32] The CNEA nevertheless plans four more power plants by 1997, with Argentina contributing significant portions of technical services and locally manufactured equipment.

Non-proliferation efforts *vis-à-vis* Argentina have been hampered because so much of its programme has developed indigenously that the nuclear suppliers have had only limited leverage over its course and because the programme has lacked dramatic events around which non-proliferation advocates could focus a concerted international campaign. The recent awarding of the contract for Argentina's third power reactor, Atucha II, demonstrates the clear limits of outside leverage over Argentina's nuclear choices. The two primary competitors were Canadian and West German firms, and the competing contract negotiations increasingly focused on the safeguards to be demanded over the new facility. Argentina planned to purchase a commercial-scale heavy-water plant as part of a package deal with the power reactor, which would complete its control over the heavy-water fuel cycle.[33] The US, although not competing for the reactor contract, sought to ensure that full-scope safeguards would be a condition of any sale, since Argentina is not a party to either the NPT or the Tlatelolco Treaty and has only International Atomic Energy Agency (IAEA) safeguards currently in force. Argentina argued against pressures for full-scope safeguards, but West Germany and Canada agreed to demand them as part of any package deal. Argentina, either on its own or in response to prompting by the West Germans, then split up the package, awarding the reactor contract to KWU, the West German firm, and the heavy-water plant to a Swiss firm.[34] The single contracts will cost $500 million more than the Canadian package, but the West Germans and Swiss will require safeguards only on their respective projects.[35] Admiral Castro Carlos Madero, President of CNEA, speculated that Argentina might alternate between West Germany and Canada in its awards for the three remaining reactors to maximize Argentina's continued independence and national control.[36]

An outgrowth of Argentina's technological leadership is its developing role as nuclear mentor to other Latin American nations. The new research reactor in Peru that was to go critical in 1979, for example, was completely designed and developed in Argentina; even the enriched uranium for the reactor is Argentine-supplied.[37] Argentina signed a nuclear cooperation agreement with Ecuador in April 1977, and its plan of action for 1978 with Uruguay follows on their 1968 bilateral cooperation agreement. Argentina and Bolivia announced a nuclear cooperation agreement in April 1978 that will involve development of a research reactor at Viaha, 70 kilometres from La Paz. Argentina has agreements for joint mining exploration with Uruguay, Peru, Bolivia, and Ecuador as part of their broader bilateral atomic cooperation accords.

Simple nationalism, as much as any desire to develop nuclear weapons free from outside interference, could explain Argentina's nuclear policy choices. Its chosen course to nuclear independence, however, maximizes its capability to acquire nuclear weapons more than other paths would, suggesting that Argentina has deliberately sought to maintain its nuclear freedom of choice.[38] The most likely path for eventual Argentine proliferation would be through a 'peaceful nuclear explosion' (PNE) comparable to India's. Argentina has already filed a reservation to the Tlatelolco Treaty maintaining the view that a meaningful distinction can be made between peaceful and other nuclear devices.[39] In terms simply of technical capabilities, Argentina could easily acquire nuclear explosive devices by the end of the 1980s, and far earlier if it undertook a crash programme. With or without the acquiescence of the major powers, Argentina has assured its own 'open option' for the future of its nuclear programme.

Brazil. Argentina's only challenger for nuclear leadership in Latin America is Brazil, and their rivalry reflects the patterns of their traditional struggle for dominance on the continent.[40]

Brazil entered the nuclear competition later than Argentina, stimulated primarily by the US Atoms for Peace programme. In 1956 President Juscelino Kubitschek founded the Brazilian Commission for Nuclear Energy, which supposedly formulates and controls all national nuclear energy policy.[41] The 1964 coup that ousted President João Goulart and installed a military government gave nuclear development a major boost, for the new military leaders revived Brazilian ambitions to continental dominance and great-power status. Nuclear energy, including development of nuclear explosive devices for peaceful purposes, formed an integral part of the military's plan for Brazilian greatness, as well as a means to reduce Brazil's heavy dependence on imported oil.[42]

The same desire for indigenous development and control that motivated Argentina propelled Brazilian nuclear development, but with less success. Its three nuclear research reactors, all based on US designs, depended on American-supplied enriched uranium, although the reactors were manufactured in Brazil by Brazilian companies and are staffed entirely by Brazilian technical personnel.[43] The ambitious nuclear power programme, by choosing light-water reactors, leaves Brazil dependent on foreign sources of enriched uranium at least until the mid-1980s and probably throughout the decade.[44] As evidence of its desire to escape eventually from such dependence, Brazil signed a nuclear cooperation agreement with France in 1967 that would, it was claimed, transform Brasilia into 'the atomic capital of Latin America' through the eventual development of the Phenix breeder reactor technology.[45]

Brazil is still awaiting completion of its first nuclear power plant, the 626 MWE Angra I. Already several years behind schedule, serious construction problems and safety hazards have plagued the builders, the American firm Westinghouse.[46] Questions about geological suitability of the site itself, which is scheduled to include two other 1300 MWE power reactors, have cast doubt on the future of Brazil's 1975 deal with West Germany for the 'largest transfer ever made of nuclear technology to a developing country.'[47]

The contract with West Germany was to provide Brazil with the entire light-water fuel cycle and eventual nuclear self-sufficiency. Brazil also signed agreements with West Germany to work on high temperature reactor technology to make use of Brazil's extensive thorium deposits.[48] By 1990 West Germany was to construct up to eight huge power reactors, each with a 1300 MWE capacity, and supply Brazil with enrichment and reprocessing technology. The plans called for Brazil to assume an increasingly large share of the construction and technical responsibilities as the projects continued. The overall cost of the package, estimated at $10 billion, has now risen to $30 billion and slipped 5 to 10 years behind its planned completion date.[49]

Economic and technological problems have combined to shake Brazilian and West German confidence in their plans, although both steadfastly maintain the project will go ahead as planned.[50] The Angra III reactor may have to be moved away from its planned location with Angra I and II because adequate foundations cannot be laid for it, and the West Germans have shown increasing concern about the overall safety of the programme. Brazil in turn is finding the projected cost of its nuclear energy less and less economically attractive – up from original estimates of $900 per kilowatt of installed capacity to at least $1700 and perhaps $3000.[51] This has led to speculation that Brazil will stop at four plants and concentrate on other sources of power to relieve its energy crisis. The tone of the new government of President Figueiredo was noticeably cooler in pronouncements about Brazil's nuclear future.[52] West Germany, however, insisted that only eight plants would justify investment in the full fuel cycle and threatened to hold up the technology transfer until Brazil reaffirmed its commitment.[53] Other reports question the practicality of the enrichment technology Brazil will acquire. Only West Germany and South Africa have chosen to pursue this aerodynamic jet nozzle process, which has yet to move beyond laboratory-scale into full commercial operation.

Finally, a Sao Paulo newspaper leaked details of the secret agreement for forming NUCLEN, the joint Brazilian-West German venture to oversee the transfer of nuclear technology that indicated West Germany retained full control of the technology and was not implementing its transfer.[54] This threatened to provoke a major scandal, for the promise of technological independence had been the primary rationale for making the deal with West Germany and defying the heavy US pressure to cancel the contract. In this case, it appears technological and economic problems, rather than political strategies, may achieve the greatest effects for non-proliferation.

The censorious US reactions to the deal – a *New York Times* editorial spoke of 'nuclear madness'[55] – and its subsequent heavy-handed pressure on Brazil and West Germany put a severe strain on US relations with both countries.[56] In the process, it confirmed Brazilian perceptions that independence in nuclear and energy matters was essential to its visions of Brazil's future role in Latin America and the world, however severe the technological difficulties. When asked if his country would consider foregoing reprocessing technology, the president of NUCLEBRAS, the Brazilian energy corporation, replied:

> To give up recycling means to have no plutonium which is also ours, right? It would be like giving up our water, the energy of our rivers, our oil, or our uranium. Plutonium is a fuel which will be produced in Brazil, in our country, There is no reason to give it up.[57]

Brazil, because its nuclear technology has developed more slowly and has come from abroad rather than developed indigenously, has not pursued the role of nuclear mentor to other Latin American or Third World countries in which Argentina has been so successful. This changed in mid-1979 with a major oil-for-nuclear assistance agreement with Venezuela. In return for 50 000 barrels of oil per day, the Brazilians will supply Venezuela with technological assistance with their plans for nuclear power development.[58] Argentina, disturbed by this Latin American Brazilian approach to the democratic regimes outside the southern cone, responded by signing a more ambitious long-term nuclear cooperation agreement with Venezuela a month later.[59]

Brazil's potential mastery of nuclear technology has also brought it a less welcome potential ally – Iraq. Iraq now supplies 40 per cent of Brazil's oil imports and Iraqi officials have made no secret of their interest in gaining access to the nuclear technology Brazil will receive from West Germany. A modest nuclear cooperation agreement between the two countries was signed in 1979, but the Brazilians are reluctant to become more heavily involved in a nuclear programme with the heavy political character of Iraq's, and will probably avoid close nuclear cooperation if they can, especially after Osirak.[60]

Like Argentina, the probable Brazilian route to nuclear weapons would be through PNEs. Brazil filed a reservation to its ratification of Tlatelolco reaffirming that a meaningful practical distinction could be made between peaceful and military explosions. Each nation, in its own way, is ensuring itself of the independent technical capacity to produce nuclear explosive devices. At the moment, Brazil lags behind Argentina in nuclear technology, but an all-out effort could close the gap. Given their long rivalry and mutual suspicion, a 'peaceful' nuclear explosion by one could trigger a comparable 'test' by the other within a short time. The perceived tie between their national self-image and the need to maintain the independence of their nuclear energy programmes has led Brazil and Argentina into a determined pursuit of the full nuclear fuel cycle, which, in turn, means a greater technical capacity to produce nuclear weapons. Their search for prestige and independence, however, runs directly counter to the current emphasis of international non-proliferation strategy on restricting the export of sensitive technology.

CONCEPTUAL APPEAL, PRACTICAL LIMITATIONS

As the discussion of Argentina and Brazil illustrates, separating the prestige states from other potential proliferators offers a useful conceptual approach to understanding proliferation in the 1980s, whatever its impact on specific policy choices. Such classification should help policy-makers in ordering priorities and assessing the probable impact of the eventual, and perhaps inevitable, spread of nuclear weapons capacity. If, as appears likely, merely technological solutions elude the grasp of anti-proliferators, a greater awareness of motives and incentives might facilitate the political solutions that increasingly appear a necessary part of efforts to control or manage proliferation.

Acceptance of open options as a strategy, however, requires acknowledgement of the grave risks run if policy-makers acquiesce in the enhancement of any nation's ability to produce nuclear weapons. Motivations may change overnight in a coup, through an election, or emergence of an unanticipated external threat; once significant nuclear capabilities are in place, the path to nuclear weapons is short and the obstacles outsiders can erect on it limited. The argument that the risks are worth taking rests on particular, pessimistic convictions about the proliferation threat in the 1980s: If new technologies are likely to put this capability in the hands of many nations in spite of the best non-proliferation efforts, if the status needs of countries can be satisfied by having this capacity and no more, if the real politico-military concern is for the development of nuclear *forces* rather than a nuclear *device*, then some intermediate position between capability and deployment may be tolerable, where perceived intentions and perceived threats do not suggest a strong urge to move from one to the other. If this appears to set a course down a slippery slope, the open options strategy assumes it is the bearing nations have had to follow since the advent of nuclear weapons; a new tack seems most unlikely and careful navigation is thus the best that can be hoped for.

An approach to proliferation based on distinguishing the prestige states from others is analogous to recommendations to concentrate on more security-minded states where motivations for nuclear weapons might be more manipulable, for both prescribe a differentiated strategy.[61] This argues again that proliferation is a regional or even subregional rather than global problem that must be dealt with selectively to have any hope of effectiveness. If discrimination is to be a permanent 'feature of non-proliferation efforts – and the nature and history of the problem suggest it will – then perhaps policy-makers should be self-conscious about it, and make a virtue of this vice, in spite of all its difficulties. The alternative is to adopt even-handed, across-the-board policies as a matter of principle and apply them differentially in practice, thereby creating resentment over the resulting hypocrisy. (Less rhetorical righteousness and more realism on the part of both anti-proliferators and potential proliferators would also help to put the perennial problem of discrimination in perspective.) Since, owing to objective differences, discrimination is likely to be a permanent part of international relations in some form, it is probably something nations can learn to live with if it is carefully rationalized and not constantly made conspicuous. In any case, it derives from an essential question non-proliferation policy must increasingly face up to: Does it make a difference to worry about a possible bomb in the basement if the basement is in Buenos Aires rather than in Rawalpindi? Again, this perspective suggests that all near-nuclear states are not the same, hardly a startling concept but one that dictates a shift in diplomatic tactics.

Evaluation of the prestige states indicates that other political and economic instruments might have positive consequences for non-proliferation, especially if used in conjunction with a policy that is more tolerant of a nuclear weapons capacity yet more intolerant of deployed nuclear weapons. Carrots, tangible and intangible, might be more effective than the sticks that make up much of current non-proliferation policy, at least the American version.[62] Bribery in the name of non-proliferation is not the answer – it makes bad policy and bad precedent – but neither is the patronizing and indiscriminate approach that seems guaranteed to offend the already very sensitive near-nuclear nations, especially the prestige-conscious ones. Diplomatic style does matter in non-proliferation efforts; it can be improved by efforts to understand and address the multiple motives for acquiring nuclear weapons.

Easing the pressure on the prestige states might also give other forces with indirect benefits for non-proliferation a chance to make their effects felt. A number of prominent analysts suggest that increased programme costs, worries about safety and health hazards since Three Mile Island, technological barriers that resist easy solutions, and less-than-projected energy requirements will combine to dampen the enthusiasm for nuclear power around the world.[63] If this disillusion with nuclear energy spreads – a controversial projection not accepted by many experts – it may diminish the desires of some states to push ahead toward the full fuel cycle. Given the alternative routes to nuclear weapons production, this would not necessarily ease proliferation pressures on security-motivated states, but it could have substantial indirect benefits in the prestige states if it leads to a slowdown in their nuclear development.

Any policy that lowered the priority to be given to the prestige states in non-proliferation efforts would have to resolve the question of how to treat safeguards. Most of the garrison and prestige states considered the most likely nuclear candidates have not signed the NPT and refuse to accept the full scope safeguards the US and some other suppliers now demand as conditions for further cooperation and exports of technology. The supplier states could retreat to acceptance of IAEA safeguards, to which most nations adhere, and work to upgrade their quality or could again discriminate, less overtly perhaps in this instance, in choosing which nations should suffer the heaviest pressure to toe the line on comprehensive safeguards. The intelligence requirements for checking compliance to ensure that states do not slip across the technological boundaries to develop nuclear weapons clandestinely would be formidable. Pakistan's recent 'end run' to acquire uranium enrichment capabilities argues against being optimistic that detection would provide the necessary warning to bring a diplomatic deterrent into action.[64] Of all the pitfalls inhibiting an open options strategy, the problems of safeguards and the means to monitor the prestige states' good behaviour pose the most serious hazards.

Balancing its advantages and drawbacks, certain features of an open options policy could enhance any non-proliferation strategy. Recognition of prestige motives as serious and enduring if it leads to a lowering of the rhetorical temperature on both sides, would be a genuine boon. Coupling a more sensitive diplomatic style with diplomatic practices to facilitate alternative routes to international status and conscious efforts to recognize these achievements could ease the prestige state's perceived need to maintain their commitment to the full fuel cycle for the sake of their national independence and pride. These slow, painful adjustments hold no non-proliferation panaceas, but they avoid the risks in the full open option strategy, while promising to ease some of the intense bitterness that so seriously undermines the present non-proliferation regime.

The early 1980s appear a bad time to launch any new non-proliferation initiatives, for the current international regime has still not fully adjusted to the impact of the 1974 Indian test. Moreover, 1980 brought new factors: the second NPT review conference, the culmination of the International Fuel Cycle Evaluation (INFCE) deliberations, and the deadline set by the US Nuclear Non-proliferation Act for nations to negotiate new bilateral cooperation agreements that include 'full-scope' safeguards or face a cut-off of American nuclear assistance. For the next few years at least, non-proliferation efforts would be better served by responding to the effects of these events, capitalizing on their success or failure and coping with their particular dangers. An open options policy, which demands firm diplomatic control and fine tuning, seems especially risky in this uncertain environment. Prescriptions on changes in policy do not preclude changes in diplomatic practice, however; the difference between good and bad diplomacy often rests as much on style as on substance. Distinguishing among types of near-nuclear nations while implementing a general non-proliferation strategy may appear a modest recommendation but it would represent a significant improvement over much current activity. If attitudes and perceptions lie at the heart of the prestige states' interest in nuclear weapons, then anti-proliferation efforts in the 1980s should concentrate at a minimum on not exacerbating, and in the long term on easing, those fundamental concerns. Meeting in legitimate aspirations of the prestige states is a wise long-range diplomatic objective for the current world powers. Thus, what is sound non-proliferation policy is good policy generally.

NOTES AND REFERENCES

1. Among the studies that list probable candidates for nuclear-weapons are Lewis A. Dunn and Herman Kahn, *Trends in Nuclear Proliferation, 1975-1995: Projections, Problems, and Policy Options* (Croton-on-Hudson, NY: Hudson Institute, 1976); William Epstein, *The Last Chance: Nuclear Proliferation and Arms Control* (New York: The Free Press, 1976); Stockholm International Peace Research Institute (SIRPRI), *The Near Nuclear Countries and the NPT* (New York: Humanities Press, 1972); and Onkar Marwah and Ann Schulz (eds), *Nuclear Proliferation and the Near-Nuclear Countries* (Cambridge, Mass.: Ballinger, 1975).

2. Of the 34 possible Nth countries reviewed by Dunn and Kahn, prestige dominated the motives of only a dozen. Dunn and Kahn, unfortunately, include a desire 'to demonstrate national viability' and a susceptibility to 'fashion' among prestige motivations. Given the countries they cite – Taiwan and South Africa – the former category seems more analogous to security considerations, while the latter judgement seems more pejorative than analytic. The remaining ten are Algeria, Argentina, Brazil, Chile, Cuba, Italy, Nigeria, Spain, Venezuela, and Zaire and, of these, two – Argentina and Brazil – are labelled 'most critical potential Nth countries.'

3. Analysts appear better able to accept fear for national survival as legitimate, even if they completely reject nuclear weapons as a cure. The view that additional proliferation might under certain conditions enhance rather than detract from international security received its first popular promotion from France's General Gallois [*Stratégie de l'âge*

nucléaire (Paris: Calmann-Levy, 1960). For a critique of Gallois' concept of 'proportional deterrence' see Raymond Aron, *The Great Debate: Theories of Nuclear Strategy* (Garden City, NY: Doubleday, 1965).

4. Committee for Economic Development, *Nuclear Energy and National Security* (New York: Committee for Economic Development, 1976) p. 11.

5. In a 1958 television interview, British Prime Minister Macmillan reported:

> The independent (nuclear) contribution gives us a better position in the world, it give us a better position with respect to the United States. It puts us where we ought to be, in the position of a great power. The fact that we have it makes the United States pay a greater regard to our point of view, and that is of great importance.

Quoted in Robert E. Osgood, *NATO, The Entangling Alliance* (University of Chicago Press, 1962) p. 243.

6. As Wilfrid H. Kohl concludes in his study, *French Nuclear Diplomacy* (Princeton University Press, 1971) pp. 41-2:

> When by 1958 a government consensus on the question had finally emerged, the political arguments in favor of developing atomic weapons appeared paramount in the minds of political leaders... it was the evolution of the international situation in the middle and late 1950s that brought the question to the fore in the high councils of government, as France sought to compensate for her diplomatic isolation and her successive defeats in colonial conflicts. The development of a French nuclear capability was seen primarily as a way to preserve France's status and respect as a front rank ally within the Atlantic alliance, along with Great Britain, the United States, and the other atomic powers. Military incentives are supplemental, rather than central, factors in the government's final choice.

7. See George Quester, *The Politics of Nuclear Proliferation* Baltimore: The Johns Hopkins University Press, 1973), and James E. Dougherty, 'Nuclear Proliferation in Asia,' *Orbis* (Fall 1975).

8. The best known work with a capabilities inventory approach to measuring power is Hans J. Morgenthau, *Politics Among Nations: The Struggle for Power and Peace*, 4th edn, (New York: Alfred A. Knopf, 1967). A recent study using this approach is Ray S. Cline, *World Power Assessment: A Calculus of Strategic Drift* (Washington, DC: Georgetown University, Center for Strategic and International Studies, 1975).

9. The NPT defines nuclear weapons states as only those nations already possessing nuclear weapons when the treaty was opened for signature in 1968. For a discussion of the NPT negotiations that highlights the non-nuclear weapons states protests against discrimination see George Fischer, *The Non-proliferation of Nuclear Weapons* (London: Europa, 1971).

10. Rikhi Jaipal, 'The Indian Nuclear Situation', *International Security* (Spring 1977) p. 47. This article contains all the major themes in the non-nuclear nations' criticisms of present non-proliferation policy; see also Jorge A. Sabato and Jairam Ramesh, 'Nuclear Energy Programs in the Developing World: Their Rationale and Impacts', Paper presented to the Royal Institution Forum on Energy Strategies for the Third World, 1979.

11. World Bank, *1978 World Bank Atlas* (Washington, DC: The World Bank, 1978). Brazil is often mentioned as a *potential* great power, largely because it has yet to consolidate its dramatic growth and extend its 'miracle' to broader segments of Brazilian society; in *per capita* GNP Brazil ranks 57th and is in the middle third among 140 nations in 1975 rankings on major social indicators [Ruth Leger Sivard, *World Military and Social Expenditures* (Leesburg, Virginia: WMSE Publications, 1978)].

12. The OAPEC nations have forced significant alterations in Western policies toward Israel and the rights of Palestinean self-determination, for example, but their political efforts have concentrated on mostly regional not international issues.

13. See Epstein and Fischer for examples of these arguments and their impact on non-proliferation efforts.

14. Jaipal, op. cit., for example, argues:

> It is a fallacy to regard the prevention of horizontal proliferation as a *quid pro quo* for vertical nuclear disarmament. Both kinds of proliferation should of course be prevented, but the fact is that there has been no horizontal proliferation of nuclear weapons so far and the prospect of it seems extremely unlikely. In any case it cannot possibly pose the same degree of threat to world peace as vertical proliferation of nuclear weapons by the superpowers who seem to escalate from one nuclear brink to another (p. 48).

15. Non-proliferation advocates were thus concerned by India's almost unscathed entry into the ranks of nuclear nations, although technically India is not yet a nuclear power because it has not moved on to a nuclear weapons programme. Of the nuclear suppliers only Canada, which had supplied the research reactor from which fuel was diverted for the Indian test, protested strongly. The US enacted only mild sanctions against India and continued to supply nuclear fuel for the Tarapur reactor [Ernest Lefever, *Nuclear Arms in the Third World: US Policy Dilemma* (Washington, DC: The Brookings Institution, 1979)].

16. American officals repeatedly state that such acceptance is already an essential feature of current policy. See, for example, Joseph Nye, 'The US Approach to Non-proliferaton – Are We Making Progress?', address to the International Conference on Non-proliferation and Safeguards, Atomic Industrial Forum, New York City, 23 October 1978. This perception is not widely shared outside the United States, however; see Michael Brenner, 'Carter's Non-proliferation Strategy: A Fuel Assurances and Energy Security', *Orbis*, (Summer 1978.

17. The treaty text is contained in SIPRI, p. 107-12.
18. This ignores the fact that India's programme, begun in 1948, ranked among the most advanced in the developing nations and compared favourably with those in several developed ones. See Jaipal, op. cit., pp. 44-6 and Lefever, op. cit., p. 27-8. The long-term implications, if not the immediate threat, remain serious, however.
19. See Nye and Warren Donnelly, 'The Nuclear Non-proliferation Act of 1978, Public Law 95-242: An Explanation' (Washington, DC: Congressional Research Service, Library of Congress, 1978).
20. Michael Brenner, 'Carter's Bungled Promise', *Foreign Policy* (Fall 1979) and Joseph J. Nye, Jr, 'We Tried Harder (And Did More)', *Foreign Policy* (Fall 1979).
21. For a discussion of the effects of proliferation in several regions, as well as its international impact, see John Kerry King (ed.), *International Political Effects of the Spread of Nuclear Weapons* (Washington, DC: GPO, 1979).
22. The US and other suppliers have on occasion shown a willingness and capacity to affect a near-nuclear nation's choices. In South Korea, for example, a concerted diplomatic effort led by the US forced the South Koreans to cancel plans for buying a reprocessing plant from France (Young-Sun Ha, 'Nuclear Future of Koran and World Order', Paper presented to the Annual Meeting of the International Studies Association, 1979).
23. Lincoln P. Bloomfield and Amelia C. Leiss, 'Arms Control and the Developing Countries', *World Politics*, vol xviii, no. 1 (1965) p. 7.
24. *Nuclear Proliferation Factbook*, prepared by the Environment and Natural Resources Policy Division, Library of Congress (Washington DC: GPO 1977) pp. 222-3. Only Peru and Uruguay are close to research reactors; Bolivia and Ecuador are just launching programmes.
25. John R. Redick, 'Nuclear Proliferation in Latin America', in Roger Fontaine and James D. Theberg (eds), *Latin America's New Internationalism: The End of Hemisphere Isolation* (New York: Praeger 1976).
26. Brazil has ratified the Treaty of Tlatelolco but refuses to permit it to enter automatically into effect (a special clause in the Treaty permits this waiver) until all the Latin states are full parties. Argentina, in spite of public commitments during the UN Special Session on Disarmament, has yet to ratify the Treaty. For a discussion of the Tlatelolco Treaty, see Jo L. Husbands, 'Nuclear Proliferation and the Inter-American System', in Tom J. Farer (ed.), *The Future of the Inter-American System* (New York: Praeger 1979).
27. Between 1950 and 1952, then President Juan Peron lavishly maintained Nazi émigré Ronald Richter in a research centre picturesquely isolated on an island in a mountain lake. Richter was dismissed when his exaggerated claims of fusion research breakthroughs eventually embarrassed the Peron regime.
28. The Argentine navy has had a continuing proprietary interest, and the CNEA has benefited from its protection. The agency had only three

directors in its first 18 years, all of them retired admirals. See John Redick, 'Regional Restraint: US Nuclear Policy and Latin America', *Orbis* (Spring 1978).

29. E.J. Elder, 'The Present Status of Research Reactor Engineering in Argentina', Paper translated from the Spanish by Dr J. G. Wilson (Washington, DC: National Technical Information Service, 1975).

30. The US complicated its non-proliferation efforts further by closing the books for orders for uranium enrichment services with the Energy Research and Development Agency in 1974, just as the first effects of the OPEC oil embargo and price increases were beginning to be felt. The US had expended considerable effort since, not always successfully, to restore its reputation as a reliable supplier (see Brenner, op. cit., 1978).

31. *Nuclear Proliferation Factbook*, p. 239.

32. The cost for the Cordoba plant rose from $320 million to $1 billion over the course of contruction and has been delayed at least 2 years (Geri Smith, 'KWU Wins Argentine Contract for Atucha-2; Sulzer to Build D$_2$O Plant', *Nucleonics Week*, 4 October 1979, p. 10).

33. Argentina was operating a prototype chemical reprocessing plant as early as 1968, but it was reported closed down (*Nuclear Proliferation Factbook*, p. 198). In 1978 CNEA director Admiral Carlos Castro Madero announced plans to reactivate the plant and to develop an expanded indigenous reprocessing capability (M.R. Benjamin, 'Argentina on the Threshold of Nuclear Reprocessing', *Washington Post*, 16 October 1978).

34. 'The Argentine Reactor Order Has Cast a Cold Spell on Canadian-West German Relations,' *Nucleonics Week*, 29 November 1979, p. 5.

35. Smith, p. 10.

36. Ibid.

37. Reports from Buenos Aires noted that the Argentine decision to send 15 kg of enriched uranium to Peru generated inquiries from a number of other Third World countries (Buenos Aires Domestic Service, quoted in the Foreign Broadcast Information Service (FBIS), 1 March 1978).

38. John R. Redick, *Military Potential of Latin American Nuclear Energy Programs.* (Beverly Hills: Sage, 1972). Quester, SIPRI, and Lefever all reach similar conclusions about Argentina's deliberate choice of an open options policy.

39. The Argentines and Indians have signed a nuclear cooperation agreement; by an unfortunate coincidence, the agreement was completed just after India exploded its first peaceful nuclear device.

40. Lefever, p. 100 and Steven M. Gorman, 'Security, Influence, and Nuclear Weapons: The Case of Argentina and Brazil', *Parameters*, (March 1979). The Gorman article discusses the conventional military balance between the two nations and possible strategic rationales for nuclear weapons.

41. CNEN has been superseded by NUCLEBRAS, with jurisdiction over specific aspects of nuclear development vested in various government-owned or managed utilities and corporations. Recently, NUCLEBRAS has moved to reassert its control. Roger Smith, 'NUCLEBRAS Will Run Brazilian Program After Angra-2', *Nucleonics Week*, 31 May 1979, pp. 5-6.

42. H. J. Rosenbaum and G. Cooper, 'Brazil and the Nuclear Non-proliferation Treaty', *International Affairs*, vol. 46, no. 1 (1970).
43. Redick, 1978, p. 52.
44. Brazilian plans to purchase enriched uranium from URENCO, the British-French-Dutch consortium, until its own enrichment facilities are completed, hit a snag in early 1978. The Dutch parliament refused to permit URENCO exports unless Brazil agreed to extensive safeguards. The Brazilians considered their arrangements with the West Germans for IAEA safeguards sufficient and refused to sign stricter agreements. The Dutch objections were eventually overruled, but while the dispute lasted, Brazilian newspapers reported British, French, and even Soviet offers to supply enriched uranium if the URENCO deal collapsed.
45. John R. Redick, *The Politics of Denuclearization: A Study of the Treaty for the Prohibition of Nuclear Weapons in Latin America* (Unpublished Ph.D. Dissertation, University of Virginia, 1970). By the late 1960s, Brazil had signed nuclear cooperation agreements with twelve countries and international organizations.
46. A series of reports began appearing in March 1978, first in *O Estado do Sao Paulo*, of major constructon accidents and flaws. A total of 71 fires were reported between June and November 1977; one $4 million warehouse blaze destroyed equipment for all parts of the Angra I project. Beyond this, foundation cracks were reported, and slight tilting of the turbogenerator building cast doubt on the geological soundness of the site. There was also a report of a 7 metre high tide almost flooding the reactor building, and various hints of industrial sabotage. Construction stopped on Angra I and II while additional pilings were driven to ensure a firm foundation for the reactors. Official comments have been confined to downgrading the seriousness of the accidents, and pointing out that other nations' nuclear projects have troubles too.
47. Norman Gall, 'Atoms for Peace, Dangers for All', *Foreign Policy* (Summer 1976).
48. *Jornal do Brasil*, 28 February 1978, p. 23.
49. Roger Smith, p. 5.
50. Brazilian President Figueiredo announced at a state dinner for visiting West German Chancellor Schmidt that 'the nuclear programme will be fully implemented' (*Latin American Political Report*, 13 April 1979, p. 117).
51. 'Change of Mood May Halt Brazil's Nuclear Plans', *Latin American Economic Report*, 4 May 1979, p. 135.
52. In June 1979, Electrobras, the energy holding company, released a report that nuclear power will not really be needed until after 2000, even in the south-east region usually forecast for severe energy shortages ['Tests Start at Angra I', *Nuclear Engineering International* (September 1979)].
53. Since the new regime cancelled the Shah of Iran's ambitious nuclear power plans – 34,000 MWE by 1995 – the West German nuclear industry badly needs the Brazilian orders to remain economically viable.
54. Henry Johnston, 'Brazil Pot Boils as German Hold on Nuclear Technology is Revealed,' *Nucleonics Week*, 30 August 1979, p. 9.
55. *New York Times*, 13 June 1975.
56. See Gall and Helga Haftendorn, 'The Nuclear Triangle: Washington,

Bonn, and Brasilia, National Nuclear Policies and International Proliferation', Occasional Paper Series (Washington, DC: Georgetown University, 1978).

57. *O Globo*, 8 January 1978, p. 6.
58. 'Venezuela and Brazil Sign Deals', *Latin American Economic Report*, 3 August 1979, p. 237.
59. *The Energy Daily*, 14 August 1979.
60. Ernest McCrary, 'Oil-for-Nuclear Trade-off Possibility Seen for Brazil and Iraq', *Nucleonics Week*, 15 November 1979, p. 1.
61. Richard K. Betts, 'Pygmies, Paranoids, Pariahs, and Non-proliferation', *Foreign Policy* (Spring 1977) p. 165.
62. US policy-makers are severely constrained, however, by the provisions of the Nuclear Non-proliferation Act of 1978 (see Donnelly) in their ability either to offer carrots or to avoid using sticks.
63. Henry Rowen and Albert Wohlstetter, *US Non-proliferation Strategy Reformulated* (Los Angeles: Panheuristics, 1979).
64. Don Oberdorfer, 'Pakistan: The Quest for the Atomic Bomb', *Washington Post*, 27 August 1979, p. 1.

Part III
The Limitations of Current Approaches

6 Nuclear Proliferation in the 1980s: Perceptions and Proposals

THEODOR WINKLER

ENTERING AN ERA OF AMBIGUITY

The explosion of a 'peaceful nuclear device' by India on 18 May 1974, must be considered a watershed in the perception of the non-proliferation issue: If the problem appeared to be a difficult but manageable one before the Rajasthan test the general assumption after the Indian step was that things were threatening to go out of control. Ever since, it has been feared that the dam could definitely break and the world would be confronted by a rapidly growing number of nuclear weapon states.

The impact of the 1974 test upon the non-proliferation strategies of the nuclear 'haves'[1] has been amplified by a combination of three separate but inter-linked factors: first, the spectacular increase the world has witnessed during the last three decades both in the number of actors on the international scene and in their technological and industrial capabilities. This diffusion of general technological potential has been paralleled by an intriguing spread of civil nuclear technology. The phenomenon was further accentuated by the energy crisis of 1973-4, which greatly accelerated the worldwide expansion of existing nuclear power programmes. Second, plutonium reprocessing and recycling – predicted since the early days of the nuclear age – has evolved from a theoretically desirable but far distant element of the nuclear fuel cycle to an actual policy-making issue awaiting a decision. An early transition to a 'plutonium economy' is today strongly advocated not only by the Europeans and Japanese, but also by the socialist bloc and some key countries of the Third World. There are fears that this might lead to a further dramatic spread of sensitive or weapons-related nuclear technologies. Finally, the motives and incentives for acquiring nuclear weapons – or for obtaining an option to acquire them – have become much more complex and heterogeneous since the circle of the nuclear threshold nations widened to include countries from the Third World.

This changing international environment has led to a revitalization of the non-proliferation efforts of the international community and to a reshaping of the non-proliferation strategies of the existing nuclear weapon countries. The record of these renewed efforts in curtailing proliferation is in some respects quite impressive: the Indian explosion was not followed by an Indian weapons programme, nor has it so far encouraged another country to follow the ambiguous road of peaceful nuclear explosives (PNEs). The number of parties to the Non-proliferation Treaty (NPT) has risen from some 83 in late 1974 to a respectable 102 by April 1977[2] – with 12 additional countries having signed but not yet ratified the treaty.

These positive developments are, however, clearly outweighed by an erosion of other elements of the non-proliferation framework that earlier had been taken for granted. Doubts have been cast on the viability and adequacy of the NPT itself. The delicate balance of the treaty and the statute of the International Atomic Energy Agency (IAEA) has been jeopardized by the reappearance of old fears and the emergence of disturbing new problems and questions: what is meant by the very term 'proliferation'? To what extent can the nuclear states prevent threshold countries from going nuclear? Can effective non-proliferation strategies and national sovereignty in the energy field be compatible at all in a time of the rapid horizontal and vertical spread of civil nuclear technology? Thus, energy requirements and new nuclear technologies have engendered a growing need for common action and wide international consensus and a renewal of the entire debate about nuclear proliferation. So far, however, conflict, not cooperation, has clearly predominated in this new debate; consensus has been eroded instead of reconfirmed. A basic reason for this development has been the absence of a common perception among the nuclear states of the proliferation issue as such. Nuclear proliferation is essentially – though not exclusively – a political problem. The fundamental task for the international community in the 1980s does not lie in further perfecting the technical barriers to proliferation (as important as such barriers may be), but rather in reestablishing some sort of a consensus about the rules of the game. Time may be running short, however, in this search for a common and widely acceptable perception of the issue at stake because the larger international environment is evolving in a way that might make the 1980s an era of ambiguity.

THE ROLE OF PERCEPTION

Should nuclear power continue to be considered a promising if not indispensable source of energy and technological expertise, the continuing spread of nuclear technology and know-how will be inevitable. Though overly optimistic nuclear energy forecasts have everywhere had to be revised downward and may continue to shrink due to a growing anti-nuclear mood in most industrialized countries, there can hardly be any doubt that nuclear power will play a sizable energy role in future decades. Investments and other stakes are simply too high to expect any other outcome. The fundamental question with respect to nuclear proliferation cannot, therefore, the whether civil nuclear technology should be allowed to spread further, but rather whether this spread will outpace efforts to adjust the international system to a changing environment. In the last analysis, no non-proliferation regime is capable of preventing the clandestine diversion of nuclear weapons material or the military exploitation of a nuclear option resulting from a peaceful nuclear energy programme. Even the most sophisticated 'safeguards' system will always remain primarily a political symbol. The ultimate goal of any non-proliferation regime must be, therefore, to inspire basic international confidence through a generally observed code of behaviour and a meaningful control and surveillance mechanism. Such confidence, however, is largely a produce of perceptions.

At least four different sets of perceptions are relevant in this respect. First, the perceptions of the nuclear states of the proliferation issue which have never been identical, often inconsistent, and sometimes clearly conflicting. Secondly, the perceptions within and among the nuclear threshold countries of what they are searching for which vary from a desire to get on the nuclear learning curve to the quest for nuclear weapons. Thirdly, the perceptions by the neighbours of threshold-state motivations which will almost certainly not be identical with the real intentions harboured by these near-nuclear countries. Finally, there are the perceptions of the international community at large as to the rules of the game. Only a common perception of the equity and desirability of the rules can give to a non-proliferation regime the indispensable seal of legitimacy that makes it acceptable to individual countries. If the rules of the game are not seen as equitable and legitimate, efforts to halt the spread of nuclear weapons will fail.

Among the different types of perceptions, those of the nuclear 'haves' obviously play a crucial role, particularly if the definition of this group should be widened to include, besides the five recognized nuclear-weapon states, the relatively small number of highly advanced countries capable of producing and supplying key elements of the nuclear fuel cycle. Their perceptions not only define their own non-proliferation policies – which in turn regulate to a very large degree the international nuclear market – but are also instrumental in the establishment and reorganization of the institutional and organizational framework through which those non-proliferation policies are implemented. Thus, they have a very considerable influence on the general international environment, if not on the perception of the international community at large of the problems posed by nuclear proliferation.

The absence of a common perception of the proliferation issue on the part of the nuclear 'haves' inevitably leads to inconsistent, if not conflicting, export and safeguards policies. Sharp disputes over what institutional framework would best manage the complex problems of the peaceful atom are another result. Whereas the United States has traditionally perceived proliferation as a danger to international stability, and therefore as a world order problem, the Soviet Union has regarded it, at least originally, in the narrower terms of national security. The geopolitical and strategic situation of the USSR – a country longtime surrounded by a belt of unfriendly, if not hostile, states and a superpower only in military terms – was the major factor distinguishing the Soviet outlook from the American one. Finding a common non-proliferation strategy between the two major nuclear powers remained inconceivable as long as the Soviet Union's major concern was a nuclear-armed Germany or Japan. The American proposal in the early 1960s for a US-European multilateral nuclear force (MLF), as a response to the French nuclear weapons programme and European perceptions of a weakening American commitment, and the Soviet reaction to this proposal illustrate well the diverging perceptions of the superpowes of the problem of nuclear proliferation.

Though the perceptions of the nuclear states have gradually changed, their views have not become fully compatible. Thus, France's position has always betrayed a mixture of resentment of the superpowers and, at least formally, an insouciance with regard to the implications of nuclear-armed world (though there was always a sharp awareness of the importance of the *'force de frappe'* in a non-nuclear continental Europe and with respect to the German rearmament). When the first Chinese nuclear test convinced the two superpowers of the need for common action (which eventually lead to the NPT) , suspicion of superpower cooperation was seemingly confirmed. This resentment has been echoed in Chinese polemics against the NPT and other forms of 'superpower obstruction' to the peaceful and not-so-peaceful uses of the atom.[3]

Thus, although a consensus on few very fundamental questions (e.g., that proliferation is destabilizing rather than stabilizing) seems slowly to emerge, the historical and continuing divergence in the nuclear-weapon states' perceptions of the problem remains a formidable obstacle to a meaningful coordination of their non-proliferation policieds, let alone to the forging of these policies into a common strategy. This is particularly deplorable considering the increasing number of actors with a voice in non-proliferation policy, including new suppliers, new recipients, and perhaps even new but unacknowledged nuclear weapon states, and the dwindling base of shared values and interests on which such strategies could be built. Efforts to achieve a further rapprochement amid the diverging views of the nuclear-weapon states and the major exporting countries on the nature of the proliferation problem deserve the highest priority in the 1980s.

THE WIDENING DEBATE

The non-proliferation policies of the nuclear states all suffered originally from two inadequacies. First, they were – except for the Soviet one – extremely non-specific. Simple opposition to a nuclear-armed world was hardly sufficient to guide action in the practicalities of day-to-day politics. And the translation of this attitude into well defined, concrete policy goals was surprisingly deficient.[4] Secondly, the tremendous efforts required of the first nuclear powers to acquire nuclear weapons, led them to overestimate grossly the complexity of that task for other countries, at least in terms of fabricating an explosive device, if not quantities of reliable warheads and delivery systems.

These defects in outlook resulted in disturbing surprises for most of the nuclear states. The Canadian nuclear cooperation with India that laid the foundation for the Indian test of 1974 is certainly the most striking example. American unhappiness with unforeseen results of the Atoms for Peace programme is well known.[5] The Soviet Union's first adventure in the field of nuclear cooperation – the assistance it gave the People's Republic of China between January 1955 and August 1960 – ended in disaster for the Soviets.[6] Its impact on the Soviet leadership must have been particularly strong since China (except for Mongolia) had been its first and only true ally and since the nuclear cooperation agreement with China was the most far-reaching engagement the USSR had even entered into in this field. Although France's involvement in the Israeli nuclear programme may have been well thought out, French nuclear deals with Pakistan, South Korea, Iraq and South Africa seem to be the offspring of an opportunistic and carefree attitude, rather than a farsighted and careful strategy.[7] Miscalculation of potential effects as well as a certain naivety is also evident in the entanglement of the Federal Republic of Germany in the South African uranium enrichment programme.[8] It is puzzling to note the apparently limited willingness or ability of the nuclear powers to learn from the mistakes of others. The various nuclear states have also drawn different conclusions from essentially similar experiences. Whereas the USSR and the United States have adopted hardware-oriented policies aimed at hampering the *capabilities* of threshold countries to acquire nuclear weapons, the Europeans show a clear preference for economic and political strategies influencing the *incentives* for 'going nuclear.' These two approaches need not be mutually exclusive. A clash became inevitable, however, when the Carter Administration combined good intentions with what has been perceived as an indiscriminately restrictive and technocratic outlook, while the Europeans seemed eager to balance the rising cost of energy through billion dollar nuclear agreements.[9] The ensuing controversy was highlighted by the sharp American reaction to the French-Pakistani and the German-Brazilian deals between the summer of 1976 and the autumn of 1977. The divergence of views was partly rooted in the inevitably different outlook a world power must have. However, it was as much the result of misunderstanding each other's intentions as of actually disagreeing on the most suitable policy.

Thus, the United States considers nuclear energy an important and indispensable source of energy in the short and medium term, and showing an impressive potential in the long run should today's research in the field of breeder and fusion reactors prove successful. It opposes at the present stage, however, nuclear fuel rod reprocessing and plutonium recycling, as well as the early introduction of breeder reactors on a commercial scale, since their economic benefits still seem marginal. Moreover, these benefits would have to be weighed against the sharply increased risk of nuclear proliferation that is linked to an indiscriminate spread of these sensitive technologies. According to the United States, available uranium reserves justify further delaying the transition to a 'plutonium economy'. New discoveries and intensified exploration will provide additional breathing space. In the US view it is, therefore, possible to continue use of the low-risk, light-water reactor for a while and to develop new fuel cycle technologies that are more proliferation-resistant.

Accordingly, Carter announced on 7 April 1977, that the United States would 'indefinitely postpone' spent fuel reprocessing and refrain from a premature commercialization of the breeder reactor, both of which produce weapons-grade material.[10] The United States expected that its European allies and Japan would consider the American arguments in their own decisions and would join the United States in its search for new approaches along less proliferation-prone lines. The US Congress went one step further in the Nuclear Non-proliferation Act (NNPA) of 1978 and required:

Full-scope safeguards, covering all of an importer's nuclear facilities, to be included in any new or amended agreement for nuclear cooperation, as well as in all existing agreements within 24 months from enactment of the law;

Cutting off cooperation with any non-nuclear weapon state detonating a peaceful nuclear explosive, terminating international Atomic Energy Agency (IAEA) safeguards, or materially violating a US cooperation agreement; and

Renegotiation of all existing cooperation agreements in the nuclear field in order to achieve conformity with a new set of criteria and conditions defined by the act (notably, IAEA safeguards, US consent to any re-transfer or reprocessing of nuclear material, and the maintaining of adequate physical security for the supplied materials).

The Europeans considered this new US policy to be a clear violation of the American commitments both under the NPT and under the numerous existing bilateral cooperation agreements. To them, the delicate balance of the NPT was put into question by the American demands that came close, whether intentionally or not, to an ultimatum. The assumption that existing uranium reserves would permit deferral of the breeder reactor and of reprocessing seemed to them unproven and, in any case, beside the point. What really mattered for the Europeans was not so much the absolute level of uranium reserves but the available supply of natural and enriched uranium. Not only did this point up the United States's poor record as a supplier, it also threatened the Europeans with an embargo precisely at the moment when the Canadian government stopped all uranium shipments to Europe – also out of non-proliferation concerns.[11]

The uncertainty introduced by these American and Canadian measures, in European eyes, could only be counterproductive. Instead of preventing a further spread of sensitive technologies, it would accelerate this dissemination for two reasons. First, with the scarce energy resources of Europe, Japan, and other parts of the world, a uranium embargo would increase the incentives for them to exploit new fuel-efficient but proliferation-prone technologies such as fuel reprocessing and plutonium recycling, as alternatives to enriched uranium.[12] Secondly, spent fuel reprocessing in most European countries is inextricably linked to the nuclear waste management issue. Any delay in its introduction might indeed prove to be a fatal blow to a European nuclear industry that is increasingly hard-pressed by environmentalists and other nuclear power opponents.[13]

Considering the extremely high interests at stake and the ever-lengthening planning periods in the nuclear industry, the American veto power over waste fuel reprocessing legislated in the NNPA would amount to nothing less than putting the entire nuclear venture in Europe at the mercy of the American president; it would permit the United States to intervene still further in European energy policy. The so-called 'denial' approach would also be counterproductive in the Third World, where the United States would inevitably be accused of imperialistic motives and a cavalier attitude toward economic development.[14] Finally, the real American motives behind this new policy were suspected of being much less altruistic than US public statements implied. A European reactor industry, almost squeezed out of the market by American offers in the 1960s of complete or 'turnkey' nuclear power plants, could hardly see anything else behind Carter's 7 April speech than an attempt to stop the more advanced European breeder reactor industry long enough to permit American technology to catch up.

The Carter administration thus had to learn during 1977 that, in politics, abrupt policy changes entail severe penalties. The early policy initiatives of the Carter administration – including those on SALT and human rights – all suffered from the fact that they were too technical, conceptual, or oriented to domestic politics and largely ignored the specific sensitivities of the overseas audience to which they were addressed.

The Europeans did not truly resent the American desire to raise barriers against proliferation however, and, after initial hesitations, they agreed to discuss a new set of export guidelines among the supplier countries in what became known as the 'London Club'. The 16-part suppliers' code was published early in 1978. Moreover, both France and the Federal Republic of Germany (FRG) responded eventually to American concerns by announcing that they would not enter into any further nuclear contracts involving sensitive technologies. In the autumn of 1978 France finally agreed to shelve its reprocessing plant deal with Pakistan. The Dutch government in January 1978 had extracted from the Brazilians their agreement to put future stocks of plutonium under international safeguards in return for Dutch enriched nuclear fuel.[15]

The Europeans remained embittered, however, by what they perceived as steadily increasing American interference in their domestic nuclear programmes. Most West European countries having ratified the NPT between 1975 and early 1977, they had expected the nuclear weapon states to live up to the treaty's essential *quid pro quo* of enjoying the freedom to develop the peaceful uses of nuclear energy for agreement not to acquire nuclear weapons. But the rules of the game set forth in the NPT proved flexible once they were accepted by the Europeans. The hard line taken on the issue by an assertive US Congress reinforced the harsh aspects of the new Carter policy. What was remembered from President Carter's April 1977 speech was therefore not the reference to possible American assistance in solving the waste management problem, but the opposition to reprocessing; what impressed the Europeans was not Carter's pledge to enlarge the American enrichment capacity, but the actual stopping of uranium deliveries. The consequence of the debate has been that the non-proliferation problem has been overshadowed by the much broader question of the future of nuclear energy. The uncertainty arising from the clash of perspectives on world energy and world security can only be considered unfortunate, if inevitable.

THE IMPACT OF AMBIGUITY

The increase in actors with stakes in the game and the diffusion of technology have led to conflicting perceptions of the issue that upset the former limited consensus and, so far, prevent formation of a new one. Nor is this the only way in which nuclear technology has factionalized international politics; it is also undermining the shared definitions of a decade ago. The Euro-American controversy reveals the growing difficulty of even defining unambiguously the very term 'proliferation'. Is it the spread of *any* nuclear activity? Is it the diffusion of the technological know-how necessary for producing weapons-grade material? Does it imply the spread not only of the know-how but also of the sensitive hardware required for that purpose? Does the testing of any nuclear device – whether 'peaceful' or not – constitute proliferation? Or is it necessary to label the device a 'weapon' and follow the test by a regular weapons procurement programme? Where do motivations come into the picture? Can intentions be neglected for the sake of a clearcut technical criterion, or is motivation the crucial element? Once a clearcut watershed, the successful testing of a nuclear device is no longer an unequivocal litmus test; it only marks a new stage in an ongoing nuclear options game. Now a distinction must be made between 'demonstrated proliferation' and 'latent proliferation'.[16] India, for example, has tested a nuclear device but stoutly denies possessing any nuclear weapons or ambitions. Yet two other countries, Israel and South Africa, are widely credited with clandestine nuclear arsenals, though they have never actually tested a bomb (assuming the phenomenon detected between South Africa and Antarctica in September 1979 by US satellites was not a test). Where does the difference lie between demonstrated and latent proliferation?

Widespread and varying types of ambiguous nuclear weapons status could lead to the worst of all possible worlds. A contest of nuclear nerves conducted by regional rivals in an atmosphere of profound uncertainty about each other's nuclear weapons capability and intentions may trigger regional and international reactions no less severe than an overt nuclear weapons programme. To the extent that uncertainty sparks worst-case planning, anticipatory reaction, preemption, and crisis decision making, nuclear ambiguity might lend itself more easily to dangerous escalation, even though, in principle, some ambiguous levels of nuclear weapons capability may be more conducive to reduction of tension than would unambiguous nuclear forces. Moreover, unsure of its rival's exact nuclear weapons status but doubting any significant nuclear deployment, a country might believe that accelerating its own nuclear programme or increasing conventional forces will deter and balance the rival's nuclear capability. In either case, high levels of uncertainty about nuclear weapons capacity seem destined to stimulate or aggravate tensions and increase instability.

A cornerstone of the non-proliferation strategies of the nuclear 'haves', and particularly of the United States, has been the effort to contain proliferation at the lowest possible level. What matters, according to this view, is preventing a country from ever getting close enough to an actual weapons capability to trigger these negative reactions, with their escalatory and destabilizing potential. This goal is certainly laudable. However, there are two very serious drawbacks.

First, the embryonic nuclear capability of a country may be perceived as credible, and thus provoke regional reactions, precisely because of the level of concern shown by the nuclear powers. The unfortunate handling of the South African nuclear crisis in August 1977 is a case in point. Open warnings to South Africa not to proceed with what major nuclear states considered an imminent weapon test may have conferred upon the country the status of an unacknowledged nuclear-weapon state. After the alarm was over, it did not matter whether South Africa had actually tested a device or not; it had been accorded the capacity to do so by no less than the nuclear superpowers.

Secondly, seeking to contain proliferation at the earliest possible stage may constitute what has been called 'proliferation oversell'.[17] If nuclear states – and again particularly the United States – show themselves too willing to buy off a potential nuclear-weapon state through increased supplies of conventional weapons, security guarantees, political concessions, or economic assistance, nuclear weapons programmes might mushroom, just in order to be cashed in later. Moreover, would the value of a nuclear option for bargaining purposes not be a function of *both* its credibility *and* the likelihood that it would eventually cause dangerous regional side effects? Yet where is one to draw the line between a straightforward civil nuclear energy programme and the quest for a nuclear option to gain diplomatic leverage? As Christoph Bertram has rightly pointed out. 'This embryonic nuclear weapon status is relatively easy to acquire since all it needs is for a government to raise suspicion in the eyes of others about its ultimate objectives – it may take no more than sending a handful of students to study nuclear physics at Massachusetts Institute of Technology'.[18] Last, but not least, can a nuclear option really be bought off? Who guarantees that the trained people, the hardware acquired, and the stockpiled enriched uranium or plutonium will not eventually be used for a nuclear weapons programme any way? Nuclear knowledge is irreversible. If capabilities are the critical factor, safeguards on nuclear facilities can hardly be a final or definite answer to the fears that a nation will one day acquire nuclear weapons.

There have been at least three instances in which the United States seems to have tried to purchase nuclear good behaviour through conventional arms deliveries: the supply of Hawk surface-to-air missiles to Israel in 1963, the proposed sale of 110 A-7 fighter-bombers to Pakistan, which was finally shelved in 1977,[19] and the attempt of the Carter Administration of spring 1979 to barter away Pakistan's fatal drive towards nuclear weapons through the proposed delivery of an inspecified number of F-5 jet-fighters. Israel has clearly been trying hard, sometimes successfully, to sell its nuclear capabilities for political gains.[20] It must be assumed that these developments have been very carefully observed by Taiwan, which is struggling for continuing American arms deliveries and political backing, and by South Africa, with its complex political and economic worries.

Nuclear power must not become a bargaining chip through concern over proliferation. The continuing spread of civil nuclear technology will inevitably allow more and more countries to enter the 'gray zone' of ambiguous nuclear status, depending as much on perceptions as on demonstrated capabilities and intentions. Any premium unduly attached to a nuclear option is, therefore, extremely dangerous. Particularly to the internationally isolated 'garrison' or 'beleaguered' countries and to nations that perceive themselves as emerging medium powers, the slippery road of the nuclear weapons option might be made to look all too attractive, a path that appears to provide both bargaining leverage with the major powers and the opportunity to go nuclear one day, if necessary.

A crucial test for the efforts to stop, or at least delay, further nuclear proliferation in the 1980s may then be the willingness to resist the temptation to overdramatize the issue. Nuclear weapons programmes will not mushroom overnight. Exaggerated fears and a nervous tendency to perceive the nuclear weapons threshold at an excessively lower level of capability might in fact nurture proliferation.

THE SEARCH FOR CONSENSUS

The period following the Indian nuclear test of 1974 has been marked by conflicting tendencies. On the one hand, a disquieting disdain has developed for the value of the institutional framework set up in the early days of international peaceful nuclear cooperation. IAEA safeguards are often not judged on the basis of their political and symbolic value, but instead are expected to provide a fool-proof technical barrier against clandestine diversion. Too easily overlooked, on the other hand, is the possibility that it might prove impossible today to sustain or recreate a framework as universal as the NPT and the statute of the IAEA.

Secondly, the revival of the proliferation issue has caused a brush-fire mentality in many quarters. Proliferation of any type has been considered a problem calling for immediate action. The results have been broad policy initatives too hastily launched that did not distinguish between the symptoms and the deeper causes of the problem. The result of this 'legislate first, convince later' approach has been unnecessary polarization, further rupturing and fragmenting whatever consensus may have existed regarding nuclear non-proliferation.[21]

Richard K. Betts is certainly right when he writes, 'There are no simple solutions feasible, no feasible solutions which are simple, and no solutions at all which can be applied across the board'.[22] It would be wrong, however, to conclude that nuclear proliferation can be solved only by a very specific, case-by-case approach. First of all, no policy approach, general or specific, is likely to succeed in an anarchy of values, interests, and perspectives, in the absence of a minimum consensus on the rules of the game. Moreover, highly differentiated approaches to potential proliferators will bring forth even more loudly the calls of discrimination provoked by non-proliferation policy to date. Finally, the advantages of conducting a general policy, albeit with qualifications, and the need to take roughly similar approaches to roughly similar circumstances suggest that broad, rather then merely piecemeal, approaches to proliferation are desirable and necessary.

In this context, it is important not to overlook the elements that may be emerging as the basis for a new non-proliferation strategy. The Indian test has brought about a growing awareness of the problems inherent in the ever-wider diffusion of the newer nuclear technology. Both the Indian decision not to go ahead with its peaceful nuclear explosions programme (though that position might change, if Pakistan forges ahead with its nuclear weapons programme), and the moratorium on the export of sensitive technologies are evidence of the considerable rethinking that has taken place. The joint export guidelines published in January 1978 by the London suppliers Club have to some degree prevented safeguards from becoming the subject of bargaining between suppliers and recipients. The reinforcement of the idea that proliferation is destabilizing, or at least not unequivocally beneficial to the proliferator, and should therefore be avoided could provide a conceptual basis for common action. Above all, there seems to be a new willingness in the international community to face and discuss the entire issue again. Coming after the long and difficult debate that led to the NPT and the polarization of recent years, such a willingness must be considered remarkable. The initial deadlock that followed the drastic American and Canadian policy initiatives has given way to a new, though still embryonic, dialogue.

This new search for consensus seems to have found institutional expression in the International Nuclear Fuel Cycle Evaluation (INFCE). Convened in October 1977 in Washington at American invitation, INFCE evaluated on a technical level existing and alternative fuel cycles with respect to their proliferation resistance. This is not an easy task.

From the beginning, the 56 countries and five international organizations that participated in this two-year venture denied that its conclusions could have any binding power. The mood at the conference was rather sober and sceptical, with marked differences in viewpoints between the North American delegations and most other participants. Yet INFCE has its merits. The European-American controversy moved from public accusations back into the conference room. The fact that INFCE's membership embraces most of the countries interested in nuclear energy contrasts this gathering with more restricted – and therefore internationally more suspect – groups like the London Club. In a world in which most Third World countries have a 'policy of not having nuclear weapons, but not a non-proliferation policy', as one observer has put it, INFCE could turn out to have been a useful tool. It permitted a broader dissemination of information on nuclear technology as it exists today and on the implications of the nuclear fuel cycle for regional and international security. It might, thereby, have contributed to a better understanding of the real dimensions and complexities of nuclear proliferation.

Though the consensus reached on key issues in the INFCE report was a narrow one, it is too early to assert that the barriers to a broader technical consensus are permanent or that INFCE will not have a positive, if unobtrusive, effect on the future decisions and actions of the participating countries. Helpful in sustaining the new dialogue would be the examination of ways to dissociate the long-term nuclear future from the shorter-term problem of curbing the further spread of sensitive nuclear technologies. In this regard, it might prove possible to proceed with the new nuclear technologies in such a way that their potential energy benefits would be realized without incurring the proliferation liabilities of their general diffusion throughout the world. Existing projects for spent fuel reprocessing facilities in Europe, for example, could be pursued with financial participation by the developing nations. In the long run, this approach might provide a more solid barrier to the spread of sensitive technologies and fissile material than the US-backed proposal for reliance on 'once-through' nuclear fuel cycles, which avoid the proliferation dangers of spent fuel reprocessing but pose the additional problem of accumulating spent fuel that could be used for weapons by a determined proliferator by building a fuel separation plant without the assistance of the supplier nations. It is efforts of this kind – threshold nuclear nations 'closing' the nuclear fuel cycle on their own initiative and with their own technology – that are most to be avoided. A Pakistani quest for an enrichment or a reprocessing plant naturally arouses suspicion, but the opening of a similar European plant, such as the British Windscale reprocessing plant, has a different impact on proliferation. To distinguish between the desirable and the politically possible, to create an improved non-proliferation system without sacrificing the flexibility that would render it generally acceptable are difficult but necessary tasks.

In order to be successful, the new search for consensus needs time to develop. Should the United States strictly live up to the terms of the Nuclear Non-proliferation Act of 1978, the initial dialogue begun by INFCE will inevitably be submerged again in polemics and prestige-laden disputes before it ever gets underway. The chance to turn INFCE or a follow-up gathering into a standing conference between nuclear and non-nuclear weapon states, between recipients and suppliers, should not be passed up. Only if the rules of the game can be defined as broadly as possible will non-proliferation policy have a chance.

POLICY RECOMMENDATIONS

It may prove useful to adopt a two-fold strategy that distinguishes between non-proliferation policies and the specific needs of a limited number of trouble spots. The general thrust of the overall strategy should be directed toward preventing an increase in the number of states with an ambiguous nuclear weapon capability and toward a new consensus on the international rules of the game for nuclear power and proliferation. The key elements can be summarized as follows:

> Building on what has already been achieved, particularly by the NPT and the IAEA.
>
> The separation of the proliferation issue as much as possible from broader questions overshadowing the international debate, such as the breeder, waste management, reprocessing, and domestic licensing problems.
>
> Increasing incentives for cooperation instead of confrontation approaches.
>
> A continuation of the new INFCE dialogue. To be successful, however, this discussion needs to evolve from a *dialogue des sourds* into a more productive exchange.
>
> More flexible approaches to the weightiest proliferation problems. Nuclear-weapons-free zones, some form of full-scope safeguard agreements outside the NPT, and, above all, more patient and tactful efforts to integrate hesitant new actors into the non-proliferation regime should play a role in these approaches.

The case-by-case component of this two-pronged effort should then try to exploit the legitimating effect a growing international consensus on the rules of the game will provide. First priority among cases of potential proliferation should be accorded to the internationally isolated countries or garrison states. Strategies will vary from case to case, but some fundamental principles should be observed:

> Efforts should focus on underlying threats and conflicts instead of short-term perceptions of security needs. The fact that none of the garrison states is likely to face overwhelming military odds in the foreseeable future should provide diplomacy the necessary time for effective action.
>
> Broad policy initiatives, such as a comprehensive approach to arms sales, an emphasis on preventive instead of corrective diplomacy,

and the conclusion of a comprehensive test ban treaty, are likely to yield better results than limited or 'band-aid' approaches.
Nuclear weapons acquisition should not pay. Instead of trying to buy off threshold countries, the nuclear states should stress the specific sanctions a nuclear decision might entail.
Discreet diplomacy is to be preferred to expressing open concerns about a threshold country's nuclear policy.

Should the nuclear 'haves' fail to improve the political and psychological climate in which non-proliferation policies are discussed, there is scarcely any chance that a technical solution to the nuts and bolts of the problem can be found. If the 1980s is not to become an era of intolerable nuclear ambiguity, then a continued search for consensus is indispensable.

NOTES AND REFERENCES

1. Nuclear 'haves' is a convenient but misleading term. Only the United States, the USSR, and France can be considered nuclear 'haves' in a broad sense that encompasses nuclear weapons status, natural uranium availability, and an advanced, independent civil nuclear programme covering the entire fuel cycle. China has a small civil nuclear power programme. Britain is a uranium importer and plays a comparatively modest role as a technology supplier. Other advanced nuclear nations are non-nuclear weapon states and usually depend for their peaceful nuclear energy programmes on uranium and/or hardware imports.
2. US Arms Control and Disarmament Agency, *Arms Control and Disarmament Agreements* (Washington, DC, February 1975) p. 92; and Congressional Research Service, Library of Congress, *Nuclear Proliferation Factbook* (prepared for the Committee on International Relations, House of Representatives, and the Committee on Governmental Affairs, US Senate) (Washington, DC: GPO, 23 September 1977) pp. 65-6.
3. Hsin Ping, 'Utilization of Nuclear Energy and the Struggle Against Hegemony', *Peking Review*, no. 15 (14 April 1978), p. 11.
4. Both the MacMahon Act of 1946 and the Atoms for Peace proposal of 1953 could be cited as examples. The rigidity of the denial approach chosen by the United States in the late 1940s (which was perhaps in some respects as much an outgrowth of the Fuchs and Rosenberg spy cases as a true non-proliferation strategy) proved to be as counterproductive as the hasty Atoms for Peace policy in its initial form, with its loosely written safeguards agreements and premature declassifications. The fact that planning horizons of government are usually limited to five to ten years may be one of the reasons for this general shortcoming of non-proliferation policies.

5. Joseph S. Nye, 'Non-proliferation: A Long-Term Strategy', *Foreign Affairs,* vol. 56, no. 3 (April 1978), pp. 603-5.
6. Gloria Duffy, 'Soviet Nuclear Exports', *International Security*, vol. 3, no. 1 (Summer 1978), pp. 84-6.
7. Pierre Lellouche, 'Frankreich im internationalen Disput über die Kernenergie', *Europa-Archiv*, no. 17 (1978) pp. 541-52.
8. For an interesting, though quite polemical, account of the German–South African relationship in the nuclear field, see Zdenek Cervenka and Barbara Rogers, *The Nuclear Axis* (London: Julian Friedmann, 1978) p. 464.
9. Stanley Hoffmann, 'The Hell of Good Intentions', *Foreign Policy*, no. 29 (Winter 1977-8).
10. *Executive Energy Documents* (printed at the request of Sen. Henry M. Jackson, Chairman, Committee on Energy and Natural Resources, US Senate) (Washington, DC: GPO, July 1978) pp. 379-80.
11. Since January 1969, when the first important US deliveries of enriched uranium for a foreign-operated power reactor took place, the following supply shocks had to be absorbed by American customers:

> 8 December 1972: the US Atomic Energy Commission (USAEC) suspends temporarily all new contracting for enrichment services and begins a revision of contracting terms. The step is related to plans of the Nixon administration to open the enrichment market to private companies.
> 11 September 1973: the old 'requirements contracts' (extremely liberal contracts permitting customers to accelerate or delay shipments without penalties according to their needs) were replaced by fixed-commitment contracts which are much more rigid and have to be signed eight years in advance of the first core delivery. Projected capacity shortages are given as the reason for this change.
> In June 1974: the USAEC closes not only its order books, but classifies retroactively as 'conditional' enrichment contracts to 45 foreign reactors scheduled to begin operations in the early 1980s.
> Between March and September 1975: US exports of enriched uranium are stopped because of the reorganization of the American regulatory procedure following the split of the USAEC into The Energy Research and Development Administration (ERDA) and the Nuclear Regulatory Commission (NRC).

See Lawrence G. Franko and A. Javier Eugueta, 'US Regulation of the Spread of Nuclear Technologies Through Supplier Power: Lever or Boomerang?', in *Law and Policy in International Business*, vol. 10, no. 4, (1978) pp. 1181-204.
12. Another counterproductive consequence of the North American efforts to put pressure on the European countries has been their attempt to diversify sources of supply. Thus, many states in the European nuclear consortium, EURATOM, have contracted for Soviet enrichment services to a very substantial degree. Moreover, imports of South African uranium have skyrocketed. Between 1965 and 1976 the FRG imported

27.2 per cent of its uranium from South Africa but intends to cover not less than 46.7 per cent of its needs from this source during the period 1977-80. *Strategic Survey 1977* (London: International Institute for Strategic Studies, 1978) p. 111.

13. The defeat of the Social Democratic Party in the Swedish parliamentary elections of 1976, has been widely attributed to the party's pro-nuclear stand. In the first popular referendum the country has ever organized, the Austrians decided, in November 1978, against opening Zwentendorf, Austria's first nuclear power reactor. In Switzerland and in the Federal Republic of Germany, law and court orders require that a solution of the waste management issue must be at hand if an operating licence for a power reactor is to be granted. Referenda on nuclear energy have been announced in Denmark and Sweden.

14. It may be an ominous sign that, in October 1978, Argentina announced its intention to construct an experimental reprocessing plant. ('Argentina Will Reprocess Plutonium', *International Herald Tribune*, 17 October 1978, p. 4). Though the most ambitious nuclear power programme announced by some Third World countries (e.g. Brazil) will, in all probability, either be scaled down or delayed considerably, one will have to reckon in the future with a growing competence of the Third World in the nuclear field.

15. *Strategic Survey 1977*, op. cit., p. 112.

16. Ted Greenwood, *et al., Nuclear Proliferation, Motives, Capabilities, and Strategies for Control* (New York: McGraw-Hill, 1977) pp. 125-6.

17. Christoph Bertram 'Proliferation Oversell', *New York Times*, 28 January 1977, p. 23.

18. Ibid.

19. Lawrence Freedman, 'Israel's Nuclear Policy', *Survival*, vol. xvii, no. 3 (May/June 1975) p. 116, and SIPRI, *World Armament and Disarmament SIPRI Yearbook 1978* (Stockholm: Almqvist & Wiksell, 1978) p. 29.

20. Yair Evron, 'Israel and the Atom. The Uses and Misuses of Ambiguity, 1957-1967', *Orbis*, vol. xvii, no. 4 (Winter 1974) pp. 1326-43.

21. Salzburg Seminar in American Studies, Session 186. Report by Prof. Porter's Seminar Group (mimeographed) (September 1978) p. 2.

22. Richard K. Betts 'Paranoids, Pygmies, Pariahs and Non-proliferation', *Foreign Policy,* no. 26 (Spring 1977) p. 159.

7 Constraints on Nuclear Power Exports and Nuclear Weapons Proliferation

ZALMAY M. KHALILZAD

Ever since the Indian nuclear explosion of 1974 and the announcement of extensive nuclear power plans by many non-nuclear weapon states after the quadrupling of the price of oil in 1973-4, there has been a great deal of controversy over the prospects for the spread of nuclear weapons.[1] Among the questions addressed in this debate are the relationship between civilian nuclear programmes and nuclear explosive production capability, as well as the role of nuclear suppliers in preventing or at least limiting and slowing the potential spread of nuclear weapons.

The projected increase in the number of nuclear power reactors after 1974 led some analysts to argue that the civilian nuclear programmes of many non-weapon states, if completed, could bring them almost within hours of a military nuclear capability – i.e., the manufacture of nuclear bombs.[2] Several nuclear industrialists and government officials in the United States and Europe, however, argued that formidable weapons could not be made from a civilian nuclear programme.[3]

Different perceptions about the relationship between a civilian nuclear programme and a nuclear weapons capability have resulted in extreme proposals for solutions, from the banning of all further nuclear reactors to immediate commitment to and export of all types of civilian nuclear facilities, without regard for the possibilities of proliferation. However, there are a number of alternatives permitting some types of reactor without necessarily bringing non-weapon states within days or hours of a nuclear capability.

CIVILIAN PROGRAMMES AND NUCLEAR WEAPONS

There are three requirements that must be met in order to build any kind of nuclear weapon: access to sufficient quantities of fissile materials; a reasonable level of skills in working with high explosives, nuclear materials and fuses; and a design for the device. From the dawn of the nuclear age, it has been recognized that designing a bomb and acquiring the non-nuclear components of a nuclear device are much easier than getting weapons-grade materials in sufficient quantities. For example, in 1945, according to physicist Robert Oppenheimer, a major contributor to US nuclear weapons programmes, 'The overwhelming part of the cost, and therefore clearly the principal industrial problem of wartime production of bombs was the building of the plants for enriched uranium and plutonium [two weapon materials]; and that the design of weapons, though it had devoted to it a good deal of high talent, was not a massive or major part of the enterprise'.[4]

Recently a number of scientists and nuclear engineers, such as Theodore Taylor, have emphasized the relative ease of designing a nuclear device.[5] There have been a number of attempts by university students in the United States to design bombs.[6] These designs were primitive, yet they support the claim that designing a crude nuclear device might not be a very difficult task for a large number of non-weapon states with adequate laboratories and trained personnel. (The United States alone trained more than 8800 students from non-weapon states in nuclear related fields between 1955 and 1974.[7]) Disclosure of key elements of thermonuclear weapons designs by the American media may have eased the design problem still further.

The two types of reactor most relied on for power generation around the world are the light-water reactor (LWR) and the heavy-water reactor (HWR). The fuel in these reactors, normally uranium enriched to some degree, must be periodically replaced with fresh fuel. The used (spent) fuel contains plutonium which can be reprocessed to separate the plutonium from other elements. A 1000 megawatt reactor can produce on the average approximately 250 kilograms of separable plutonium. Because the spent fuel, when taken from reactors, is very hot and radioactive, it must be allowed to cool in a pond before reprocessing. During this period, which generally lasts about 100 days, some of the more radioactive nuclides decay, which simplifies subsequent handling and chemical reprocessing. Before reprocessing, the fuel rod jacket or 'cladding' is removed, the fuel rods are dismantled, and reprocessing, or plutonium separation, follows.

Another weapon or 'fissile' material besides plutonium is highly enriched uranium. Uranium, as mined, cannot be used as fuel in the light-water reactors on which an increasing number of non-weapon states are becoming dependent. While the concentration of uranium-235 is about 0.7 per cent in uranium as mined, LWR fuel requires a concentration of about 3 per cent. At present, three major methods for enriching the concentration of uranium are in use: gaseous diffusion, gaseous centrifuge, and the Becker or jet nozzle process. These technologies permit uranium to be enriched 3 per cent for power reactors and to weapon-grade levels. A non-weapon nation may purchase an enrichment facility as part of a civilian nuclear fuel cycle. Access to highly enriched uranium by non-weapon states poses potential proliferation problems similar to those posed by access to plutonium.

Two kinds of fissile material that have generally been used for making nuclear explosives – plutonium-239 and uranium-235 – are thus derivable from reactor fuel before or after its use. Those non-weapon states that cannot produce these materials themselves might be able to arrange to acquire them in sufficient quantities abroad.[8] Of course, some could arrange for the theft of weapons material from other countries where physical security is inadequate, as reportedly Israel has already done. Alternatively, they might either purchase one or a number of complete nuclear explosive devices or arrange for their theft from the weapon states. Reportedly both Egypt and Libya at different times have unsuccessfully tried to purchase nuclear weapons.[9] The focus of this analysis, however, is on the extent to which constraints on civilian nuclear exports can restrict the more probable spread of the capacity or materials for production of nuclear weapons through the international nuclear energy trade.

Nuclear safeguards have been devised by the International Atomic Energy Agency to detect diversion of nuclear materials from peaceful uses and to provide timely warning; i.e., adequate time for the international community to respond before the diverted material has been used to produce a weapon. Even when effectively applied, the present IAEA safeguard procedures however detect diversion only after the nuclear material balance has been closed and all inspection data have been evaluated. This process could take many months. Much of the Agency's safeguard information is based on reports provided by each state and on records kept at the facilities in each state. The effectiveness of IAEA safeguard procedures is also closely related to the effectiveness of national systems for the accounting and control of nuclear material and on the extent to which the member states enable the Agency to carry out the planned verification activities in a timely fashion. Thus, a non-cooperating state could substantially reduce the effective operation of the IAEA safeguard system.

Since the present international agreements do not forbid work on the non-nuclear parts of nuclear explosive devices, non-weapon states with enrichment or reprocessing plants of their own could work simultaneously on testing and construction of the non-nuclear parts of nuclear devices and on the accumulation of plutonium or enriched uranium without violation of any international safeguards. Much of the distance toward acquiring a nuclear device could thus be traversed without the actual diversion of nuclear materials which the safeguards are intended to detect, and without a violation of IAEA standards. A bomb could then be assembled in anywhere from a few hours to a few days, depending on the technical capacity of the country concerned. Yet the completion of the IAEA inspection of nuclear facilities could take several months and therefore might not provide timely warning to the international community. Without enrichment or reprocessing, on the other hand, countries depending on LWRs and HWRs will not have direct access to separated, fissionable material and cannot come very close to a nuclear weapon capability. IAEA safeguards are likely to be more effective here since they will have time to work.

Some analysts and nuclear reactor vendors have argued that the plutonium from spent fuel of LWRs and HWRs is not usable in effective weapons.[10] Yet recently declassified information has put this argument to rest. According to a document released in 1977, the United States has successfully exploded a nuclear device using plutonium from a power reactor.[11] At least one non-weapon state, Pakistan, apparently believes that plutonium from power reactors will provide an effective nuclear device. Former Pakistani Prime Minister, Zulfikar Ali Bhutto, sought to purchase a French reprocessing plant, although its role in the Pakistani nuclear power programme is highly questionable. This plant would have reprocessed the spent fuel of a 125 megawatt electrical [MW (e)] power plant near Karachi.[12]

If uranium enrichment and spent fuel reprocessing facilities are commonly accepted as necessary or desirable features of every nation's nuclear energy programme, the possibility exists that countries will develop the capacity to manufacture one or more nuclear devices in a very short period – hours to days – without abridging international safeguards. A good case can therefore be made that, in order to decrease the probability of a non-nuclear weapon state acquiring this threshold weapons capacity, the suppliers of nuclear power technology should ban the export of both enrichment and reprocessing plants, their critical components or know-how.

EXPORT MORATORIUM EFFECTIVENESS

At present, a number of countries, including the United States, the Soviet Union, the Federal Republic of Germany, France, Great Britain, Canada, Sweden, Israel, South Africa, Japan, Italy, the Netherlands, the People's Republic of China, and India, are in a position to export either reprocessing facilities or enrichment plants or both. Historically, the United States propagated the notion that reprocessing reactor fuel was essential to the nuclear industry. It declassified the Purex separation process and did not object, in the 1960s, to the acquisition of reprocessing facilities by non-weapons states such as the Federal Republic of Germany, Japan, and India. However, the Indian nuclear explosion prompted greater concern about nuclear weapons proliferation, and in 1976 President Ford declared a moratorium on domestic reprocessing. He also sought international agreement among major suppliers not to export enrichment and reprocessing facilities to non-weapons states. Ford's policies were continued by President Carter.

The United States succeeded in arranging a series of meetings among the principal Communist and Western nuclear technology suppliers in London (the London Club).[13] The participants agreed in 1977 on a moratorium on the export of enrichment and reprocessing facilities for the near future. After the London meetings, France cancelled the sale of the reprocessing plant to Pakistan, to which it had agreed in 1976.[14] It has been speculated that the Federal Republic of Germany might similarly rescind its plan about supplying a reprocessing plant and an enrichment facility to Brazil.

The People's Republic of China (which can supply both reprocessing and enrichment facilities), India and Israel (both of which can export reprocessing facilities), and South Africa (which is said to have an enrichment capacity) did not take part in the London talks and thus are not restricted from exporting these critical facilities or providing reprocessing or enrichment services to other countries.[15] Compared with the London club, these countries have very limited export capabilities and thus far have been reluctant to export their technologies to other countries.[16] But, if all the participants of the London meetings maintain their decision not to export reprocessing and enrichment technologies, those suppliers outside the London arrangements may in the future seek a significant economic and political gain from selling 'sensitive technologies' – as defined by the London Suppliers Club – to some non-weapon states.

Export constraints such as those agreed on in London, despite certain limitations, will increase the costs, risks, and time for non-nuclear weapon states, especially those least industrially developed, to acquire a nuclear weapons capability and are thus effective in discouraging some countries from striving for such a capability. [These constraints, of course, would not affect those non-nuclear weapon states, such as the Federal Republic of Germany, that can produce these sensitive technologies domestically without great additional cost.] The moratorium on the export of reprocessing and enrichment facilities is intended to provide the international community with the time to explore safer and more proliferation-resistant nuclear fuel cycles and technology transfer regimes.

If an export constraint in the form of a moratorium has the benefit of deterring or retarding the proliferation of nuclear weapons, what are its economic and political costs? Naturally, it means losses in foreign trade revenues and in sales for the exporting countries and their nuclear industries and this has been a source of contention among the suppliers group. The importing countries also object to the moratorium; they make the following arguments on behalf of the worldwide diffusion of reprocessing technology, in which they are often joined by some of the supplying nations and firms:

First, reprocessing is economical in the sense that the fuel value of the recovered material would be higher than the cost of obtaining it by reprocessing.

Second, reprocessing is needed to prepare for the anticipated commercial introduction of breeder reactors.

Third, the export of reprocessing facilities is in conformity with the obligation imposed on the suppliers by the Non-proliferation Treaty to share nuclear power technology. In this context, it is also argued that a moratorium will further aggravate North-South relations.

Reprocessing for current reactors. The estimated costs of reprocessing increased from $30 per kilogram in 1974 to $280 in mid-1976 (in constant dollars). In negotiations between COGEMA and JAPCO, the price of separating a kilogram has been reported to range as high as between $500 and $700 (in constant 1977 dollars).[17] These increases raise serious doubts as to the economic wisdom of investing in reprocessing. Several studies have shown that the future costs of reprocessing and of producing plutonium fuel will exceed those for fresh uranium, even when carried out in a large-scale plant, such as the one that was under construction at Barnwell, South Carolina, in the United States with a planned capacity of 1500 metric ton units per year.[18]

For most other countries reprocessing in the immediate future will be more uneconomical because of the smaller units required for many non-weapon states, due to their lower demand for plutonium fuel, and even more so for countries such as India, Argentina, and Pakistan, which have heavy-water reactors that leave less plutonium in the spent fuel. The 1977 Canadian cost estimate for HWR fuel reprocessing clearly supports this point. In the Canadian calculations, 5.5 grams of fissile plutonium are added to 1 kilogram of natural uranium. Two kilograms of spent fuel at 2.7 grams of fissile plutonium per kilogram of spent fuel must be reprocessed to obtain the 5.5 grams of plutonium, at a total cost of $160 ($80 per kilogram). Adding to this excess fabrication cost of $35 per kilogram brings the total cost for mixed oxide fuel to $195. At a uranium oxide price of $40 per pound (the present cost of uranium, which some expect to go down), on the other hand, HWR fuel obtained without reprocessing would cost only $139 per kilogram. Reprocessing thus yields a 50 per cent increase in effectiveness at a cost penalty of 70 per cent – not a wise economic investment.

In the case of LWRs, upon which most non-weapon states are coming to rely, the economics of reprocessing spent fuel, while better than that for HWRs (because 1 kilogram of LWR spent fuel contains about 7 grams of plutonium, while HWR spent fuel produces about 2.7 grams per kilogram), is still subject to a great deal of uncertainty and confusion. Even two years ago, when the estimated cost of reprocessing was considerably lower than the present one, reprocessing and recycling were thought to be a more expensive means of obtaining fuel than uranium enrichment.[19] It appears that, given the present comparative costs of reprocessed fuel and fresh fuel, a moratorium on the export of reprocessing plants for the coming decade would not involve large economic sacrifices for the importing countries. Even if reprocessing were marginally economical, a 10-year moratorium would not be very costly in terms of the cost per kilowatt hour of delivered electricity from nuclear plants.

Reprocessing for breeder reactors. For many years, considerable benefit has been anticipated from the commercialization and adoption of fast breeder nuclear reactors of the type that require reprocessing – since they are far more fuel-efficient than conventional reactors. The hopes for breeders mirror those placed on nuclear power in general in the 1950s. It is expected that breeders will supply cheap and abundant electricity, provide an important alternative to the expected scarcity of fuel for conventional reactors, and bring about energy independence. Like the early estimates of the spread of conventional nuclear power plants, recent estimates by fast breeder advocates generally reveal great enthusiasm about the extent of the future diffusion of fast breeders in the world.

It is questionable, however, whether the production of power and fissile material through fast breeders will ever become economical. The breeder reactor's future depends on a number of uncertain considerations such as capital costs of various breeder and conventional reactors, future technical development, the cost of the reprocessing of irradiated fuel, and the price of uranium, to name only a few. Even if breeders someday become economically competitive with other energy sources, it is uncertain when that day might be. The breeder projections have been slipping, and it appears that even in the supplier countries they are unlikely to become economical in the immediate future. A variety of doubts have caused the United States to announce a domestic moratorium on plutonium breeders. In the case of potential importers of breeder technology, the arrival of the breeder is likely to come later if ever.

Even if breeders should become economical for most non-weapon states, they would likely be imported from abroad rather than produced domestically. If an international market develops for breeders, a market will probably also develop for plutonium, since some non-nuclear weapon state importers would want to import plutonium for their imported breeder reactors. Alternatively, the importing non-nuclear weapon states might engage the services of foreign reprocessing facilities for separating plutonium from the spent fuel of their own LWRs, after they have begun the construction of breeders. Or domestic reprocessing by the importer may seem desirable in order to acquire some degree of fuel independence for their breeders. Optimistically, it would take almost 10 years to build a breeder reactor and about five to construct a reprocessing plant. Hence the construction of reprocessing facilities could be delayed without much cost until the construction of fast breeders has begun in the importing countries. The simultaneous construction of both, on the other hand, would only provide the non-nuclear weapon states with considerable time for stockpiling plutonium.

In any case, potential breeder importers do not need to construct reprocessing plants in the immediate future in order to have breeder programmes later on. Yet many non-nuclear weapon states, such as South Korea, Pakistan, and Iran, that have expressed interest in importing reprocessing facilities do not have any known specific breeder plans.

A commitment to plutonium breeders, while their economics remain uncertain, involves risking substantial resources, on the order of billions of dollars. Thus, a moratorium on reprocessing until technical and cost-benefit issues are resolved would not be very costly for potential breeder importers because of the probable higher costs of investing in an unproven and uncertain technology.

Political costs. Although the moratorium on the export of reprocessing and enrichment facilities will not be economically very costly for the importing countries, it has exacerbated North-South relations. There are several points of contention between suppliers and importers over the transfer of nuclear technology; first, whether restrictions on the export of certain facilities are a violation of obligations under the NPT; second, whether these restrictions are a violation of sovereignty of the importing countries; and third, whether they maintain the technological and energy dependence of the rest of the world on the industrialized suppliers.

Many analysts in the supplying countries, as well as in the importing ones, see the NPT as a straightforward agreement between the nuclear-weapon states and the non-nuclear weapon states, obligating the former to provide technological help to the latter. The imposition of moratoria on the export of facilities such as reprocessing and enrichment is regarded as a violation of Article IV of the NPT. Former Iranian Prime Minister Amir Abbas Hoveyda accused nuclear suppliers contemplating such moratoria of 'being selective in the implementation of the NPT'.[20] Many participants in the Shiraz Conference on the Transfer of Nuclear Technology in April 1977 expressed the fear that the American nuclear export constraint proposals would shake the NPT system.[21] Such a situation, it was thought, would lead to the withdrawal of many member states from the treaty. [These views have at times been expressed most forcefully by countries that have not joined the NPT system, such as Pakistan and India.[22]]

The NPT articles are vague enough, however, to allow for a variety of interpretations. Article IV obligates all members of the NPT regime to 'facilitate and have the right to participate in, the fullest possible exchange of equipment, materials and scientific and technological information for peaceful uses of nuclear energy.'[23] This article forms the basis of the claim for the import of sensitive technologies by the non-nuclear weapon states who are members of the NPT. At the same time, however, Article IV requires conformity with Articles I and II, which obligate the nuclear weapon states not to 'in any way assist, encourage, or induce non-nuclear weapon states to manufacture or otherwise acquire nuclear weapons or other nuclear explosive devices.'[24] Thus, a question may legitimately be raised whether helping non-weapon states to come within hours of a nuclear explosive capability through the transfer of certain technologies is not assisting them to acquire nuclear weapons and thus to violate Article I of the NPT.

Article III of the NPT requires effective safeguard application to any transfer of a nuclear-related technology to a non-nuclear weapon state. In that reprocessing and enrichment technologies impede the application of effective safeguards, a case could be made that the transfer of such technologies may be a violation of Article III as well.

Clearly, there is a variety of possible interpretations of the obligations imposed by the NPT on the sellers and buyers of sensitive nuclear technologies. The moratorium on reprocessing and enrichment facilities, however, has already placed an additional strain on North-South relations. Some in the less industrialized countries, such as Cyrus Manzoor of the Iran Atomic Energy Commission, have argued that the 'unbounded' flow of technology to these countries is a *sine qua non* for successful industrialization.[25] Technology, including nuclear power is regarded as the vehicle for development. Thus, it is held, the manipulation of any technology results in the manipulation of the development and industrialization of the industrializing countries. Some have charged that the developed countries have used the medium of technology control to promote and sustain their global hegemony. Pakistan, among others, has accused the developed countries of technological apartheid and neo-colonialism, because of the imposition of a moratoria on the export of certain technologies.[26]

Part of the drive to acquire sensitive technologies, especially enrichment facilities, by the non-weapon states is to assure fuel availability through autonomy. Some policymakers in the supplying countries, while pushing for a moratorium, have not responded with equal vigour and sensitivity to this legitimate need of the buyers of power reactors for uninterrupted supplies of nuclear fuel at fair prices. For many years, it has been expected that dependence on nuclear power would bring about energy independence. Abba Eban of Israel in 1956, for example, forecasting the international future of nuclear power, argued that 'a genuine equality of nations, unknown in the era of coal and oil, will then become possible, replacing some of the present tensions between the suppliers of vital fuel and those dependent on their supplies'.[27] Yet dependence on LWRs has disappointed this hope by leading to a very real dependence on those countries that have enrichment facilities. For importers, then, this dependence on the Western suppliers for reactor fuel is a source of deep concern. Assurances of a continued supply by the United States, for example, are not considered completely convincing, as contracts have been suspended before and they are susceptible to reversal by the US Congress, 'which is notoriously sensitive to determined partisan or special-interest pressure'.[28] The suppliers, it is feared, may also be tempted to use their leverage on fuel for other goals.

Thus, a moratorium on the export of enrichment technology arising from proliferation concerns is increasingly likely to be the target of substantive criticism by the importers of LWRs, if it does not deal with the problems associated with dependence on a few countries for fuel. To expect the industrializing importers to accept dependence for nuclear fuel on a few industrial countries, while the latter states regard dependence on foreign oil supplies as threatening to their economic, political, and military well-being, would appear to the developing world to be yet another manifestation of the international double standard.

In order to deal with this problem, the international community, with the help of nuclear suppliers and the IAEA, should consider the creation of an International Slightly Enriched Uranium Bank under IAEA control. This bank would have enough LWR fuel on hand at all times to meet the needs of non-weapon states for five years. The non-weapon states, after the first fuel load, would receive the necessary slightly enriched uranium in exchange for the spent fuel from their LWRs at prices that would not increase annually at rates higher than the average worldwide inflation rate. The spent fuel would be shipped to the weapon states in proportion to their fuel contribution to the bank. Since the transaction would take place through the bank, the supplying countries would not be able to adopt a policy of selective embargo. An international nuclear fuel bank would be economically feasible, since the fuel costs are relatively small in proportion to the investment costs of a complete nuclear power programme. Because the fuel is not very bulky, transportation and storage costs are not likely to be prohibitive.

Alternatively, the international community should consider selling shares in the existing or the future enrichment facilities of the nuclear weapon states to the non-nuclear weapon states in proportion to the needs of their nuclear programme. Although at present there is no international slightly enriched uranium shortage, the weapon and non-weapon states could start discussions regarding the international expansion of existing national plants and the creation of new internationally-owned enrichment facilities in the nuclear weapon states. Such an international arrangement should be flexible enough to allow the participation of new members and the cancellation, deferment, and trading of shares among member states.

Multinational ownership of enrichment facilities is being tried in France. Iran, for example, has acquired a 10 per cent share in the EURODIF gaseous diffusion enrichment plant there. Other share-holders include non-weapon states such as Spain, Italy, and Belgium. A similar arrangement is expected in the case of the COREDIF enrichment facility, also to be constructed in France. Other nuclear weapon states, especially the United States – the world's largest supplier of slightly enriched uranium – might seriously consider following the French lead in selling shares to non-nuclear weapon states in its existing and future enrichment facilities.

*   *   *   *   *

Constraints on the export of reprocessing and enrichment facilities by major suppliers will make it harder for non-nuclear weapon states to acquire a nuclear weapons capability based on their civilian nuclear power programmes. Without export constraints, many non-nuclear weapon states could come to the brink of a nuclear weapons capability without violating international safeguards. Export constraints, however, are not a panacea for the problem of non-proliferation. They do not deal with the reasons why the non-weapon states may want to produce nuclear weapons and do not affect those non-nuclear weapon states that can produce proliferation-sensitive technologies domestically at a tolerable cost. Restrictions on the nuclear technology trade will be most effective against the least developed countries unable to develop their own facilities. For those countries in the middle of the technical capability continuum, constraints increase the risks, costs, and time required to produce these sensitive facilities at home. In some cases, the problems might deter them from developing weapon-related nuclear systems, though, in the case of others, political considerations may increase the incentives for indigenous development of critical facilities.

On economic grounds, the moratorium on the export of reprocessing and enrichment plants will mean the loss of some export earnings for the suppliers. For the importers, on the other hand, no significant economic losses are likely. However, the imposition of export constraints has contributed to the deterioration of North-South relations. The deterioration in relations will increase unless the producers respond to the legitimate demands of the developing or importing countries for access to slightly enriched uranium at fair prices without any serious danger of interruption.

NOTES AND REFERENCES

1. According to 1975 projections, by 1985 a large number of states (almost forty) were expected to have access to enough chemically separable weapon material (plutonium) for a few bombs in the spent fuel of their civilian nuclear power plants. Albert Wohlstetter, *et al., Moving Towards Life in a Nuclear Armed Crowd?* (Los Angeles: Pan Heuristics, 1976) pp. 1-8. The International Atomic Energy Agency estimated in 1976 that by 1990 the less industrial countries alone were expected to have an installed capacity of 150,000 megawatts electrical [MW (e)]; Rurik Krymm and George Woite, 'Estimate of Future Demand for Uranium and Nuclear Fuel Cycle Services', *The International Atomic Energy Bulletin*, vol. 18, no. 516 (1976) p. 71.

2. Thomas Schelling, 'Who Will Have the Bomb?', *International Security*, vol. I, no. 1 (1976) p. 77. Albert Wohlstetter argued in 1977 that under existing nuclear export rules, 'a non-weapon state can come closer to exploding a plutonium weapon today without violating an agreement not to make a bomb than the United States was in the Spring of 1947, when the world considered us not only a nuclear power but the nuclear power'. Albert Wohlstetter, Spreading the Bomb Without Quite Breaking the Rules', *Foreign Policy*, no. 25 (Winter 1976-7) p. 88.

3. Former French Foreign Minister Louis de Guirringaud has argued that plutonium from civilian reactors 'could not be used for military

purposes' [New York: Service de Presse et d'Information, no. 76/95 (1976) p. 3.] According to Leny Abordarham of Framatome, the French reactor exporting company, the worst way to make a bomb is to buy a light-water reactor, the reactor which most non-weapon states are purchasing. *Nucleonics Week*, 3 June 1976. In February of 1978, Walter Marshall of the United Kingdom Atomic Energy Commission argued that nuclear weapons were not 'related to nuclear power at all'. *The Reuters Applied Atomic Report*, 28 February 1978, p. 2.

4. Robert Oppenheimer, 'The Environs of Atomic Power', *Atoms for Peace* (New York: The American Assembly, 1957) p. 21.

5. According to Taylor, 'Under conceivable circumstances, one person who possessed about ten kilograms of plutonium oxide and a substantial amount of high explosives could, within several weeks, design and build a crude fission bomb' In O. Marwah and A. Schultz, (eds), *Nuclear Proliferation and Near Nuclear Countries* (Cambridge Mass.: Ballinger, 1975) p. 117.

6. In 1974, an MIT student was hired by a television station to design a bomb for a programme on nuclear proliferation. In 1977, a Princeton University student was said to have designed one as well.

7. Dixey Lee Ray, 'Multinational Nuclear Power – Peaceful Use or International Terror?', *Pan American Magazine* (October 1974).

8. In the past the United States has exported 697 kilograms of highly enriched uranium and 104 kilograms of separated plutonium to Japan and 2710 kilograms of highly enriched uranium and 349 kilograms of separated plutonium to the Federal Republic of Germany. Large quantities of highly enriched uranium have also been shipped to Italy, Rumania, and Spain.

9. It is reported that in 1965 Egypt wanted to purchase a nuclear weapon from the Soviet Union but was rebuffed. *New York Times*, 4 February 1966. Libya has also attempted to purchase a nuclear device from the People's Republic of China. Originally reported by H. Hykal in the Cairo Documents, quoted in *New Outlook* (October 1974) p. 39.

10. Those who argue that power plant plutonium is not usable in effective weapons, state that this plutonium contains a high percentage (20-30 per cent) of plutonium-240. The presence of large quantities of plutonium-240 in the spent fuel or power reactors is due to the long irradiation time necessitated by the economical operation of power reactors. This argument has several major flaws. First, since the isotopic composition of plutonium in the spent fuel depends on the period of fuel irradiation, a country çan operate its power reactors in such a way as to produce large quantities or rather pure high-grade plutonium. This would involve some departure from theoretical norms for reactor operation and some economic cost. In many countries, reactors have been operated quite differently from the norms. Present international agreements do not require economic operation of reactors.

Second, recently released information shows that there is a considerable latitude in regard to the level of purity of plutonium-239 required for explosives. In the United States, plutonium containing up to and including 8 per cent plutonium-240 can be used to make nuclear weapons.

Sources: (a) 'Spent Fuel and Radioactive Waste', Staten Offenlige Utredninger, document no. 32 (Stockholm: Libervulag, 1976) p. 43; (b) G. Hildebrand, 'The Fuel Cycle and the Export Situation', Lecture, Mülheim, 30 April 1976; (c) Carl Walske, 'Nuclear Energy Environment in the United States', Paper to a Conference in Madrid, Spain, 4 May 1976.

11. Energy Research and Development Administration, *News Release*, 4 August 1977.
12. *Financial Times*, 5 October 1978.
13. Those attending the London meeting included the United States, Great Britain, the Federal Republic of Germany, the Netherlands, Sweden, Canada, the Soviet Union, the Democratic Republic of Germany, Poland and Czechoslovakia.
14. *San Francisco Chronicle*, 24 August 1978.
15. A document released in 1974 by the CIA reports: 'We believe Israel has produced nuclear weapons'. DCI NIO 1945-74, 4 September 1974.
16. The PRC has been reluctant to help others (for example, Libya) acquire a nuclear weapon capability. Until 1981 it emphasized nuclear self-reliance. India, too, has been reluctant to provide help in sensitive areas to other countries. Besides, it is dependent on the United States for the fuel of some of its reactors and thus may be reluctant to risk an American fuel embargo by exporting reprocessing know-how to other countries. Israel and South Africa are both pariah states and are unlikely to favour the proliferation of nuclear weapons to the rest of the world which is largely hostile to them. Israel's dependence on the United States for military and political support makes it further unlikely for that country to risk America's serious displeasure by exporting sensitive nuclear technologies.
17. Albert Wohlstetter; *Proof of Evidence on Behalf of Friends of the Earth at the Windscale Inquiry on British Nuclear Fuel Limited's Planned Expansion of Reprocessing Facilities*, 5-6 September 1977.
18. Vince Taylor, *The Economics of Plutonium and Uranium* (Los Angeles: Pan Heuristics, Report to Energy Research and Development Administration, Contract 49-1-3747, 1977).
19. Vince Taylor, 'Economic Aspects of Nuclear Proliferation', in *Moving Towards Life in a Nuclear Armed Crowd?*, op. cit. chapter IV.
20. *Energy Daily*, 12 April 1977.
21. Ibid.
22. The German Atomic Forum in its 1977 meeting in Mannheim expressed sentiments similar to those of the Shiraz Conference: 'No reprocessing will lead to the end of the NPT'. Ibid.
23. Anne W. Marks (ed.), *NPT: Paradoxes and Problems* (Washington, DC: Arms Control Association, 1975) Appendix I.
24. Ibid.
25. Cyrus Manzoor, 'The Politics of Technology Transfer', op. cit.
26. *Nucleonics Week*, 21 April 1977.
27. IAEA, *Debate on the Statute*, October 1976.
28. Shahram Chubin, paper presented to the Conference on Managing in a Proliferation Prone World, December 1977.

8 A Critique of the Technical Approach

CYNTHIA CANNIZZO

There are two approaches to the problem of nuclear weapons proliferation: the technical-economic and the political. The former focuses on the 'dis-economies' of nuclear power and of producing nuclear weapons as a spin-off from commercial nuclear power, and on depriving the near-nuclear states of the technology, technical means, and materiel needed to produce nuclear weapons, as the way to control proliferation. This paper refutes the technical approach as a complete solution and then develops a possible political approach which incorporates technical constraints as a partial solution. To this end, it seeks to answer the following series of questions: Do we really have to worry about nuclear weapons proliferation? Will technical strategies suggested for non-proliferation work? Why or why not? What strategies might be effective?

To begin with, there is little real evidence to support the exaggerated concern for nuclear weapons proliferation, at least to the extent that some fear, that is, scores of nuclear armed states emerging on the horizon. Most people believe that nuclear weapons proliferation is a problem, citing increased probability of an accident, difficulties for the US and USSR in determining where an attack (or a hypothetical stray missile) is coming from, increased chance of weapons falling into terrorist hands or being used to influence domestic politics, and most importantly, the increased chance of nuclear weapons being used in war by states that have not had the long learning the US and USSR have regarding their non-utility. More generally, it has been argued that nuclear weapons proliferation will increase international tensions, will make wars more destructive in shorter periods of time, will increase regional instability by perturbing regional balances of power, will reduce Western and especially American control over international crises, and will weaken existing alliance systems.

On the other hand, nuclear weapons proliferation may have a stabilizing influence, since it would bring equality among nations; would satisfy those who condemn the present world nuclear regime as discriminatory and would make the acquiring governments and their neighbours more cautious. In addition, there is the notion that since nuclear deterrence has worked for the superpowers, there is a good chance that it could work, albeit at a lower level of weaponry, for other antagonistic states.

This paper does not argue that proliferation does not contain some dangers, but rather that those dangers do not apply equally to all non-weapons states and that they are not global in scope. Problems and dangers are certainly inherent in the possession of nuclear weapons, yet we cannot assume that all states will fall prey to proliferation. To show that this is indeed the case, we need to answer three questions: if a state has the technology, will it acquire nuclear weapons? If a state acquires nuclear weapons, what kind of weapons are likely to be acquired? And, if a state has nuclear weapons, will it necessarily use them in a crisis situation?

First, it is clear that the mere ability to make a nuclear weapon does not inexorably lead to their production. 'For years there have been governments, maybe a score of them, that had jurisdiction over the physical facilities and the personnel with which to construct nuclear weapons. As far as we can tell, they either found it good policy to resist the temptation to mobilize those nuclear resources, or they were not tempted'.[1] To put the issue more precisely, ''Going nuclear'' is a matter not of capability but of intention,' and '. . . political will is the key, rather than mere competence'.[2]

Capability and intention are obviously intertwined, for without the capability all the intention in the world will not build a bomb (assuming the current nuclear weapons states continue to refuse to sell ready-made nuclear weapons). However, the argument here is that capability alone is not enough either; a state must also want to have nuclear weapons and make a conscious decision to acquire them. The decision to 'go nuclear' is a complex political question, involving domestic as well as international considerations. This political decision can only come into play once the technology and materials are available. Or, a state could decide to acquire a nuclear weapons capability, and to do so, pursue the prior step of acquiring the technology and materials. Since technology is the prior step, the advocates of technical-economic solutions feel that, by denying the technical means, the bandit states driving for a nuclear-weapons capability can be 'headed off at the pass'. However, as we shall see below, the bandits are already at the bank vault.

A number of lists of near-nuclear states are available with a common core of twenty-three, as shown in Table 8.1 These are the candidate states that are likely to have the capacity to produce nuclear weapons by the mid 1980s (if not before) unless controls are implemented now. By assuming that all these 23 states will, in fact, acquire nuclear weapons, the alarmists predict a 'nuclear armed crowd'.

TABLE 8.1   The twenty-three near-nuclear states

Argentina	Mexico[a]
Austria[a]	Netherlands[a]
Belgium[a]	Pakistan
Brazil	Philippines[a]
Federal Republic of Germany[a](FRG)	South Africa[b]
India[b]	Sweden[a]
Indonesia[a]	Switzerland[a]
Iran[a]	Taiwan[a]
Israel[b]	Yugoslavia[a]
Italy[a]	Egypt[a]
Japan[a]	Vietnam[a]
South Korea[a]	

Notes:

[a] Signatories to the Non-proliferation Treaty (NPT)

[b] These states are classed as potential weapons states since no definite evidence is available for current weapons possession, although a presumption of possession is clear.

It is my contention, though, that not all of these candidate states wish to join the club. As a means of divining intent, we can use the signing of the Non-proliferation Treaty (NPT) as an indicator of a state's intention *not* to produce nuclear weapons. By that criterion most of the candidates can be removed from consideration, leaving us with Argentina, Brazil, India, Israel, Pakistan, and South Africa – a mere handful indeed. Of course, treaties are easily abrogated by unilateral withdrawal; the NPT review conference in 1980 might have provided a convenient forum for states to change their minds. We should, therefore, probably add to our list of potential proliferators those current NPT signatories presumed likely to withdraw at some future date; this group could include Iran, Japan, Taiwan, and South Korea. We now have a list of ten proliferators – not very comforting to those for whom even one more nuclear weapons state is anathema, but still far from the horrifying scenario of twenty or thirty new nuclear powers.

As another indicator of intent to acquire, the presence of a long-standing conflict would clearly provide an incentive for weapons. All ten states on the shortened list of near-nuclear states are engaged in or threatened by such rivalries: Argentina-Brazil; India-Pakistan; Israel-(Arab states); Iran-(Iraq; Saudi Arabia; USSR); South Africa-(Black Africa); Japan-(PRC; USSR); Taiwan-(PRC); South Korea-(North Korea; PRC). Some of these are more serious than others, but all would appear to be more intense than the conflicts faced by the other thirteen states (with the exception of the FRG-USSR, but West Germany is clearly behind the US nuclear shield.). Thus, the ten candidates seem much more likely to be the new nuclear weapons states than the remaining thirteen. Hence when we worry about nuclear weapons proliferation, our attention should be focused on this limited set of states and not diverted to more global scenarios.

This is not to say that intentions cannot change over time; the possibility remains of states withdrawing from the NPT. Should the Vietnamese-Cambodian clashes escalate, with increasing participation of the People's Republic of China (PRC) for Cambodia, it is conceivable that Vietnam would seek Soviet aid, possibly in the form of nuclear weapons technology. If the Camp David accords fall due to Israeli intransigence or if the moderate post-Sadat group fails in Egypt, Egypt would probably speed up her nuclear weapons research. If the NATO alliance clearly begins to disintegrate, or the West Europeans perceive an obvious weakening of the US nuclear commitment, the West Europeans – primarily the Federal Republic of Germany (FRG), Italy, and Belgium – are likely to follow the French and British lead in acquiring national nuclear forces. However, these scenarios are all predicated on major shifts in the status quo, and we must first deal with the world as it is today, and secondarily worry about tomorrow. We will return to these second-line states (those with the capability but no current incentive), and proceed to the second questions: what type of nuclear weapons are the ten front-line states (those with the capability *and* the incentive) likely to acquire?

Assuming that this handful of states does indeed acquire nuclear weapons, it is unlikely that such weapons would be in the strategic category. Although there is apparently some controversy on this point, the weapons are most likely to be small, tactical (kiloton ranges), fairly reliable and few in number.[3] The first nuclear weapons of these new states would thus be roughly similar to the first US bomb – a crude, yet reliable and effective device with an explosive force of approximately Hiroshima size (20 kilotons) and designed for aircraft delivery. Such weapons could, of course, inflict a great deal of local damage – such as razing Damascus or Pyongyang – but they would not create the type of global holocaust associated with a superpower strategic exchange. The loss of such locales would be national disasters, of course, with the human misery and collateral damage truly regrettable. Countervalue strikes (against urban centres) in the Third World are certainly not more morally or legally acceptable than they are in the US-USSR context. However, the probable level of damage and capacity for the annihilation of an entire country would be only a fraction of that implicit in the current inventories of the US and the USSR. The superpowers will remain for some time the only states capable of unleashing global Armageddon.

This assumes, of course, that a regional nuclear exchange would not escalate into, nor engender, a US-USSR strategic exchange. Although fears of entanglement and escalation are not groundless, the probability of such an eventuality is all but miniscule. Neither the US nor the USSR have seriously threatened the use of their nuclear arsenals over a local conflict, aside from political signaling. It is even doubtful that the superpowers will send troops to such hot spots. Thus, to raise the spectre of escalation from localized tactics to super strategies is to be alarmist.

With regard to the third question, even if the states acquire such 'tactical' nuclear weapons, some relatively cogent arguments can be made to the effect that the weapons would not necessarily be used in a crisis situation. We have seen the number of nuclear weapon states (NWS) increase from one in 1945 to five known and eight possibles today, but we have not seen a repeat performance of Hiroshima and Nagasaki – despite a number of very intense crises involving one or more of the nuclear states. Hence, it is possible to practice restraint. This might not always be the case, of course, especially given the history of actual armed conflict by many of the candidate states, a history of direct confrontation being something the nuclear powers have carefully sought to avoid since conventional war is generally assumed to be the step prior to nuclear escalation. Furthermore, because the destructive capability of these new nuclear states would be less than that of the current powers, and in many instances the state with potential nuclear weapons is not facing a nuclear armed opponent but one that is relatively strong in conventional capabilities, there might be more of an incentive for these new nuclear weapons states to use their arms. Hence, the hesitation born of the fear of the destructive potential and the assured second strike would be much less pronounced for these states. Although the current regimes in most of the candidates are considered moderate and rational, some are subject to internal disorders and the probability of a radical clique – one that might use nuclear weapons – assuming power cannot altogether be discounted. Yet, the fact remains that current nuclear weapons states have not used their arsenals and, more importantly, that the potential proliferators have been known to show restraint and, by-and-large, to avoid civilian targets in their conventional wars. Thus, use is not automatic once the capability has been attained.

Despite the fact that the previous arguments have tried to show that we do not have to be doomsayers on nuclear proliferation, a number of caveats were raised that indicate we should be attempting to find ways of controlling or at least regulating proliferation.

WILL TECHNICAL STRATEGIES STOP PROLIFERATION?

The effectiveness of technical strategies needs to be considered separately for the front-line and the second-line states. In addition, given the multiplicity of such approaches, a more precise specification of 'technical strategies' is required. The most common and reputably discussed technical solutions include (a) moratoria on the export of nuclear-weapons technologies and essential fuels (i.e., the 'trigger' list of sensitive nuclear technologies agreed to by the London Suppliers' Club), usually for 5-10 years; (b) renegotiation of the NPT to distinguish more clearly between military and civilian technologies; (c) an international fuel bank; and (d) assumed inherent constraints on indigenous production (see Khalilzad, this volume, for a full explication of this fourfold strategy).

Let us first consider these steps for the non-nuclear states, *excluding* those ten on the proliferation list. Generally speaking, these constraints could effectively slow down, if not halt, the acquisition of nuclear weapons by the vast majority of states without engendering too many dangerous side effects. These states are mainly interested in nuclear power for electricity and as long as they receive a fair deal under the NPT (the renegotiation) and a guaranteed access to fuel (the bank) and non-military technology (the NPT) they are not likely either to produce nuclear weapons or become anti-status quo. The moratorium on trigger items along with the difficulties of producing a nuclear weapon on one's own without access to weapons-grade fuel and the trigger technology, would help to ensure against a state deciding to embark on a nuclear weapons option at some future date. Thus, such a strategy – assuming the technical details could be worked out so that states do have access to peaceful technology and fuels – would not alienate anyone in this group under present circumstances but would deprive them of the capability to produce nuclear weapons in the future.

However, the story is somewhat different with the ten probable proliferators. Most of these states are, or aspire to be, regional leaders. Also, as we saw above, these states face hostile neighbours, and in the case of some (Israel, South Korea, Taiwan, South Africa) their very existence as independent states is threatened. What effect could such a technical strategy have on these front-line proliferators?

First, although these states, as we will see below, can now 'go-it-alone,' cheap and easy access makes the nuclear options more available and in less time. Presuming that these states are interested in acquiring nuclear weapons primarily for security and secondarily for prestige, the moratorium could breed frustration and hatred. Such policies could produce 'resentment, along with mounting determination by the "nonaligned" to seize the political initiative' from the suppliers.[4] Such a conclusion is consistent with sociological studies on the 'revolution of rising expectations'. Additionally, the international atmosphere is already quite charged with accusations of continued exploitation and dependence-inducing policies on the part of the developed world, and a moratorium on exports would be just one more step. The front-line states could, with some effort, mount a propaganda campaign against the restraints along these lines, thereby gaining support of states not initially resentful. The frustration and bitterness could 'further accelerate the nationalistic trend to construction of independent indigenous fuel cycle capabilities... and lose or reduce the likelihood of gaining acceptance for effective international controls and safeguards'.[5] Thus, not only would these ten states go ahead and acquire nuclear weapons, they would be in a position to pass on the technology to other states that might want it in the future, and the present suppliers would be powerless to act.

Second, a complete renegotiation of the NPT would probably take several years; the original was at least six years in the making (dating from the 1964 US proposal to the Eighteen Nation Disarmament Conference (ENDC) which included provisions dealing with peaceful uses) and represents carefully balanced compromises of views and interests. To attempt to change it is to ask for its end. Furthermore, it is not self-evident that it needs to be renegotiated. The Preamble (particularly paragraph seven) and Article I are not inconsistent. Although the distinction between peaceful nuclear reactors, devices, explosions and military ones may have become blurred in practice, they remain analytically distinct. The problem is with the application of the treaty, and this is a matter of interpretation. The time of negotiators at the scheduled five-year NPT review conferences would be better spent on clarifying that distinction rather than attempting to rewrite from scratch. Further, if agreement on the trigger list can be extended and expanded to this end, such would provide for a more solid suppliers' front. Without a solid front, the agitation of the ten potential proliferators could drive a wedge and break the NPT apart.

Third, is the question of indigenous production. Is it really so difficult to 'home-grow' nuclear weapons as some physicists and engineers would have us believe? I think not. To produce nuclear weapons without outside assistance would require a supply of uranium, some method of enriching this to weapons-grade, and an industrial base for construction of the device and delivery vehicle. A small team of highly skilled persons with diverse technical backgrounds along with supporting staff and machinery is all that is necessary for the encasement, triggering mechanism, delivery vehicle, etc.[6] Argentina, Brazil, Pakistan, and Iran are the only ones of the candidate states that probably do not, at this time, have such a capacity; however, they are working on it. Delivery vehicles are already in the hands of these states, in the form of any number of fighter planes, attack planes, and even transports or commercial aircraft. Most of these planes can be modified relatively easily and cheaply to carry nuclear bombs. Thus, acquisition essentially hinges on obtaining weapons-grade fuels for these ten states.

Of the candidate countries listed before, Argentina, Brazil, India, Japan, Korea, and South Africa all have naturally-occurring uranium; only Israel, Pakistan, Iran, and Taiwan have to import uranium supplies. However, these latter countries currently have in place some form of nuclear reactor and hence some stock of basic fuel already on hand. Furthermore, a state does not need the extensive facilities associated with the generation of civilian nuclear power to obtain enriched materials for at least several weapons. All ten of these countries have research reactors which provide a relatively cheap means of producing the needed material.[7] Thus, all the candidate states meet the necessary requirements, and an embargo on materials and technology would not affect their weapons production capacity very much, if at all, although production would be easier in the absence of such restrictions.

Hence, of the states we have previously identified as those we need to worry about, none would be seriously affected by either embargoes or renegotiation of the NPT and most have the capacity to produce rather quickly at least a few, relatively reliable, small nuclear bombs complete with delivery systems without further assistance. Those that do not quite have the engineering capacity for the more complicated process could still acquire such knowledge from the other nuclear pariah states.

Moratoria and negotiations might be able to 'buy time', say five years (more than enough time for the ten potential weapons states to secure their bombs) but only at the expense of finding the world worse off than before since there would be heightened resentment towards, and a subsequent questioning and weakening of, the leadership of the current suppliers. Thus, not only would there be several additional nuclear weapons states, but these states would not be inclined to listen to other nuclear powers, whether the issue be one of restraint on use or restraints on further proliferation.

In sum, a technical approach could help prevent borderline or second-line states from exercising a weapons option in the future, but at the same time could have dangerous effects on the policies of the near-term proliferators. For these ten states, a very different type of technical strategy is called for – a regulatory rather than prohibitory one. However, these ten could still develop nuclear weapons (albeit 'safe' ones), and the possibility for further proliferation would remain. Thus, we need to ask why technical strategies aren't truly effective and what kind of strategy could be?

WHY WON'T TECHNICAL STRATEGIES WORK?

The technical approach to non-proliferation is likely to fail – especially for the front-line states – because it basically does not recognize and deal with the essential politics of the problem for either the suppliers or the recipients.

On the supplier side, states are faced with strong pressures from their domestic nuclear industries to export. These pressures arise from profits, export earnings, employment, economies of scale, markets for obsolescing equipment, and so forth. The stronger these internal pressures and the more commercially-oriented the executive, the less likely a state will be to enter into multilateral control arrangements. For example, in the US between 1977 and 1981 there were relatively strong pressures, but a chief executive who did not like exporting nuclear materials. On the other hand, France in the same period had a strong domestic industry and an amenable national leader. With such differing levels of belief in the value of restrictive, technical policies, it will be difficult for the suppliers to create and maintain a united front.

Another problem on the supplier side is the question of leadership. The role of the US in establishing standards and trends in any area, but especially economic ones, has been deteriorating for the past decade or so as Europe's has been revived. The Europeans have never been particularly fond of their somewhat subservient economic role, and, now that they are strong once again, US leadership efforts are severely questioned. This attitude was clearly displayed at the trilateral economic summit in Bonn in 1978 and by the FRG's righteously outrageous reaction to US attempts to stop the sale of sensitive nuclear power technology to Brazil.

As damaging and fragile as politics among the suppliers may be to technical strategies for non-proliferation, the politics of acquisition present an even more formidable obstacle. Although actual acquisition of nuclear weapons depends on having the appropriate technology, the motives and incentives for acquisition are basically political. Bureaucratic momentum and the technological imperative could conceivably bring a state to the threshold without any conscious decisions being taken by the government. Upon finding itself in such a position a state could conceivably decide 'Why not?' and build a bomb. However, it is difficult to imagine a government making such an off-hand decision, especially given the potential consequences.

Yet the bureaucrats and technocrats can wield a great deal of political clout; the issue is not as simple as portrayed above. Suppose a state has acquired either a power or research reactor. In such a case there would be an associated group of scientists and bureaucrats with vested interests. Both groups would desire an expansion of nuclear experimentation, technology, institutions, etc., and could probably bring this about. The physicists and engineers might even develop (although not test) a nuclear weapon, all without government involvement or top-level decisions. It would probably be at the testing step that the government would have to become involved and would have to make a decision. Even if the various objective and discernible motivations discussed below are only weak initially, the lobbies and influence that vested interest could bring to bear might pressure the government to go ahead and exercise its nuclear option. Thus, technical constraints now could preclude the development and expansion of the nuclear lobby to some extent, thereby decreasing the probability that a state would eventually acquire nuclear weapons.

However, surreptitious means could be used, and technical constraints cannot totally constrain 'natural' tendencies to expand. Even in the bureaucratic-technological juggernaut, it is politics that provides the driving force. Thus, unless a non-proliferation strategy addresses the political incentives – especially for the ten probable proliferators – it is likely to be ineffective. 'The emphasis has to shift from physical denial and technological secrecy to the things that determine incentives and motivations and expectations'.[8] Thus, we need to ask what those motivations are and what strategies could curb them and halt proliferation.

POLITICAL MOTIVATIONS AND STRATEGIES FOR PROLIFERATION

The major incentives for acquiring nuclear weapons are security, influence, status and prestige, and the international climate.[9] The ten candidate states all appear to be susceptible to these incentives to greater or lesser degrees, so strategies designed to remove the incentives may be effective.

The primary reason for acquistion is security. All the candidate states face a very real external threat, and nuclear weapons are seen as a means of countering that threat. In many instances, this threat takes the form of an actively hostile opponent that is well-armed conventionally, has an equivalent (or greater) population and resource base, and a nuclear-armed backer (USSR or PRC). Thus, for states such as Israel, South Africa, Taiwan, and South Korea, a long, protracted conventional war is risky business. Nuclear weapons are seen as a way to balance the situation.

As an alternative to nuclear weapons, security could be provided through large scale sales of conventional arms, as has been done for Israel, South Korea, and Iran.[10] This would have to include basically unlimited quantities of sophisticated weapons systems, spare parts, and service. Great power (i.e., American) guarantees might also be reassuring, as the US has done for Israel and South Korea. Such a guarantee, to be effective, should be composed of: (a) a formal declaration of support that is periodically buttressed by public statements; (b) relatively major economic invetments – through arms sales as well as private investments; and (c) a visible military presence either through nearby naval deployments or preferably actual ground and air combat troops that manouevre and exercise with the local troops.

Second, states may decide to acquire nuclear weapons as a means of acquiring (or maintaining) influence and leverage *vis-à-vis* other states. This is clearly one of the reasons that France chose to have an independent nuclear force and that India chose to explode a nuclear 'device'. Although many, if not most, governments probably want more influence, the top ten potential proliferators would appear to need it more than others. For example, South Africa could clearly use a powerful lever to help regain trading privileges and to lift the various barriers that currently keep her isolated from world affairs. Iran, although clearly now in grave domestic difficulty, has always aspired to regional leadership. Regional leadership is also a goal of Argentina and Brazil, as well as Japan. Japan might also gain some bargaining leverage in her negotiations with the Soviet Union over trade and the Kurile Islands. South Korea, Taiwan, and Israel all probably want some independent means of assuring continued US support, and Pakistan needs a lever *vis-à-vis* India.

Are there other ways to buy such influence? Probably not. Nuclear weapons are potentially a cheaper and easier route than massive conventional forces or economic development. Further, the nuclear option is less likely to cause substantial disruption of the public sector and among the people. Thus, the desired influence would have to be 'given' to those potential proliferators by those concerned if this is to be a viable route. Much of the scrambling of the current NWS in the diplomatic persuasion field has been of the negative sort: 'if you do, we'll stop this, cut off that, punish you'. This could be changed to 'if you don't, we'll start this, give you that, reward you'. However, this would constitute 'pre-nuclear' blackmail and could not guarantee that a state would not eventually exercise its option. It might also have the undesirable side effect of spurring a number of other states to advance their nuclear programmes in order to join the pre-nuclear blackmail gang. The dilemma is either to use punishment and ostracization which might push a state over the edge or to give in and try to appease these states, which can't assure they will reject the nuclear weapons option forever. As usual, the solution is likely some delicate, middle balance: consultation but not automatic concessions or rejections on matters directly affecting the nuclear candidate state or its region. Another aspect of this would be seriously to negotiate new voting systems in some of the major financial and technical agencies of the UN as part of the New International Economic Order (NIEO). Such negotiations would concern giving certain of the candidate states (i.e., Japan, Iran, Argentina, Brazil) more decision-making authority; some of the privileges and rights of Israel, South Africa, and Taiwan should also be restored within the UN system.

Third, states desire nuclear weapons for status (states wanting the bomb simply because it is a prestigious thing to have) as well as the more legitimate desires to be recognized as regional leaders and powers discussed above. To counter such lesser and more diffuse aspirations a new climate would need to be created, perhaps through UN channels and through bilateral diplomacy of the current nuclear-weapons states. Emphasis should be shifted to other symbols of status and power, such as headquartering of various agencies, holding chairmanships of various organizations and conferences, best hospitals, lowest illiteracy rate, human rights awards, progress in alleviating internal income disparity, increase in agricultural production, and so forth. This could introduce an element of healthy competition in these crucial areas of human development, with concomitant recognition and status to the more progressive governments. This is perhaps somewhat similar to helping individuals find their niche – we all can't be rich and famous, but we can all do what we do best and that often carries a large degree of satisfaction.

Along with this good faith bargaining, the current NWS might use some selective dissuasion. Rather than pontificating that nuclear weapons 'aren't good for you', stressing dis-economies, world public opinion, and so forth, the NWS could try a bit of counter-extortion, but not by means of trade embargoes. Economic sanctions have a notoriously bad record of success. As pointed out earlier, most of these states have bitter regional enemies. Thus, the NWS should indicate their willingness to provide assistance to this enemy, including nuclear weapons technology, should a contender actually exercise its nuclear option. Perhaps in some ways Bhutto's promise that Pakistanis would eat 'leaves and grass' to obtain nuclear weapons capability has helped to slow down or at least depublicize India's programme. How much greater impact such statements would have if the NWS agreed to help. In essence, the NWS should clearly indicate that no more proliferation is desired, but if a state decides to conjure up the evil genie, the NWS will abandon non-proliferation in favour of controlled and regulated (by them) proliferation.

Another aspect of the status motivation is the alleged 'horizontal-vertical linkage'. This argument suggests that as long as the US and USSR continue *their* nuclear arms race (vertical proliferation), they have no right to insist that other states do not acquire nuclear weapons (horizontal proliferation). Furthermore, as long as the superpowers devote so much time and attention and so many resources to their nuclear weapons programme, the status and prestige of being a member of the nuclear club will also continue. This horizontal-vertical proliferation linkage has been enshrined in Article VI of the NPT. One of the many rumblings before the NPT review was that if the SALT II accord was not perceived as a meaningful and sincere attempt at arms control, the supplier nations might find themselves with no one to talk to about non-proliferation. This argument contends that the way to slow, control, and discourage horizontal proliferation is to slow, control, and discourage vertical proliferation. The current nuclear weapon states – especially the US and the USSR – must lead the way in arms control and disarmament just as they have led the way in armaments. This implies the successful and meaningful conclusion of a number of outstanding negotiations, including START, INF, MBFR, and the Comprehensive Test Ban Treaty (CTBT).

Lastly, states acquire nuclear weapons as a hedge against a generally hostile and uncertain environment. The international world is seen as the anarchic feuding and violence of Hobbes: *realpolitik* is more than a theory; it is reality. Thus, a change in the international evironment is indicated. The steps suggested under status and prestige could go a long way towards developing such a new climate. 'Active and concerted attention needs to be devoted to resolving the more acute regional conflicts, as well as improving international mechanisms for crisis-management, pacific settlement, and peace-keeping'.[11] Improvements in and proliferation of verification and early-warning monitoring systems would further help to bolster feelings of security since a state would have knowledge of the degree to which its opponent was adhering to an arms control agreement. In the event of defection and imminent warfare, the state would also have more time to mobilize its defences, either through military means or through international peace-keeping machinery.

These are, of course only first steps. An expansion of trade, aid, and realistic, good-faith bargaining in the NIEO negotiations would be additional actions. The main objective is to shift from an atmosphere of distrust and hostility to one of trust and good will. The major powers must realize that, no matter how unfortunate for them, they can no longer indulge themselves in attempts to dictate the foreign and domestic policies of the entire world.

Nevertheless, there must be scepticism even about these political solutions. Changing the international environment could take generations and even insignificant steps toward nuclear arms control and disarmament take years. Although the alternate status symbol effort has been helpful in depoliticizing some UN agencies, to expect that it would be equally effective in the broader, more entreched arena of nuclear weapons is optimistic, if not naive. Similarly, the aura of influence associated with nuclear weapons has been built and magnified for 30 years and will probably take as long to build alternate means of leverage and influence, especially if the current NWS insist upon retaining their nuclear weapons. Also, the line between appeasement and rejection of potential proliferators is difficult to discern and partly in the eye of the beholder.

The counter-blackmail strategy might work. However, it could have serious side effects. First, states would probably 'go underground' with their nuclear programmes, and the only evidence available on capability would be rumour. Second, it would negate most, if not all, of the benefits gained by attempts to change the international climate. And third, counter-blackmail could eventually lead to the 'nuclear armed crowd' that it was designed to prevent. Lastly, it is doubtful that the superpowers will ever acknowledge as fact the linkage between vertical and horizontal proliferation. The US-USSR nuclear arms race is an old and hallowed tradition, a big power, bilateral prerogative that is deeply rooted in a major ideological struggle. They will, undoubtedly, continue to conclude arms control agreements that suit themselves, regardless of world opinion.

Thus, we are left with a need for alternate methods of guaranteeing security. However, even this strategem may fail. The approach of supplying conventional arms merely substitutes one form of arms race for another and precision-guided munitions (PGMs) can be as devastating as tactical nuclear weapons. Such a situation could also be destabilizing, as one side or the other might be more tempted to resort to force if the threat of nuclear war is *not* present. Furthermore, with the spiralling costs of conventional arms, going nuclear may soon become the cheaper alternative. And lastly, some states, such as

Israel, may never feel secure without nuclear weapons.

What about security guarantees? Here, too, we encounter grave difficulties. All ten of the front-line states with the possible exception of Pakistan are in the US and Western 'camp,' while their opponents are supported by the USSR or the PRC. Hence, US guarantees raise the spectre of cold war crises and confrontation, working counter to the revival of détente. Further, with the latent isolationist stance of the US public with regard to military policy, any significant increase in foreign commitments is likely to meet stiff opposition. This was clearly evidenced in the hue and cry over arms sales to Iran, the wavering of support for the Shah, and the generally enthusiastic response to plans for bringing the 2nd Division home from Korea. Outside of the long-standing guarantees to Western Europe and Israel, US credibility on this score has been lacking.

Given the ineffectiveness of technical constraints and the probable infeasibility of removing political incentives for the ten prime proliferators, the ineluctable conclusion seems to be that preventing nuclear weapons proliferation is impossible. Therefore, it seems reasonable that attention should be focused on *regulation* of proliferation and on *dis*incentives for *use*.

REGULATION OF NUCLEAR WEAPONS PROLIFERATION

Regulation of proliferation has two basic aspects: (1) making public the acquisition of nuclear weapons along with their destructive potential; and (2) encouraging safe, reliable, and secure weapons systems.

Public explosure. Known nuclear weapons are more subject to verification (by national technical means) and monitoring than are secret, hidden weapons. Hence, largely observable, varifiable systems are to be preferred to obscure ones, so that, if weapons spread, there is a way of ascertaining with greater surety than currently exists which states do and do not have nuclear weapons.

There are two concrete steps to be taken in pursuit of this goal. The first makes use of the concept of the international nuclear fuel bank. Rather than setting up restrictions that require states to return as much fissile material as they withdraw, simply charge them for that portion not recycled, with the caveat, however, that it is presumed until proven otehwise that non-returned fuel has been diverted to warhead production. From the amount diverted a rough estimate can be made of the destructive potential of the weapons built with this material. Regular reports of the bank's activities would include such estimates, as well as estimates of nationally produced weapons-grade materials based on what we currently know of a state's reprocessing and enrichment facilities.

Such reporting cannot by itself curb proliferation, but it would provide the opponents of the nuclear-armed states with more accurate estimates of capabilities. It could also provide the basis for private, probably bilateral, diplomacy to pressure the expansion downward.

The second track of public exposure depends upon another regulatory approach: encouraging safe, reliable, and secure nuclear forces. This step involves making certain nuclear-weapons technology available at low cost. States that avail themselves of such technology, and it would be in their own self-interest to do so, can obviously be assumed to be producing nuclear weapons with ascertainable characteristics. Again, it is assumed here that increased knowledge of a state's nuclear capacity is stabilizing. Further, by luring these states into the open, their systems become verifiable and subject to monitoring. This improves the probability of negotiating stable arms control agreements.

Encouraging secure weapons systems. Since the basic assumption of this paper is that no external pressures are going to halt the acquisition of nuclear options by the front-line states, we should explore ways in which acquisition can be manipulated to encourage more stable systems. Although the determination of stabilizing or destabilizing is to some extent in the eye of the beholder, objectively speaking, systems that are safe in terms of possible accidents, that are reliable (i.e., go off only when and where they are supposed to), that are less vulnerable to sabotage, terrorists, or conventional attacks, and that provide ample decision time are more stabilizing than other systems. Unsafe, unreliable, and vulnerable systems could invite a preventive attack or encourage a preemptive strike to avoid the preventive attack.

In addition to the problems of safety, reliability, and vulnerability, non-regulated proliferation could create other difficulties. For example, if the reliability is in question, a state would probably opt to build as many as possible to ensure that 'enough' would be available in the event of war. If accuracy is low, yields would likely be increased to compensate.

Thus, the proliferation of unstable, secretive, and potentially provocative systems that are likely to result if current policies of the NWS continue are not in the interests of anyone, whereas regulated proliferation is or could well be. The reduction in the probability of accidents is to everyone's benefit. The potential proliferators would benefit from increased security and stability, as would their opponents. Even the current NWS stand to gain since they would retain some control over the situation.

Hence, my argument suggests the opposite of the technical approach. That is, the current NWS should provide such technology that would advance the safety, reliability, and invulnerability of new nuclear weapons systems.[12] This does not necessarily entail providing technology essential to the creation of a nuclear weapon. The technology involved would be in the areas of command, control and communications; sophisticated fusing and timing devices; secure storage areas; hardening; mobility, and dispersal. Only in this way can the NWS hope to encourage systems that are to every one's benefit (relatively speaking) and discourage secrecy, rumour, and worst case planning that would otherwise abound. In this manner the newly nuclear armed states would have a relatively reliable and secure last resort or second strike capability. Hence there would be no rational reason to use these weapons unless on the verge of defeat. On the other hand, no state would rationally wish to attack knowing it could not neutralize the nuclear weapons of its opponent and therefore could not probably win. Men and governments are not always rational, but we cannot plan against the irrational and unpredictable. If we can remove the rational element of war – the ability to achieve a political objective – the world will have made a significant step forward.

Another possible step in encouraging the acquisition of safe, reliable, and invulnerable nuclear systems would be for the NWS to encourage and aid those states acquiring technology to orient their defence planning towards what could be termed a mission approach.[13] Under such an approach the goal would be to (a) first define the various missions a state's forces must be capable of performing and then (b) design a force structure using a mix of moderate numbers of high-accuracy, high-reliability nuclear weapons and sophisticated conventional systems that could accomplish those missions. This could preclude the unmitigated purchase and production, both overtly and covertly, of both conventional and nuclear systems.

Furthermore, such a force structure can be designed defensively, based on damage-limitation and denial as underlying deterrent doctrines. The new NWS should be provided with active air-defence, strong conventional forces, and some passive civil defence programmes. The current NWS could, and probably should under this plan provide such systems to the new NWS's antagonists.[14] Having roughly equivalent, defensively-oriented force structures on both sides should provide a stable deterrent situation in the area. Since the tensions generated by escalating and occasionally unstable conventional arms races and secretive acquisition of nuclear weapons would be reduced, it should then be possible to proceed with negotiations between the new NWS and its neighbouring enemies to try to alleviate the basic conflicts and tensions between them. Such a step could take a long time and be exceedingly difficult in some cases. Yet the fact that peace negotiations between Egypt and Israel are proceeding – albeit not quite apace – lends hope to the outlook, as does South Africa's reluctant acceptance of negotiations over the future of Namibia. Both of these successes have been accomplished, not by ever more stringent isolation, but by increasing attention paid to the real fears of these states and by including them in decisions and negotiations. Once a state has been totally islated, the world loses all leverage over it. Thus, the potential proliferators should be drawn back into the world community on a variety of issues and sincere, face-to-face negotiations begun with their opponents. Such negotiations can be under third party (i.e., US, USSR, or another major power) auspices, through regional organizations, or through the UN. The most important requirement is that negotiations be held and credible rewards offered for success. Rewards would probably take the form of funds and technology for development.

In sum, then, the combination of defensive military technology and negotiations seems the most promising way of providing disincentives for the use of nuclear weapons by future proliferators.

CONCLUSION

I have identified three basic strategies for avoiding the worst consequences of nuclear proliferation: employing technical constraints; encouraging regulatory restraints; and creating an atmosphere conducive to negotiations. Outlined below are the various elements of each strategy that were previously found to be at least partially reasonable.

I.   Technical constraints
A. A moratorium on exports of 'trigger list' items.
B. An international nuclear fuel bank.
C. Clarification of the NPT.
D. Restrictions to be observed voluntarily with the consent of consumers; states not desiring nuclear weapons will not buy 'trigger list' items.

II. Regulatory restraints
A. Non-malicious public exposure.
    1. Through reports of the fuel bank on who's diverting.
    2. Through reports of the suppliers on who's buying what sensitive technologies.
B. Provision, upon request, of technology assuring safe, reliable, and secure nuclear weapons if a state already possesses the basic technology to produce nuclear weapons.
C. Force-planning conferences to encourage states to acquire moderate numbers of highly accurate and reliable systems as an alternative to either nuclear weapons or massive conventional forces.

III. Negotiating atmosphere
A. Deterrence through provision of defensive technology to the nuclear weapons state and also its opponent.
B. Negotiations to stabilize and resolve regional conflicts.

These strategies should be pursued simultaneously whenever possible. But technical constraints should be abandoned if they have counterproductive political ramifications and interfere with regulatory and disincentive strategies. Such constraints are delaying actions and can be helpful, but they cannot solve the underlying problem of proliferation; only political solutions will solve political problems.

NOTES AND REFERENCES

1. Thomas Schelling, 'Who Will Have the Bomb', *International Security*, vol. I, no. 1 (Summer 1976) p. 80.
2. Lincoln Bloomfield and Harlan Cleveland, 'Swords into Plowshares: A Scenario', *Christian Science Monitor*, 9 February 1978, pp. 12-13, and Albert Wohlstetter, 'Spreading the Bomb Without Quite Breaking the Rules', *Foreign Policy*, no. 25 (Winter 1976-7) p. 148.
3. Schelling, op. cit. See also C. Starr and E. Zebroski, 'Nuclear Power and Weapons Proliferation', paper delivered to the American Power Conference, 1977, p. 11.
4. Lincoln Bloomfield and Harlan Cleveland, 'After SALT, What?', *Christian Science Monitor*, 8 February 1979, pp. 14-15.
5. Starr and Zedbroski, op. cit.
6. Schelling, op. cit., p. 78.
7. Starr and Zebroski, op. cit.
8. Schelling, op. cit., p. 80. See also Karl Kaiser, 'The Great Nuclear Debate', *Foreign Policy*, no. 30 (Spring 1978) p. 108.
9. These motives are agreed on in the non-proliferation literature; see the previously cited works by Schelling, Wohlstetter, and Kaiser; see also Frank Barnaby, *Preventing Nuclear Weapons Proliferation* (Stockholm International Peace Research Institute, 1975).
10. Leslie Gelb, 'Arms Sales', *Foreign Policy*, no. 25 (Winter 1976-7) pp. 2-23.
11. Barnaby, op. cit.
12. Hal W. Maynard, 'In Case of Deluge: Where Nuclear Proliferation Meets Conventional Arms Sales', Los Alamos, California: Los Alamos Scientific Laboratory (unpublished mimeo) (July 1977).
13. Christoph Bertram, *Arms Control and Technological Change, Adelphi Paper*, no. 146 (London: International Institute for Strategic Studies, 1978).
14. Providing the presumed opponents of nuclear proliferators with both first- and second-strike capabilities is consistent with Alton Frye's only partly facetious admonition in 'How to Ban the Bomb, Sell It', *New York Times Magazine*, 11 January 1976, pp. 11ff.

Part IV
Alternatives for the Future

Part IV

Alternative Policies for the Future

9 Beyond Dependency: the Future of the Non-proliferation Treaty

GLORIA DUFFY

'When this Treaty comes into force', Lyndon Johnson wrote to the president of the Senate and the speaker of the House of Representatives in January 1968, 'it will be for all the world the brightest light at the end of the tunnel since 1945'.[1] The Treaty on the Non-proliferation of Nuclear Weapons (NPT), United Nations Ambassador Arthur Goldberg told the General Assembly three months later, would 'assure that control over nuclear weapons, with their catastrophic power of destruction, shall spread no further among the nations of the earth'.[2] Who profits more from the treaty – nuclear or non-nuclear nations – Soviet Deputy Foreign Minister Kuznetzov asked the General Assembly rhetorically. 'All states stand to gain from the Treaty on the Non-Proliferation of Nuclear Weapons', he said. Thus, all would find adherence to its principles advantageous.[3]

More than a decade has passed since the NPT was signed with such high hopes on 1 July 1968, in Washington, London and Moscow. Through the early part of the decade this treaty, trading the promise of the nuclear states to dispense peaceful atomic aid and control their own arms race for renunciation of nuclear weapons by non-weapons countries, remained the central symbol of hope that the spread of nuclear weapons might be confined to five countries.

The NPT has received curiously little attention in the late 1970s, considering the limelight once again cast upon the threat of nuclear proliferation.[4] Alva Myrdal, the Swedish disarmament negotiator who was instrumental in drafting the treaty, was moved in 1976 to observe that 'the NPT is now in much disrespect and its practices in great disarray'.[5]

197

Hope that a broad agreement commanding the allegiance of most, if not all, nuclear and non-nuclear countries to halt the spread of nuclear weapons has ebbed slowly over the past 10 years. India's explosion of a nuclear device in 1974, a mere four years after the treaty took effect, dramatically pointed up the failure of the agreement to win support from countries closest to making nuclear bombs. The complexity of changes in the international nuclear economy and technology of nuclear power, which seem to suggest a new trend toward proliferation, also partly accounts for inattention to the treaty. The wave of concern in the 1970s about nuclear spread has by-passed the comprehensive, legalistic approach of the treaty to explore instead more subtle economic and technical strategies to cope with challenging nuclear developments.

The Non-proliferation Treaty does not entirely deserve the oblivion toward which it seems headed. The provisions are vague, and the obligations the treaty places upon parties are open to interpretation. It is still, in both symbolic and tangible senses, a remarkable and useful document.

The NPT has high symbolic value. It represents a formal consensus among 102 countries that the further spread of nuclear weapons is to be avoided. The pact signifies a commitment by several countries with the technical wherewithal to build atomic warheads – Japan and West Germany, most notably – not to cross the nuclear firebreak. Renunciation of nuclear weapons by these countries, in turn, relieves certain of their neighbours of fears that could lead to nuclear armament.

The treaty has upon occasion been used as a symbol inside a signatory country by factions arguing against acquiring nuclear forces. Parliamentary discussions periodically resurface in Japan over whether Article 9 of its constitution does or does not proscribe defensive nuclear weapons.[6] Senior officials consistently repeat in these debates that Japan has ratified the NPT and is thus devoted to the 'three non-nuclear principles' – never to manufacture nuclear weapons, to possess them, or to allow them to be introduced on Japanese territory.[7]

Most concretely, the NPT obligates many countries that would not otherwise be bound to open their nuclear operations to International Atomic Energy Agency (IAEA) safeguards. The inspection of nuclear sites and accounting of nuclear materials provided by the agency, while imperfect measures, are a boon to the safe management of nuclear energy throughout the world.

The accomplishments of the NPT in slowing the spread of nuclear weapons are difficult to measure. Like judging the value of nuclear deterrence for preventing war between the superpowers, it is unclear whether the process of weapons proliferation might have accelerated in the absence of the agreement. But without the treaty, any non-proliferation regime would lack a central, formal symbol setting forth the goals of the process.

Any international agreement is, however, a crystallized superstructure that rests upon a substructure of relations among the parties it binds. When concluded in 1968, the NPT did represent a bargain more or less in the interests of both weapon and non-weapon countries, as the Soviet delegate said. Today the ground under the treaty has shifted so radically that even the symbolism of the document appears increasingly hollow.

THE MAKING OF THE NPT

Logic might imply that initial impulses toward a non-proliferation treaty came from weapon nations alarmed about nuclear spread to non-weapon states. In fact, the first serious inclination toward an agreement restricting the development of nuclear weapons arose from concern in non-weapon nations over the nuclear policies of the superpowers.

Between 1958 and 1961, Ireland and a handful of other countries seemingly uninterested in nuclear weapons for themselves first introduced resolutions in the United Nations calling for a non-proliferation agreement. Lobbying efforts by these non-nuclear countries grew partly from apprehension about American proposals to give West Germany a finger on the nuclear button through involvement in a European Multi-Lateral Nuclear Force in 1959.[8] French atmospheric testing in the Sahara Desert in 1960 and 1961 and the Cuban crisis of 1962 brought the nuclear activities of the superpowers too close to home for many non-weapon states, accelerating the non-proliferation drive.[9]

While for non-weapon countries the nuclear problem took on a special significance only in the early 1960s, the nuclear powers felt an ongoing and somewhat natural sense of alarm about proliferation. Non-weapon countries worried that the superpowers would inject their nuclear forces destructively into regional relationships. The nuclear powers, on the other hand, feared that the spread of nuclear weapons, either through policies of countries among their own ranks or through indigenous developments in non-nuclear states, would interject disturbing new elements into international political relations. Aside from obvious concerns about nuclear terrorism and escalation of local conflicts into nuclear wars involving the superpowers, a disjunctiveness in power relations implied by proliferation has been regarded with concern by the nuclear weapon powers.

The prospect that small countries, lacking the economic, demographic, or conventional military elements of international power, by concentrating resources upon the central goal of constructing nuclear bombs, might suddenly obtain influence outside the traditional context of international relations, has been a less than comforting prospect to the countries that currently dominate the international scene.

Both sides had an interest in non-proliferation, but in the early 1960s the threat seemed more immediate to the non-weapon countries. Bowing to considerable pressure from the non-weapon powers, the United States and the USSR finally agreed in 1965 to accept some restrictions on their nuclear programmes. As a price for curtailing their activities, the superpowers were able to achieve the extraordinary coup of exacting a commitment from the majority of non-nuclear weapon countries to renounce nuclear weapons, while making only slight concessions themselves. While the nuclear weapon powers did address several special concerns of the non-nuclear weapon countries in order to strike the bargain, the only concrete, enforceable promise in the treaty was given by the non-weapons states.

It is a matter of no little curiosity that any non-weapon state at all signed such a treaty. What could Persian, Nigerian, or South Korean diplomats have told their governments between 1968 and 1970 that convinced them to accede to the NPT?

In a few cases, particularly Sweden, debates revolved around the uselessness of nuclear warheads for small countries and the danger of a nuclear weapons spread for all mankind.[10] The majority of non-weapon countries, however, may have simply made tough-minded judgments that nuclear weapons could not be developed for many years. The risks to nuclear energy programmes of not joining the treaty were too great and the benefits of maintaining a weapons option were too small not to accede to the treaty.

For a smaller group of countries, the calculus tilted in the other direction. Seventeen countries investing in nuclear power have declined to ratify the NPT. These countries may never have cherished and may still not cherish aspirations to build nuclear weapons. Their leaders recognized that not only could the weapon powers determine the types of nuclear aid they would provide through the treaty, but also that remaining outside the treaty would give them greater leverage for affecting superpower behaviour than would signing the NPT.

The existence of the International Atomic Energy Agency (IAEA) distinct from the treaty structure was a further reason the benefits of remaining outside the NPT regime seemed greater than the risks of signing for several countries. Rejection of the NPT seemed to pose little danger to nuclear energy programs. Countries interested in nuclear power have been able to gain the same civilian aid from weapon states through ratifying the statute of the IAEA as by acceding to the NPT, without restricting their indigenous programmes from military uses. Today the IAEA statute claims 109 ratifications, while the NPT has only 102. Many of the countries absent from the ranks of NPT adherents have participated enthusiastically in IAEA-supervised transactions since the agency's inception.[11]

A DE FACTO NON-PROLIFERATION ORDER

The fact that 17 nations with expanding nuclear power programmes remained outside the NPT did not seriously hamper the effective functioning of a non-proliferation regime until the mid-1970s. The dependency of the non-weapon countries upon the weapon powers for nuclear technology ensured that most non-nuclear nations would have difficulty making weapons, even should they so desire. Because the dependency for many years applied to all non-weapon countries, the nations that elected not to sign the NPT were affected equally with the NPT countries by the *de facto* situation.

This dependency was no premeditated scheme on the part of the weapon powers but merely a relationship of economic rationality and technological necessity for the non-nuclear weapon states. As long as low-enriched uranium from the United States was cheap enough and as long as the capability for manufacturing power plant components remained the province of the supplier states (also the countries most interested in non-proliferation), the dependency served the purposes of both parties. The individual legal and contractual obligations between weapon states and non-nuclear countries, based upon dependency, made the non-proliferation system successful.

The weapon countries had a formidable check over the behaviour of their non-weapon partners – virtually complete control over the sources of nuclear material and technology.[12] Weapon countries could simply withhold supplies of weapons-capable technologies, among other strategies, to ensure that the non-weapon states did not become weapon states.

TECHNOLOGICAL AND MARKET CHANGES

A crucial problem for non-proliferation, as for arms control more broadly, is that the regime rests upon a foundation of shifting technology and, in this case, of shifting energy economics. The paths along which technology has developed to make nuclear power more economical for non-weapon countries are the identical roads that will lead those countries away from dependency upon the suppliers. Blurring the distinctions between civilian and military nuclear power operations, this same technology could give non-nuclear countries a weapons option.

The key to a nuclear weapons programme is the ability to obtain fissile material of an appropriate quantity and quality for fabrication into warheads. In practice, this means amassing stockpiles of either highly enriched uranium-235 or plutonium. When uranium is enriched to about 90 per cent in the U-235 atom, the fission reaction is intensified to a point where an explosion becomes possible. The process for enriching uranium to weapons-level is essentially the same as the present procedure for enriching to 3-4 per cent the uranium in the U-235 atom for use in civilian power reactors. The major difference is the time and intensity of exposure of the uranium to the enrichment process.[13] Thus, any country that has access to uranium enrichment facilities can theoretically obtain weapons-grade material. Twenty kilograms of uranium fuel enriched to 90 per cent in the U-235 is required to make a nuclear warhead.[14]

Enough unfissioned uranium and newly generated plutonium remain in the spent fuel rods removed from reactors to encourage separating the various elements in the waste product of the reactor for later use. Any country that can reprocess spent nuclear fuel theoretically has access to plutonium. Roughly 5 kilograms of plutonium diverted from reactor waste could provide a country with a nuclear warhead.[15]

The drive for energy self-sufficiency, set in motion by the 1973 oil embargo, encouraged countries to invest in nuclear power. The conventional wisdom throughout the world nuclear industry has been that 'front-end' and 'back-end' closure of the nuclear fuel cycle, achieved by developing uranium enrichment and plutonium reprocessing capabilities, respectively, would render nuclear power more economical and less dependent upon outside sources of fuel. Even more significant economies and self-sufficiency would follow, the theory held, when conventional power reactors yielded to a second generation of fast-breeder reactors that would run by consuming the net surplus of plutonium they produce over what they use.[16]

The nuclear industries of the supplier countries communicated the inevitability of these developments to their fledgling counterparts in non-weapon countries. The shock of the 1973 oil crunch wrought by the Organization of Petroleum Exporting Countries (OPEC) reinforced the impression that it would behove countries investing in nuclear power to obtain their own enrichment and reprocessing plants, so as to avoid the OPEC-like control of the nuclear technology suppliers over critical elements of the fuel cycle.

A tacit agreement prevailed for many years among the nuclear-material-exporting countries to prohibit the sale of reprocessing and enrichment technologies to non-weapon nations. Historically, the United States has dominated the world market for supply of nuclear power plants and fuel.[17] As the uncontested source for nuclear power goods, the United States was able to maintain tight control over dissemination of advanced fuel cycle technology.

But the US monopoly began to fragment in the early 1970s. French and West German manufacturers began to compete with Westinghouse and General Electric for reactor sales to non-nuclear weapon countries. As competition among the suppliers grew, the provision of reprocessing and enrichment technologies became a bargaining chip in negotiations for reactor orders with consumer countries.

In 1975 the West German firm Kraftwerk Union announced its 'deal of the century' – sale of reactors, nuclear fuel reprocessing and enrichment plants to NUCLEBRAS, the Brazilian state atomic energy agency. France followed in 1976 with an offer to sell a reprocessing plant to South Korea and a sale to Pakistan.

A number of indigenous enrichment and reprocessing plants are also either operating or planned today. Israel has reportedly developed a highly secret enrichment facility for preparation of its nuclear weapons material.[18] South Africa is building a pilot enrichment facility at its Valindaba nuclear production centre.[19] The Tokai-Mura reprocessing plant in Japan began operating in 1977. India reprocesses nuclear fuel. And Brazil, West Germany, Israel, Italy, Argentina, Taiwan, Spain, Sweden, Pakistan, Yugoslavia and Canada are among the non-nuclear weapon countries now either constructing or already operating pilot reprocessing plants.[20]

The military implications of the nuclear technology today desired by the non-weapon countries has created a central paradox for the weapon states in adhering to the NPT. These countries are finding that Article IV of the treaty, mandating nuclear assistance, and Article I, prohibiting the weapon states from aiding non-weapon state military nuclear programmes, may have become contradictory propositions. The technology that non-weapon states now request for peaceful uses could contribute to weapons programmes in the future.

Even more confusing, weapon countries have no way of knowing which of the policies they could promote on nuclear technology transfer might enhance the prospects for proliferation, and which might decrease the incentives. If the nuclear states deny technology under Article I, will they thereby deny the non-weapon countries the capability to make weapons, or will they instead promote proliferation by increasing the incentives for fuel cycle self-sufficiency?

In the face of such uncertainty, after initial dissension among themselves, the nuclear countries seem to have concluded for the present that Article I takes precedence over Article IV. Through the London Suppliers Group, the International Nuclear Fuel Cycle Evaluation (INFCE), and unilateral restrictive policies like that of the Canadians, they have halted technical assistance at a level of technology that does not include facilities with dual civilian and military uses. The nuclear powers have decided that the price implied in the transfer of the next generation of nuclear technology is just too costly.

RECREATING DEPENDENCY

Advancing technology and the direction of the world nuclear market now threatens the dependency structure and, with it, the overlying non-proliferation regime. At present, the nuclear countries are responding to this challenge by trying to recreate a dependency once again based upon economic rationality and technological necessity for the non-weapon states. The joint nuclear export policies of the London Suppliers Group and the emerging strategy of the United States to develop and market 'proliferation-resistant' nuclear fuel cycles to forestall fuel cycle closure in the non-weapon states imply continued dependency.[21] The nuclear countries seem to hope that the majority of non-weapon states will once again choose to accept aid with nuclear power, as defined by the suppliers, over self-contained fuel cycles with nuclear weapons potential. In this way, the dependency relationship could continue to uphold the NPT regime.

A sharp division of opinion runs through recent discussions of nuclear proliferation. Can the nuclear weapon countries convince the non-weapon states to subscribe to a non-proliferation set-up proscribing the development of indigenous enrichment, plutonium reprocessing, and, more distantly, breeder reactor technologies using plutonium? Counting the indigenous fuel processing capabilities already in being and understanding the strength of the drive toward nuclear self-sufficiency in non-weapon countries provide hints of the answer to the question.

Once the state of technology no longer makes dependency necessary, non-weapon countries show every intention of pursuing fuel cycle developments that promise to lead to self-sufficiency. It is difficult to overemphasize the strength of the commitment to this goal in the non-weapon states.

To quote from a summary of the April 1977 Persepolis Conference of Non-Nuclear Countries on the Transfer of Nuclear Technology given by the then head of the Iranian Atomic Energy Organization:

A common thinking among the participants was that a closed fuel cycle and the use of breeders were an essential condition for the economic competitiveness of nuclear energy.

Many nations felt that reprocessing of spent fuel is the only feasible route to safe ultimate disposal of radioactive wastes. They observed that some nations are legally commited to that route.

The curtailment of progress towards the closing of the nuclear fuel cycle and the implementation of the breeder reactor, and the restriction of information exchange in those areas, were not, however, regarded as effective ways of preventing proliferation. They may, in fact, prove to be counterproductive.[22]

Non-NPT countries, sceptical of dependency from the beginning, have already chosen to develop seven indigenous nuclear facilities, as well as solicit a variety of safeguarded or unsafeguarded weapons-capable technologies from weapon states that would sell. In one striking case, Pakistan began constructing in 1979 a uranium enrichment plant to produce highly enriched uranium. The facility was assembled through purchasing unrestricted components from private companies in West Germany, Britain, and elsewhere. The Pakistanis have apparently attempted to duplicate the enrichment process developed by URENCO, a consortium of private Dutch, British, and West German nuclear companies.[23] The Pakistani plant was constructed without overt aid from the supplier countries and is not subject to external safeguards.

The all-important enrichment and reprocessing technologies are thus gradually passing out of the control of the nuclear supplier states. Without control, the nuclear powers have no sure-fire guarantee that NPT signers will uphold their promise not to use the technologies to develop varying degrees of nuclear weapons capability. And the practical inhibitions to weapons are reduced for the non-signers who have made no diplomatic pledge against them.

Were the individuals who negotiated the NPT for the weapon states unaware that the direction of technology was toward dual civilian and military capabilities? Certainly not. As William Foster, director of the US Arms Control and Disarmament Agency, told the Senate Foreign Relations Committee in 1968:

> It might be useful to point out, for illustrative purposes, several activities which the United States would not consider *per se* to be violations of the prohibitions in Article II. Neither uranium enrichment nor the stockpiling of fissionable material in connection with a peaceful program would violate Article II so long as these activities were safeguarded under Article III. Also clearly permitted would be the development, under safeguards, of plutonium fueled power reactors, including research on the properties of metallic plutonium, nor would Article II interfere with the development or use of fast breeder reactors under safeguards.[24]

The nuclear weapon countries accepted a very narrow definition in the NPT of what constitutes evidence of a nuclear weapons programme in non-weapon countries and what actions would aid such a programme on the part of the weapon countries. The meaning of 'manufacture' of nuclear weapons in the treaty language, Foster testified, included only production of items that could have relevance to a weapons programme alone.[25] Attempts were made by the weapon countries to define the relevant activities more broadly during the negotiations, but unsuccessfully. The prevailing mood of acceptance of the restricted definition was expressed by US Ambassador Arthur Goldberg:

> If we insist upon a perfect treaty – each Member with its different ideas of perfection – then we shall be unable to move forward, for there is no perfection in this world. If after careful deliberation we insist that the last grain of uncertainty be removed, then we shall be unable to move forward, for there is no complete certainty in this world.[26]

It must seem to the non-weapon countries that the nuclear states are attempting to broaden retroactively the definition of the goods they are prohibited from transferring under Article I of the treaty. If self-sufficiency has become a goal that supersedes economics and efficiency for the non-weapon states, then the nuclear countries will have considerable difficulty selling their alternative-fuel-cycle/no-plutonium schemes, particularly in view of the fact that indigenous facilities are now under way in several countries. (See Table 9.1)

Responding to technological and market changes by devising new types of dependency, the weapon countries may now risk losing the commitment of a wider group of countries to the principles of the NPT. The official communiqué of the April 1977 Persepolis conference threatened that some of the 102 nations that signed the NPT may now withdraw because they feel they can 'no longer benefit from the accord'.[27]

WHAT CAN BE DONE?

The terms of the NPT call for a review conference to measure the usefulness of the agreement five years after it takes effect. If a majority of parties desires, a second review can be called another five years hence.[28] The first review convened in May 1975. It was an acrimonious affair. The United States and the USSR were commonly vilified by the non-weapon countries for lagging in controlling their strategic arms and not fully sharing their nuclear technology.[29] There was even greater acrimony at the review conference held in August 1980, when the US worked to prevent passage of a final resolution desired by the non-weapon states.

Coincidentally, INFCE in February 1980 issued its report on two years of technical discussions aimed at forestalling the growth of a

TABLE 9.1 Operating nuclear facilities not subject to IAEA or bilateral safeguards as of 31 December 1976[a]

Country	Facility	Indigenous or imported	First year of operation
Egypt	Inshas	Imported (USSR)	1961
India	Apsara research reactor	Indigenous	1956
	Cirus research reactor	Imported (Canada/ USA)	1960
	Zerlina research reactor	Indigenous	1961
	Purnima research reactor	Indigenous	1972
	Fuel fabrication plant at Trombay[b]	Indigenous	1960
	Trombay reprocessing plant	Indigenous	1964
Israel	Dimona research reactor	Imported (France)	1963
	Reprocessing plant (assumed)	Indigenous (in collaboration with France)[c]	–
South Africa	Pilot enrichment plant	Indigenous (in collaboration with FRG)	1975
Spain	Vandellos power reactor	Jointly operated With France	1972

[a] Excluding the five nuclear weapon states recognized by the NPT. A previously unsafeguarded reprocessing facility in Argentina (Ezeiza Nuclear Centre, laboratory scale) has been dismantled. Consideration is being given to the construction of a new reprocessing plant in this country (see Stockholm International Peace Research Institute, *World Armaments and Disarmament*, SIPRI Yearbook 1977, p. 47, table 2.5).
The unsafeguarded reprocessing facility at the Bhabha Research Centre, India, is currently closed down for reconstruction, and is therefore not included in the list.
There may be more unsafeguarded facilities than those listed here.
[b] Producing fuel for research reactors.
[c] Assistance by Saint Gobain Techniques Nouvelles.

Source: Stockholm International Peace Research Institute, *World Armaments and Disarmament, SIPRI Yearbook 1977*, p. 51.

plutonium-centred energy economy. INFCE working groups on reprocessing and breeder technologies that would not produce pure plutonium presented the findings for which the United States had asked weapon countries and non-weapon countries alike to postpone their own developments in these fields for two years. The interaction of INFCE results and the NPT Review Conference made the spring of 1980 a crucial time for non-proliferation, but no progress was made.

The weapon countries face two challenges. First, preventing defections from the NPT – an increasingly serious prospect – is of paramount importance. If a primary motivation of NPT signatories was to obtain nuclear aid to enhance energy self-sufficiency, then the non-nuclear weapon countries will take seriously the suggestion that the way the weapon countries have chosen to favour Article I over Article IV means the NPT no longer confers the benefits of peaceful nuclear technology. Unless, on careful study, the INFCE report is perceived as offering alternative fuel cycles attractive from a self-sufficiency as well as an economic standpoint, the long-term results of INFCE are unlikely to change the desire of non-weapon countries for elements of the plutonium fuel cycle.

The threat of withdrawal from the treaty must be taken seriously. The 1985 Review Conference might well be the grandstand from which a group of non-weapon countries choose to dramatize their exeunt from the treaty. If they pull out, not only might these countries suspend IAEA safeguards covering their plants, but they would also, of course, no longer be bound by their pledge not to manufacture nuclear weapons.

The refusal of the countries most likely to develop nuclear weapons to sign the NPT is the agreement's signal flaw. Countries for whom the costs of not signing the document were relatively small in terms of loss of nuclear aid and ostracism by the nuclear states, and for whom the benefits of staying outside appeared worthwhile, have remained apart from the treaty framework. Three nuclear powers – China, France, and India – as well as most of the near-nuclear countries – Argentina, Brazil, Israel, Pakistan, South Africa – have either not signed or not ratified the NPT.

Broadening the number of countries that accede to the treaty is thus the second issue facing the weapon states. As more countries attain the ability to manufacture nuclear weapons, their pledge not to use the weapons-capable facilities to make bombs and their submission to safeguards to ensure that they keep the pledge become all the more important. The suggestion is often made that demonstrations of good faith by the nuclear countries on their portions of the NPT bargain would go a long way toward encouraging the withholding non-nuclear nations to sign. Alva Myrdal of Sweden frequently speaks for the non-nuclear weapon countries in discussions about nuclear arms. Stopping the spread of nuclear weapons, she has said, 'can only be done if the "haves" pay the price they should have paid from the beginning to make the other nations satisfied with being "have-not"'.[30]

NUCLEAR AID

The most important price the weapons state were supposed to pay to the non-nuclear countries was sharing their nuclear technology in general, as mandated in Article IV, and sharing the benefits of peaceful nuclear explosions in particular, as specified by Article V. The non-nuclear countries frequently charge that the weapon countries have not been forthcoming in sharing their peaceful nuclear technology. In general terms, that charge is patently absurd. Nuclear aid from the weapon to the non-weapon countries has, in fact, been substantial.

From 1962 to the present, the nuclear countries concluded 41 agreements for assistance to the developing nations, 36 of which are still in force and 14 of which are with the United States.[31] By 1980, developing countries will be operating 39 research and power reactors received from the nuclear states; 14 of the power reactors, as well as most of the research reactors, have come from the United States.[32] Under the Atoms for Peace programme between 1956 and 1962, the United States gave one-half of its $9 million in grants for research reactors to developing countries.[33] The US Agency for International Development (AID) nuclear assistance programmes have multiplied the early Atoms for Peace commitments many times over – $80 million had been dispensed to developing countries by 1977.[34] The US Export-Import (ExIm) Bank had by 1977 made direct loans of $2.2 billion and financial guarantees of $1.3 billion to developing countries for nuclear imports.[35] The US Department of Energy and its predecessors had given $23 million in direct nuclear assistance to developing countries by 1977.[36] With ExIm loans and guarantees, Atoms for Peace, AID, and the Department of Energy, between 1956 and 1977, the United States alone among the nuclear states had contributed more than $3.5 billion to developing country nuclear power programmes.[37] In addition, the United States has trained over 5000 developing country nuclear scientists and technicians to date.[38]

In general terms, the record of the nuclear countries in aiding the developing nations with nuclear power is actually quite good. It is in the realm of particular technologies, those that have a potential role in nuclear weapons manufacture, that the problems arise and the criticisms of the non-weapon states are somewhat better founded. Although Brazil, Iran, and India are today receiving French aid with experimental fast breeder reactors, the weapon states have not as a rule been willing to share technologies with civilian applications that also have military uses – primarily the breeder, enrichment, and reprocessing. Nor have they been willing to help the developing countries with peaceful nuclear explosions, since the technology for such is the same as for an atomic bomb.

The hope of nuclear aid today does not provide a strong incentive for the most recalcitrant states to join the NPT. Treaty or no treaty, the nuclear suppliers have shut the door to the next generation of nuclear technology to control the dissemination of military capabilities. Different export policies, however, have undercut the barriers to achieving other levels of nuclear know-how and capacity. Despite adoption of a 'trigger list' of 'sensitive technologies,' the Nuclear Suppliers Group has consistently voted down proposals to make 'full-scope' safeguards a condition of nuclear sales. Non-signers of the NPT are thus still able to import much of their conventional nuclear supplies from the weapon countries. This fleeting dependence of the non-weapon countries can and should be used by the weapon nations to strengthen the NPT regime.

Interestingly enough, it is the Soviet Union that provides a model for using nuclear aid to prod non-signers to accede to the agreement. In 1977 the USSR concluded an agreement to export research and power reactors to Libya. The Soviets demanded that the Libyans ratify the NPT before finalizing the deal. The Libyans signed. This was perhaps a special case. Such strong-arm tactics may not work unless the country at which they are directed has no other alternative for buying nuclear power goods. But if all the nuclear suppliers agreed to make accession to the treaty a precondition of further exports of nuclear goods, non-signers would have little choice but to join.

ARMS CONTROL

The second price the nuclear-weapon states were supposed to pay for limiting the spread of nuclear weapons was Article VI's demand that the superpowers negotiate in 'good faith' to end their nuclear arms race. The connections between non-proliferation and central arms control – the Strategic Arms Limitation Talks and Comprehensive Test Ban negotiations today – are often cited, but rarely explored. In fact, the main connections may be perceptual rather than direct.

One school of thought holds that progress in the SALT negotiations would actually enhance the motives for present non-nuclear countries to obtain the weapons. Reductions in superpower arsenals might be thought to reduce the nuclear/non-nuclear gap, and encourage middle-sized powers to think that it would be easier for them to 'catch up' and threaten the major nuclear countries. At the same time, it is argued, renunciation of nuclear weapons by non-nuclear countries depends upon their perception of the credibility of the superpower arsenals in protecting them. Superpower arms control might lead smaller countries to mount their own nuclear deterrents.[39]

The second of these two propositions is particularly suspect. Presumably, the motivation of non-weapon countries to build their own deterrents would only be thought to increase if one side in the SALT negotiations were to concede great advantage to the other, thus casting doubt upon the conceding side's ability to protect its allies. Even if arsenals of weapons were to decline, as long as the relative nuclear balance between the United States and the USSR remained constant (one of the primary operating principles of SALT) then the security of the non-weapon states could certainly not be thought to decrease.

The suggestion has repeatedly been made, most vociferously at the 1975 NPT Review Conference, that a guarantee not to use nuclear weapons against non-weapon states by the nuclear powers could relieve the security concern of the non-nuclear countries. But for the most part, the non-nuclear countries are worried about the nuclear potential of regional rivals, not about the superpowers. Security guarantees from the nuclear countries would likely have little more than a marginal effect upon the motivations of countries to make nuclear weapons.

A more generally valid observation is that superpower arms control would help promote wider adherence to the NPT, since the non-compliance of the United States and the USSR with Article VI serves as an excuse for non-weapons states to withhold ratification. While undoubtedly a meaningful SALT agreement would take away one of the underlying rationales for non-accession to the treaty, and reduce the demonstration effect of the superpower arms rivalry on threshold nuclear states, any impact is once again likely to be atmospheric rather than direct.

But is there any doubt that atmospherics can be critical in international politics? Progress in SALT carries important symbolic values for non-proliferation. The SALT negotiations are a living statement to the non-weapon countries of the extent to which the superpowers have been bedeviled by a costly, seemingly irreversible arms race. The existence of the talks, even their very difficulty, carries lessons for non-weapon countries of the problems they are likely to encounter down the nuclear trail. The United States and the USSR could add pointedly to the message conveyed by the spectacle of their nuclear trials by emphasizing the disadvantages nuclear weapons might present for small powers.

If the United States and the USSR agreed to diminish significantly their nuclear arsenals, they would signal their recognition that nuclear weapons are not usable or credible tools of national power. They would indicate that they accept the crystal insight of American diplomat George Kennan:

There is no political or ideological difference between the Soviet Union and the United States – nothing which either side would like, or would hope, to achieve at the expense of the other – that would be worth the risks and sacrifices of a military encounter.... It would be cheaper, safer, and less damaging over the long term for either side to yield on any of the points of difference between them rather than to accept the disaster which modern war would spell.[40]

Delays in the US–USSR talks, on the other hand, will have a negative demonstration effect by strongly underlining the conviction of non-nuclear-weapon states that both countries are still convinced enough of the utility of nuclear weapons that they have refused to make the compromises necessary to continue the talks.

DEPENDENCE OR SECURITY?

Among the mixed motives for moving toward advanced fuel cycle technologies, hence weapons capabilities, a drive for energy security ranks high. A few countries, Pakistan most visibly, may seek nuclear weapons directly. But the much broader group of nations may simply drift toward a weapons capability by seeking advanced fuel processing technology to ensure energy self-sufficiency.

If the root of the drive to nuclear power and thence to a plutonium economy lies in a quest for energy security, then the weapon countries would do well to address this underlying impulse rather than concentrating on its symptoms. Viewed in this context, the present policies of the nuclear suppliers, attempting to prolong dependency of the non-weapon countries, are precisely wrong-headed.

The non-nuclear countries are slowly discovering that nuclear power may not be a very good solution to energy dependency. Uranium and power plant component manufacture are still closely controlled by the supplier states. Capital costs are rising. And the weapon countries are endeavouring to extend control to fuel processing in the future. Only movement to reliance upon local and ideally, renewable energy sources will really provide as great a degree of energy self-sufficiency as is possible in this interdependent world.

The most promising strategies to deal with nuclear proliferation may thus lie not in the NPT, or even in the kind of policies now subsumed under the confrontation-fostering rubric of non-pro-liferation. In the long run, promoting the energy independence of the non-weapon countries is among the best strategies the nuclear countries could undertake to arrest nuclear drift and undercut the reluctance of non-nuclear countries to affirm the principles of the NPT.

NOTES AND REFERENCES

1. Letter from President Johnson to the President of the Senate and Speaker of the House of Representatives: Non-proliferation of Nuclear Weapons and Extension of ACDA, 24 January 1968. *Weekly Compilation of Presidential Documents*, 29 January 1968, pp. 122-3.
2. Statement by US Ambassador Arthur Goldberg to the First Committee of the General Assembly: Non-proliferation of Nuclear Weapons, 26 April 1968. *Documents on Disarmament, 1968* US Arms Control and Disarmament Agency Publication 52 (September 1969) p. 221.
3. Statement by First Deputy Foreign Minister Vasili Kuznetzov to the First Committee of the General Assembly: Non-proliferation of Nuclear Weapons, 26 April 1968, ibid., p. 243.
4. Major studies of the NPT are included in the bibliography.
5. Alva Myrdal, *The Game of Disarmament* (New York: Pantheon Books, 1976), p. 182.
6. Michael Pillsbury, 'A Japanese Card?', *Foreign Policy*, no. 33 (Winter 1978-9) p. 13.
7. Ibid., p. 7.
8. John H. Barton and Lawrence C. Weiler (eds), *International Arms Control: Issues and Agreements* (Stanford University Press, 1976) p. 295.

9. Ibid.
10. See Jerome Garris, *Sweden's Debate on the Proliferation of Nuclear Weapons*, California Arms Control and Foreign Policy Seminar (June 1972).
11. Most of the non-NPT countries investing in nuclear power ratified the IAEA Statute at the 1957 conference which established the Agency. Chile and Colombia ratified in 1960, the Congo in 1961, Libya and Algeria in 1964.
12. See Gloria Duffy and Gordon Adams, *Power Politics: The Nuclear Industry and Nuclear Exports* (New York: Council on Economic Priorities, 1978) pp. 48-55, for a complete breakdown of worldwide reactor sales 1953-76.
13. Victor Gilinsky, 'The Military Potential of Civil Nuclear Power', in Mason Willrich (ed.), *Civilian Nuclear Power and International Security*, (New York: Praeger, 1971), p. 23.
14. Ibid., p. 9.
15. Ibid.
16. When a Ford Foundation study [*Nuclear Power Issues and Choices* (Cambridge, Mass.: 1977)] appeared that was critical of the economic benefits of the breeder and plutonium recycle, Atomic Industrial Forum, the industry lobby in the United States, produced a cirtique of the Ford study. It said, in part, 'When breeder introduction is delayed, prices roughly double; eliminating the breeder altogether results in a tripling of prices [of nuclear electricity]'.
17. The United States took 100 per cent of the world market for nuclear reactor exports in 1966, 78 per cent in 1972, 16 per cent in 1976, and zero in 1977. Kidder, Peabody, 'Worldwide Nuclear Reactors', Industry Analysis, Research Department, 19 April 1977.
18. An open-source reference to the Israeli plant was unearthed in 'How Israel Got the Nuclear Bomb', in *Rolling Stone Magazine*, 1 December 1977, p. 38.
19. See *Nuclear Proliferation Factbook*, Subcommittee on International Economic Policy and Trade, Committee on International Relations, US House of Representatives, 95th Congress, First Session, 23 September 1977, p. 171-91.
20. Ibid., pp. 195-214.
21. According to US government officials, these alternative nuclear fuel cycles include, 'the tandem fuel cycle, various co-processing schemes, homogeneous reactors, the spectral shift reactor, and the thorium-uranium cycle'. See Joseph S. Nye, 'Time to Plan for the Next Generation of Nuclear Technology'. *Bulletin of the Atomic Scientists*, (October 1977) p. 41.
22. Address by Ambassador Akbar Etemed, president, Atomic Energy Organization of Iran, to the Salzburg Conference on Nuclear Energy, 6 May 1977.
23. 'US Aid to Pakistan Cut After Evidence of Atom Arms Plant', *New York Times*, 7 April 1979, p. 1.
24. Statement by ACDA Director William C. Foster to the Senate Foreign Relations Committee: Non-proliferation Treaty, 10 July 1968. *Non-*

proliferation Treaty: Hearings Before the Committee on Foreign Relations, United States Senate, Ninetieth Congress, Second Session, pt. 1, p. 39.

25. Ibid.
26. Statement by Ambassador Arthur Goldberg to the First Committee of the General Assembly: Non-proliferation of Nuclear Weapons, 26 April 1968. *Documents on Disarmament, 1968*, US Arms Control and Disarmament Agency (September 1969) p. 233.
27. 'Nuclear Allies Unhappy', *New York Times*, 10 April 1977, p. 3; 14 April 1977, p. 7; 15 April 1977, p. 12.
28. Foster, op. cit., p. 8.
29. For a summary of the 1975 NPT Review Conference discussions, see William Epstein, *Retrospective on the NPT Review Conference: Proposals for the Future*, Occasional Paper no. 9, (Muscatine, Iowa; The Stanley Foundation, 1975).
30. Myrdal, op. cit., p. 191.
31. Stockholm International Peace Research Institute, *World Armaments and Disarmament, SIPRI Yearbook 1977* (Stockholm; Almqvist & Wiksell, 1977) pp. 40-1.
32. *SIPRI Yearbook 1976* (Cambridge, Mass.: MIT Press, 1976) p. 43.
33. US Comptroller General, 'US Financial Assistance in the Development of Foreign Nuclear Energy Programs', Report ID-75-64, GPO, 28 May 1975, p. 60.
34. Ibid., pp. 14-16.
35. Hon. Clarence D. Long, 'Nuclear Proliferation: Can Congress Act in Time?', *International Security* (Spring 1977) p. 56.
36. US Comptroller General, op. cit., pp. 19-20.
37. Long, op. cit., p. 62.
38. Ibid.
39. George Quester, *The Politics of Nuclear Proliferation* (Baltimore: Johns Hopkins University Press, 1973) p. 29.
40. George F. Kennan, *The Cloud of Danger* (Boston: Little, Brown 1977) p. 169.

10 Revising the NPT Regime

RICHARD K. LESTER

For over a decade, the Nuclear Non-proliferation Treaty (NPT) has played a central role in efforts to prevent the spread of nuclear weapons. In the years since its negotiations, the treaty has been the subject of a great many scholarly discourses, legal analyses, and politically motivated affirmations and denunciations. Recent upheavals in international nuclear relations have generated intensified speculation on its possible role in a future non-proliferation regime.

The NPT is, in addition to its titular purpose, an internationally negotiated framework for the development of the peaceful uses of nuclear energy. From the outset of the nuclear era, it was recognized that many of the technological steps necessary for the production of nuclear energy for peaceful purposes were essentialy indistinguishable from stages in the production of nuclear weapons. After early proposals for international ownership of all nuclear materials and equipment were rejected, and subsequent attempts to limit the spread of nuclear technology through a policy of secrecy had demonstratably failed, the world, at the prompting of the United States through its Atoms for Peace programme, embarked on a period of controlled cooperative development of nuclear power.

Central to this development regime were international safeguards, which provided a mechanism for external verification of international undertakings by recipient nations not to divert nuclear supplies intended for peaceful use to military activities. Implemented at first on a bilateral basis, and subsequently by the International Atomic Energy Agency (IAEA), these safeguards served two corollary purposes: recipient nations could demonstrate to their suppliers and the rest of the world the integrity of their motives in importing nuclear supplies, and the nuclear industries of the supplier countries could engage in commercial ventures overseas and contribute to the development of foreign nuclear power systems in the knowledge that their exports were not undermining international security objectives.

217

As nuclear technology spread, and the future role predicted for nuclear power continued to expand, a growing number of nations developed the ability to engage in a wide range of nuclear activities without external assistance. It became increasingly clear that verified promises of peaceful use applying only to imported nuclear supplies could not provide enough assurance that ostensibly peaceful nuclear programmes would not also serve military ends. This recognition was a key factor in the development of the NPT.

In this context, the treaty can be regarded as the culmination of efforts to implement an international cooperative regime for the controlled development of nuclear energy. Thus, in partial return for the solemn undertaking of the non-nuclear weapon parties not to acquire nuclear explosives from any source, the treaty affirms the right of all parties to receive the benefits of peaceful applications of nuclear technology, as well as the right to participate in the fullest possible exchange of materials, equipment, and technology for peaceful purposes. As in the previous phase of nuclear energy development, however, assurances of peaceful intentions by sovereign governments were again not sufficient to offset the inherent ambiguity of nuclear technology; hence international safeguareds – in this case to be applied to all the peaceful nuclear activities of non-weapon parties – remain a principal component of the NPT regime.

Safeguards, then, can be viewed as an embodiment of a consensus view that sovereign undertakings not to engage in the military applications of nuclear technology, even if binding under international law, are not by themselves enough to dispel fears and eliminate the resulting instabilities within the international community. In a more unfavourable light, however, they may also be perceived as manifestations of distrust shown by a dominant group of sovereign states (the weapon states) toward another, less powerful group.

Whether or not the latter perception is accurate, it is undeniably true that the NPT affords unequal status to weapon and non-weapon states. It is probably also true that the weapon states active in drafting the teaty were able to secure such widespread adherence to it partly because of the virtual monopoly that they maintained not only over weapons-capable technologies but also over supplies of nuclear facilities and materials more narrowly suitable for peaceful uses.

Since then, however, the dynamic characteristics of nuclear technology and industrial performance have succeeded in moderating certain features of the gap between weapon and non-weapon states, while simultaneously introducing new divisions into the NPT structure.

In recent years, the nuclear-weapon countries, notably the United States, have been matched and in some cases surpassed in nuclear export markets by non-weapon supplies. At the same time, as technological capabilities have spread, increasingly strident objections have been raised to the deployment of certain elements of the nuclear fuel cycle, particularly those facilities associated with the reprocessing and recycling of plutonium. These objections have developed as a consequence of growing doubts about the ability of international safeguards to function satisfactorily in a future economy relying heavily on plutonium-fuelled nuclear power reactors.

International safeguards do not prevent diversion of civilian material to military uses; they deter it by the threat of timely detection. The US government and others have taken the position that the widespread adoption of plutonium as a commercial fuel would gravely reduce the chance that diversions could be detected in time for the international community to do anything about it. Then the deterrence effect of safeguards would be lost. As a result, the major suppliers, in the form of the London Suppliers Group, have adopted collective guidelines that effectively call for increased restrictions on the transfer of 'sensitive', or nuclear-weapons-prone, facilities, equipment, and materials. Simultaneously, some of these suppliers have individually sought to exert additional control over the nuclear energy programmes of other nations by applying increasingly stringent conditions on their exports. One intent of these controls has been to discourage the construction of indigenous reprocessing plants in nations that do not already possess them.

These actions have three important consequences for the NPT. First, they amount to a *de facto* redrawing of the threshold line that has separated peaceful and tolerably ambiguous applications of nuclear technology from intolerably ambiguous and unequivocally military applications. For instance, the benefits of plutonium recycling, which have been regarded as a logical and inevitable outcome of most national nuclear programmes almost from the outset of the nuclear era, are now seen by supplier governments as being outweighed by the risks and costs. These governments emphasize both the increased temptation to divert civilian plutonium to military uses and the destabilizing propagation of suspicions about the intentions of a nation possessing commercial plutonium-handling facilities, whether or not such suspicions are in fact warranted.

Second, with the new emphasis on export restrictions, recipient nations perceive supplier governments again to have struck unilaterally the delicate balance sketched in the treaty between their responsibilities to the cause of non-proliferation, on the one hand, and to the deveopment of peaceful nuclear energy in non-weapon parties, on the other (the Article I versus Article IV dilemma).

Third, the questioning of the effectiveness of safeguards raises renewed doubt about the value of the renunciation of nuclear weapons required by accession to the NPT – doubt which had led to the development of a safeguard system in the first place.

A fourth consequence is perhaps of even greater significance. Consensus among the major supplier nations themselves has been elusive, and even now is far from complete. The US-led initiative to curb the use of plutonium has constituted a direct attack on the nuclear power industries of the major industrialized nations of Western Europe and Japan, of which plutonium provides the only route to fuel cycle autonomy. The differences have been particularly acutely felt in that these nations are heavily dependent on the United States and Canada for nuclear fuel, and it is partially this import dependence that plutonium is thought to alleviate.

Under the compromise that now seems to be emerging, the United States and its fellow proponents of fuel cycle restrictions appear to be prepared to acknowledge the inevitability of reprocessing and plutonium utilization in the industrialized nations (with dual importing and exporting status) in return for an agreement by the latter group to apply restraints on transfers of sensitive fuel cycle technology in its nuclear export dealings with less developed countries. Whether this arrangement will in fact prove to be capable of healing the differences among the suppliers in the long term remains to be seen.

The net effect of these developments has been to strain the fabric of the NPT regime, both within the heterogeneous group of suppliers and between the suppliers and recipients. Indeed, the recent 'revisionist' initiatives of some of the key supplier nations have been seen in a number of other nations as an attempt by a small oligopoly effectively to reconstruct the hegemonical but deteriorating framework for nuclear energy developement envisaged at the outset of the NPT negotiations, using methods, moreover, that are seen to contravene the suppliers' obligations as treaty parties.

Thus, the classic Article I versus Article IV dilemma can be restated in a broader context: if it is true that the spread of nuclear technology is undermining efforts to prevent the spread of nuclear weapons, it may also be true that the response of a group of suppliers to its particular perceptions of the consequences of the spread of nuclear technology may itself be undermining the NPT – a central component of the overall non-proliferation regime.

To be sure, self-serving political rhetoric sometimes obscures certain causal relationships and artificially enhances the contribution of others. For example, the recent non-proliferation-related initiatives of the suppliers have coincided with a widespread reappraisal of the future course of national nuclear energy programmes. Thus, non-proliferation or economic motives alone do not drive the policies of the supplier states, as is sometimes alleged. Other problems, not related to proliferation, are contributing to growing doubts about the value of a plutonium-fuelled nuclear power economy. Furthermore, those nations with significant nuclear programmes that have not become parties to the treaty were unlikely to accede even in the absence of recent developments, while so far there has not been a major initiative by one or more of the non-weapon parties to withdraw from the NPT. So the purported impact of the developments of the past decade may not be as great as is often suggested. Nevertheless, there are other, subtler ways in which the recent general erosion of confidence in international nuclear relations could affect adversely the working of the NPT.

DECISIVE ISSUES

As government attitudes toward the NPT continue to evolve, three interrelated questions seem likely to form the framework for policy deliberations. How resilient is the treaty? How important is its role likely to be in any future non-proliferation regime? Could it be improved by modification, or could it be replaced?

As far as resiliency is concerned, the stresses created by recent attempts to re-establish the proliferation threshold have already been examined. A different set of issues concerns the durability of the treaty in the event of an act of proliferation by a party or, for that matter, by a non-party. In practice, of course these two sets of issues are closely linked. For instance, to a significant extent the recent non-proliferation initiatives of the supplier states were implemented in response to the Indian detonation of 1974. Similarly, the impact of future proliferation events on the NPT may be measured as much in terms of the subsequent re-evaluations by suppliers of their obligations as treaty parties (and the consequences of such re-evaluations) as by the immediate international security implications of the event. While the nuclear threshold aspect of NPT resilience would certainly decline in importance as more nations attained nuclear fuel cycle sulf-sufficiency, the rate at which nuclear dependence relationships are being eroded is frequently exaggerated.[1]

It is difficult to assess what the relative importance of the treaty will be in the future, although at least two trends suggest that it will decline. The treaty itself is extremely short; In fact for a set of issues of such complexity it is extraordinarily short. In practice, it has been supplemented by an extensive network of regional, bilateral, and trilateral cooperative and safeguards agreements among individual supplier and recipient nations and the IAEA, together with the agency statute itself. This network provides the substance of the NPT regime. In addition, in recent years, the major suppliers have jointly (through the London Suppliers Group) and individually (through domestic legislation and new and modified agreements for cooperation with recipients) attempted to strengthen controls over nuclear energy. This has led to suggestions that these measures, rather than the NPT itself, constitute the framework within which the international development of nuclear energy will take place. Although most of the suppliers have emphsized their commitment to the principles affirmed in the treaty, there has been increasing acknowledgment in some supplier nations of the advantages to be derived from a flexible approach to non-proliferation policy, which probably can best be achieved through bilateral or multilateral channels, and avoids or at least obscures the over discriminatory quality of the NPT.

In parallel with these developments, the spread of nuclear technology has created the conditions for an increasing number of countries to be able to construct facilities necessary for the production of nuclear weapons without relying on external assistance, either in the form of nuclear energy-related imports or as direct transfers of military technology. There is increasing evidence to suggest that future non-proliferation efforts will be obliged to focus more heavily on the political and strategic motivations and incentives for proliferation or non-proliferation, which the NPT and its associated agreements address only in the most general way and to a very limited extent. The primary non-proliferation policy instruments of the future may therefore consist, on the one hand, of political commitments, conventional arms transfers, and security guarantees, and, on the other hand, of unilateral or collective measures designed to increase the penalties associated with the act of proliferation.

Despite the possible reduction in the contribution of the NPT to an overall non-proliferation regime that may accompany these trends, the treaty continues to represent a commitment on the part of well over 100 non-weapon nations not to acquire nuclear weapons from civilian nuclear energy facilities, indigenous facilities, or from any other source. The treaty also represents a commitment by these nations to accept safeguards on all peaceful nuclear activities. It is hard to imagine any non-proliferation regime in which such commitments, each of which attests to an unusual degree of voluntary abrogation of national sovereignty, would not play an important role, or in which such commitments could be obtained or maintained in the absence of a formal treaty.

AN IMPROVED TREATY?

The third and last question is whether the treaty could be improved on, either by modification or by replacement. While it is probably impossible to answer such a question precisely, a useful insight may be obtained by reviewing several important changes that have occurred since the original NPT negotiation and that would seem to bear on the prospects for a re-negotiation.

First, there have been attempts by some governments to redefine the proliferation threshold; these attempts have had several consequences, one of which has been to increase the level of tension in international nuclear relations.

Second, in parallel with, but not entirely as a result of the international spread of nuclear technology, there is a tendency to regard the production of nuclear weapons as a decreasingly difficult task. Nations that may have formerly regarded nuclear weapons production as beyond them may now see it within reach. Yet the prestige attached to nuclear weapons possession that might otherwise have been an important incentive to proliferate may now be diluted.

Third, perceptions of the role of nuclear energy in meeting national and global energy requirements have undergone a number of changes. The first half of the decade was a period of general optimism, but in a number of countries disillusion has set in within the last few years. Large-scale reactor deferrals and cancellations and major reductions in power plant ordering levels have marked this period, particularly in the industrialized countries. Many reasons underlie these trends, including the general absence of proven methods for high-level waste disposal; increasing concern over the soaring capital costs and over health, safety, and environmental risks of nuclear power plants and their associated fuel cycle facilities; and generally reduced economic growth and associated reductions in electric power demand projections. In many countries, these factors have led to an increase in the levels of activity of groups opposed to nuclear power, and to hesitancy within governments facing the task of formulating and implementing nuclear power policies.

On the other hand, prompted by the oil embargo of 1973-4, by the increasing concentration of the world's oil supplies in the politically volatile Middle East, and by the emergence of the United States as a major oil importer, concern about the security of energy supplies in general has been growing in many nations. Nuclear energy, which in some areas (particularly Western Europe) has long been seen as a means to reduce dependence on interruptable external sources of supply, is now being reaffirmed in this role. Furthermore, several separate factors have combined to make the security of international supplies of natural and enriched uranium increasingly uncertain. As a result, the position taken by a number of governments has been to emphasize the role of the plutonium fuel cycle in reducing their vulnerability to the threat of interruptions and to onerous political conditions imposed on imported energy supplies.

Thus, in the years since the negotiation of the NPT, several issues have emerged to influence profoundly perceptions of the role of nuclear energy. Since about 1975, the most noticeable effect has been a worldwide reduction in nuclear power programme targets. But perhaps equally important, from the point of view of a potential NPT renegotiation, considerable differences among the various governmental perceptions of the configuration and contribution of the world's nuclear energy industry have also developed over the same period.

Fourth in this list of important developments since the original NPT negotiation, major nuclear energy supply industries have been built up in several nations. The past decade has seen the erosion of US hegemony in the supply of nuclear facilities, equipment, and services, and the emergence of major competition, particularly from the advanced industrial nations of Western Europe. Furthermore, a group of nations with smaller nuclear industries that are capable of contributing significantly to their domestic power programmes and of competing in international markets in limited sectors is also beginning to emerge. The foundations for many of these national industries were laid in a period of relative optimism about the future of nuclear power. In the current situation of retrenchment, the pressure on suppliers to sell, domestically or internationally, is considerable, and apparently in some cases is a matter of industrial survival. Already existing differences among suppliers can only be exacerbated in such circumstances.

Fifth, progress on superpower arms control has been far slower than non-weapon states hoped at the time of the NPT negotiation, and despite the fact that growing and increasingly sophisticated superpower nuclear weapons arsenals probably add little, if anything, to the proliferation incentives of individual non-weapon states, failure to limit vertical proliferation would almost certainly affect the prospects for renegotiation adversely.

Finally, and more generally, the past decade has seen a major increase in the discussion, disputes, proposals, counterproposals, and confrontations in a great variety of international forums that are sometimes collectively referred to as the 'North-South dialogue'. Characteristic of this dialogue has been the tendency to link issues and problems that had previously been raised and discussed individually. In the current international climate, it would seem far less likely that a negotiation could be effectively limited to the issues originally included in the NPT to the extent that this was possible a decade or so ago. Consideration of nuclear energy and weapons proliferation issues would almost certainly be linked to general international problems of technology transfer, trade relations, and global redistribution of wealth. In such circumstances, a renegotiation of the NPT would inevitably lead to problems of extraordinary complexity. On the other hand, it is by no means clear that a general willingness to deal with the question of nuclear weapons proliferation in a much broader context would not, in the long run, lead to a more effective international non-proliferation regime.

Attempts to renegotiate or replace part or all of the NPT, therefore, would likely be fraught with difficulty, and the outcome – including the probability of retaining the fundamental conditions in the current treaty – would be highly uncertain. The functions served by the current treaty will almost certainly continue to be generally perceived as being too valuable to forgo. Nevertheless, to survive in a workable form, the treaty will require continuous support and reaffirmation. As a corollary, and in recognition of the dual role of the NPT as an instrument of non-proliferation and a framework for the development of nuclear energy, each government that has chosen to adopt a position of support for the treaty, whether nuclear weapon state, non-weapon state, supplier, or consumer, bears the responsibility of gauging the impact of its nuclear policies, civilian or military, domestic or international, on the NPT regime before it implements them.

TOWARD A NEW REGIME

But beyond these general conclusions, the preceding analysis also invites speculation as to the flavour, at least, of a future non-proliferation regime incorporating the treaty. Indeed, the same trends that have demonstrated the fragility of the NPT in a dynamic environment also suggest what may be required in addition and how it may be achieved.

First, it is clear that the success of any non-proliferation regime will require that the NPT and its subsidiary agreements be amply augmented by continuing efforts to minimize political and strategic incentives to proliferate. An immensely wide range of policy instruments are available for this purpose – economic, political, and military commitments and assistance, implemented bilaterally or regionally, together with collective measures to increase international penalties arising from the act of proliferation. Few of these policy elements will be related to the nuclear power industry *per se*. Indeed, the success of a future non-proliferation regime will depend largely on the extent to which it is embedded in a much broader context than the relationship between nuclear power and nuclear proliferation which figures so prominently in the NPT itself. This is so not only because of the inherently political character of the proliferation problem and the increasing accessibility of technology suitable for producing nuclear explosive material, but also because the role of nuclear power in meeting the world's energy needs will itself be tightly circumscribed for the foreseeable future.

For those aspects of a non-proliferation regime that do concentrate on the nuclear power-weapons proliferation relationship, the task will be to supplement the current set of arrangements without destroying what has already been achieved. Thus, efforts to extend the near-universal consensus on the undesirability of proliferation that is at the heart of the NPT to a codification of 'permissible behaviour' in the field of nuclear power within the same, legally binding international framework should be avoided. They will almost certainly be fruitless; and, more important, they will threaten the original consensus, whose sustenance is essential to any successful non-proliferation regime.

Instead, additional efforts to channel international nuclear development along particular lines, away from potentially destabilizing configurations, should be on a less universal and more *ad hoc* footing; for example, in the form of understandings, agreements, and entrepreneurial arrangements between pairs or groups of nations. Issues will be resolved less by precedent than on their particular merits.

Such an approach will not be inherently unmanageable. Contrary to the view popularly held earlier in the decade, when proliferation concerns underwent a renaissance and the foundations of the current difficulties were laid, the world is not about to be overwhelmed by a flood of commercial reprocessing plants, plutonium, and other sensitive facilities and materials. The transition to a plutonium fuel cycle, if it materializes, will come slowly; slowly enough at the outset to deal with each development individually. In fact, such an approach is not only manageable, but essential. Each decision affecting the development of nuclear power is made within a particular security context and with a particular set of energy policy objectives in mind. Therefore, solutions cannot be legislated across the board.

To be sure, there will be the risk of discriminatory practices. But it will be far easier and less divisive to create a complex but malleable network of international arrangements lacking perfect internal consistency than to obtain universal agreement on generally applicable rules for nuclear development. What such rules might gain in universality they will more than lose in the vagueness and ambiguity needed to achieve a consensus.

Flexibility will be essential. The network of controls, incentives, and disincentives that is superimposed on the existing NPT regime must be capable of adapting to a dynamic environment of shifting technological capabilities and of shifting political, economic, and military states of nations. At the same time, new non-proliferation-related initiatives must be assessed not only in terms of their internal costs and benefits but also by their impact on pre-existing non-proliferation structures – most importantly, the NPT regime itself. Here again, however, a network of arrangements, the individual elements of which have only limited application, seems to show advantages over a more formal, universally applicable, and intellectually more pleasing structure, both in term of its greater flexibility in fluid surroundings and in terms of its lower cumulative stress on the existing NPT regime.

Such a system will be untidy and will make weighty demands on nuclear technology suppliers and consumers alike. The suppliers will be obliged to scrutinize their own domestic nuclear power industries, including the manufacturing industries, as intensively as they would those of the recipients. Preferably in consultation with each other, they will rationalize their own industries in line with a realistic appraisal of future prospects, in addition to requiring it of others. Actions of this kind will require a much greater degree of introspection by the suppliers than has been apparent in the past; in forums such as the London Suppliers Group, the emphasis traditionally has been on the nuclear power programmes of others. At the same time, the suppliers must also exercise responsibility in the realm of technology and materials transfer, not only from the perspective of international security but also with due regard to their role in establishing stable and reliable international trading relationships.

A sense of responsibility will also be required from other nations. Those requesting or otherwise acquiring sensitive fuel cycle facilities and materials must realize that they have the responsibility of assuring their neighbours and the rest of the world of their peaceful intentions – a responsibility that, in practical terms, may very well transcend commitments that would have to be made under the existing NPT regime.

All nations, whether suppliers or consumers, must realize that there is no final solution to the problem of developing a successful non-proliferation regime in the broadest sense. To achieve even temporary success will require a degree of international cooperation hitherto unprecedented in intensity and continuity. Presumably the objective merits such an effort.

NOTES AND REFERENCES

1. See, for example, Gloria Duffy, in 'Beyond Dependency: The Future of the Non-proliferation Treaty' in this book. In fact, the end of nuclear dependence is not imminent. For many countries, the promise of energy self-sufficiency through the plutonium fuel cycle may turn out to be illusory. The ability to manufacture breeder reactors seems likely to be limited to a handful of countries for the foreseeable future. Reliance on these countries for supplies of the generating facilities themselves and, in some cases, for operation and maintenance services is an aspect of dependence that is too seldom discussed. Furthermore, fuel cycle economics may be such that the cost premium required for purely national facilities, and therefore for full fuel cycle independence, is too high to justify the perceived benefits of such independence for most

countries. In sum, it is important not to confuse the relatively rapid spread of sensitive technologies with the much slower growth in the number of situations in which national commercial enrichment and reprocessing facilities would be appropriate.

11 The View from the Third World

FERGUS CARR

National development revolves around economics, yet is fundamentally political. The New International Economic Order sought by developing countries certainly concerns issues of trade but essentially seeks a just order of economic affairs in which both rich and poor countries have rights of decision. The pursuit of development is the search for and assertion of both political and economic sovereignty in the state system. This basic direction permeates the various Third World states' perception of proliferation.

The Third World states approach proliferation with a belief in the necessity for equality. Proliferation is construed as both a vertical and horizontal problem. India, a leader in formulating the Third World position, consistently attacked vertical proliferation:

> It is important and urgent to concentrate all our efforts in the direction of permanently eliminating the danger of nuclear war. The nuclear weapon states have a primary responsibility in this regard and we expect them, therefore to take the lead in this matter.[1]

This view has dominated the Third World approach to non-proliferation since the debates of the late 1960s over the Non-proliferation Treaty (NPT). It was a central theme at the NPT Review Conference 1975, where the non-aligned countries failed in their efforts to secure a deadline for the cessation of underground nuclear tests and the reduction of nuclear arsenals.

THE NPT DEBATE

The relationship of vertical to horizontal proliferation was a central

230

issue in the approach of the non-nuclear weapon states to the NPT debate in 1968. India found that the NPT 'as it stood did not give a real genuine and credible guarantee to non-nuclear countries against nuclear attack'.[2] A General Assembly Resolution pointing to the absence of such guarantees was offered by Ethiopia, and supported by Ceylon, Japan, Kenya, Nepal and Pakistan. African diplomats expressed reservations in response to South Africa's rejection of the NPT.[3] Algeria pointed with scepticism to the Treaty's supposition that its three co-sponsors would never be aggressors.[4] Thailand found that the Treaty offered no security against potential Chinese Communist aggression,[5] and Pakistan stated that its position would depend on its 'own enlightened national interest and national security in the geographical context of the region in which Pakistan is situated'.[6]

The co-sponsors of the Treaty, the United States, the USSR, and the United Kingdom, responded to these concerns with Security Council Resolution 255 on 19 June 1968. The Resolution was to 'provide or support immediate assistance to a non-nuclear weapon state subject to attack or the threat of attack with nuclear weapons'. Parthasarath expressed the Indian view of this Resolution:

> I should like to emphasize that any security assurances that might be offered by nuclear weapon states could not and should not be regarded as *quid pro quo* for signature. The threat of nuclear weapons to non-nuclear states arises directly from the possession of such weapons by certain states. That threat has nothing to do with signature or no signature of a particular NPT. That threat has existed in the past and would continue to remain so even after the NPT has been concluded until such time as the nuclear menace has been eliminated altogether.[7]

The Indian argument further suggested that the Security Council Resolution was a violation of the United Nations Charter, for 'when the Security Council is called upon to make a determination in accordance with Article 39 of the Charter, it does not first enquire as to whether a certain state has subscribed to a certain treaty or not'.[8]

The Indian position was of course determined by its prior rejection of the NPT, but even states such as Iran, which signed the Treaty, pointed to the weakness of the Resolution.

> Who will feel safer because of these words? Here is no guarantee, no assurance in form or words of obligation to anyone. This is a declaration of intention, not an assurance.[9]

The Algerian Ambassador, T. Bouattoura, pointed out that a Security Council measure is subject to veto and stated that 'the Resolution was either superfluous or inadequate because neither China nor France was prepared to become a party to the NPT'.[10]

If the problem of security guarantees could not be settled between the nuclear weapon states and the non-nuclear weapon states, neither could it be settled among the latter group on their own. The Conference of Non-nuclear Weapon States in September 1968 failed to achieve a collective decision on security. While all agreed on the need for security guarantees to cope with the inequalities induced by vertical proliferation, such guarantees could not be sought for non-signatories of the NPT and they would thus be unequal.

Third World statesmen also strongly affirm their right to participate in measures to curb the arms race. Indonesia's Sukarno summarized their position, stating that 'This problem is of such vital importance for the whole of mankind that all mankind should be involved in its solution'.[11] Their involvement has, however, only created frustration. While the non-aligned countries have succeeded in broadening membership of the United Nations Disarmament Conference and committees on disarmament since the early 1960s, their ability to change the structure of these bodies is limited. For example, Mexico sought to widen the scope of the Thirty Nation Geneva Disarmament Conference (now the Committee on Disarmament) by ending the co-chairmanship of the United States and USSR. The superpowers did not however relish the idea of non-nuclear states rotating the role of chairmen.[12] Not until 1978 did the nuclear giants agree, under pressure at the UN Special Session on Disarmament, to permit rotation of the chairmanship.

While the nuclear weapon states clearly hold the key to measures of arms control, their policies affect the attitudes of the non-nuclear weapon states towards economic issues, as well as security. The traditional Third World assessment of the non-security costs of vertical proliferation was expressed in the UN General Assembly as early as 1961:

> Indeed, is there a single new country which has not felt it an affront to its own poverty that such vast sums should be swallowed up by armaments which are particularly costly in view of their rapid obsolescence? Besides constituting a permanent threat to life itself on our planet, the manufacture of these weapons ties up productive forces and thus jeopardizes the prospect of a better life for us all.[13]

The Third World States made their respective decisions on the NPT in view of three basic factors: the Treaty's ability to curb proliferation, its cost to their security, and its cost to their development. The approach of certain states was pragmatic. Ethiopia found that the acute political differences among the nuclear powers 'prevent us from taking a broad and comprehensive approach to non-proliferation and compel us to consider the present approach as a partial and practical approach short of the ideal goal'.[14]

For other states, particularly those with peaceful nuclear aspirations, the NPT could only constitute discrimination and could therefore not be signed. Even though the NPT enshrined the principle of the peaceful atom, essential to attain Third World consent, it meant for certain states a restriction on their sovereign right to independent development. Brazil and India pointed to the asymmetry of obligations in the NPT. The nuclear 'haves' could retain weapons, were not subject to the safeguard system and could develop peaceful nuclear explosives (PNEs). Non-nuclear weapon states had to forgo weapons and PNEs and submit to inspections, conditions the Brazilian delegate to the Geneva Conference described as 'a new form of dependence which is certainly inconsistent with our aspirations for development'.[15] Brazilian Foreign Minister Pinto stated:

They insist on imposing on us a system of international control which would be discriminatory since it would divide the countries of the world inexorably into two categories: Those entitled to utilize nuclear energy for all purposes, even for military ends and those that cannot develop all the full uses of the atom, even for purely peaceful purposes. This is what Brazil cannot accept or agree to.[16]

Indian Minister for External Affairs Bhagat gave his government's view: 'The balance of responsibilities and obligations was not equal as between the nuclear and non-nuclear powers. With its discriminatory approach the treaty was not in India's national interest'.[17] Prime Minister Indira Ghandi's defence of the Indian PNE emphasized the idea of an imbalance of rights between nuclear and non-nuclear countries. She asked in 1974. 'Is it the contention that it is all right for the rich to use nuclear energy for destructive purposes but not the right for a poor country to find out whether it can be used for construction'.[18]

Whether party to the Treaty or not, the equal right to nuclear technology has been a common theme of the non-nuclear states. The case was put most vigorously by states ambitious to develop such technology. Of fourteen resolutions approved at the Non-nuclear Weapons States Conference in 1968, seven related to the peaceful use of the atom and the transfer of technology.

K.P. Jain of India reiterated Third World views in 1977 when he said that:

> The international community demands the prevention of proliferation of nuclear weapons, but it has also insisted on the proliferation of science and technology, including nuclear science and technology for peaceful purposes. The developing countries have made the transfer of such technology to them a cornerstone of their fight for the achievement of a just economic order.[19]

Has the Third World, though, been able to determine how the proliferation of nuclear technology could occur without encouraging the proliferation of weapons; how an equitable nuclear order can be a stable order?

THIRD WORLD INITIATIVES

The Conference of Non-nuclear Weapon States in 1968 considered three draft resolutions on security, and resolutions on disarmament, safeguards and nuclear-free zones to curb weapons proliferation yet ensure the proliferation of nuclear technology.[20] The resolutions included a series of proposals to create financial and institutional resources to facilitate the transfer of nuclear materials, plants, and knowledge.[21]

One draft security resolution sought to make Security Council Resolution 255 a juridical undertaking by the weapon states, which would reduce incentives to further proliferation. A draft introduced by several Latin American nations proposed that the UN, the IAEA, and the weapon states create a 'multilateral instrument' to take appropriate measures to ensure the security of the non-nuclear weapon states.

A draft proposed by African states suggested a protocol to the NPT in which nuclear weapon states would undertake not to attack each other or non-nuclear weapon states and to come to the immediate assistance of any state attacked by either nuclear or conventional weapons. A Pakistani draft directly proposed a juridical undertaking by the nuclear weapon states to protect the security of non-nuclear weapon states party to the NPT. The Latin American, African and Pakistani drafts were accepted as working documents for the Conference. While gaining committee approval, all three were rejected at the Plenary session.[22]

The disarmament resolutions focused on vertical proliferation and called for US-Soviet bilateral negotiations at an early date on intercontinental ballistic missiles, anti-ballistic missiles, the cessation of the arms race and nuclear disarmament.[23] The Eighteen Nation Disarmament Conference was urged to negotiate the prevention of further weapons deployment and weapons production, a comprehensive nuclear test ban and the elimination of nuclear weapons.[24]

The Conference called for all non-nuclear weapon states not party to the NPT to accept IAEA safeguards.[25] A demand was made for a modern and efficient safeguards system to be employed by both suppliers and Third World states under the auspices of the IAEA.[26] The nuclear weapon states were also asked to accept safeguards.[27] The Conference considered nuclear weapons-free zones the most effective means to counter proliferation, combining security and economic benefits. Indeed, the Treaty of Tlatelolco signed in 1967 by 21 Latin American countries and creating the Latin American nuclear weapons-free zone, must be regarded as a significant Third World initiative to curb proliferation. Despite efforts by Mexico to broaden the Treaty, Argentina is not a party and Brazil has not ratified following her signature. Moreover, neither Brazil nor Argentina construes the Treaty as prohibiting PNEs as does Mexico.[28] The Conference nevertheless urged all states not bound by the Treaty of Tlatelolco to initiate or continue studies for the establishment of nuclear weapons-free zones.[29]

THIRD WORLD RESPONSE TO NEW NON-PROLIFERATION POLICIES

The Third World's role in non-proliferation since 1968 has been basically reactive to initiatives taken by the United States individually and the nuclear exporters collectively. Following the 1974 Indian PNE and attempts by countries such as Brazil, Iran, Pakistan, South Korea and Taiwan to attain reprocessing plants, the Ford and then the Carter Administration enacted a series of new bilateral and multilateral non-proliferation policies.

The proposed French sale of reprocessing facilities to South Korea and Taiwan were prevented by American pressure, but not Brazilian or Pakistani purchase of the sensitive plants.[30] Pressure increased to tighten export restrictions, and the Nuclear Suppliers Group was created by multilateral action in 1975. Today the Group includes all significant nuclear exporters except South Africa.[31] In January 1978, the Suppliers Group adopted a series of rules to follow in sales of all sensitive materials. The rules require importers to renounce formally the use of imports for a nuclear explosive, peaceful or otherwise. IAEA safeguards must extend to all imports, local copies and transfers to third parties. Transfers must be approved by the original suppliers. Imports must also be placed under 'adequate physical protection'. In the event of any violation of the agreement or safeguards by importing countries the NSG members have declared that they would collectively withhold supplies.[32]

President Carter's policy initiatives have gone considerably further.[33] The President announced on 27 April 1977 that America would not export reprocessing or enrichment plants, significant quantities of plutonium or highly enriched uranium and would require new export contracts. He stated that all importers should be party to the NPT but, in the interim, IAEA safeguards would have to be placed on all nuclear facilities and materials, existing, copied or produced, for an indefinite period. The United States would have to approve all third party transfers and any reprocessing of nuclear waste, and no importer could explode a nuclear device peaceful or otherwise. In the event of a violation of the contract or safeguards, all US cooperation would cease. The US would accompany these measures, however, by ensuring an adequate supply of enriched uranium for civil reactor programmes.[34]

The 27 April export policy announcement followed the President's domestic policy statement of 7 April which announced the decision to defer indefinitely commercial reprocessing and the commercial use of breeder reactors, the most productive source of plutonium-238.[35]

Third World reaction to these initiatives has not been favourable. Principal objections have come from the near-nuclear states, but the principle of a curb on technology has brought opposition from a wide group of countries. The Suppliers Group has been referred to as a 'cartel' and a new form of 'imperialism'. At best countries like Iran are 'suspicious of club diplomacy'.[36] The idea of technically preventing proliferation has been dismissed. Munir Ahmad Khan, Chairman of Pakistan's Atomic Energy Commission has said that 'Nuclear proliferation cannot be prevented by putting an embargo on the supply of material, equipment and technology by the advanced countries to the developing countries'.[37] The Indian position was expressed by External Affairs Minister Vajpayee: 'our view is that non-proliferation of nuclear weapons should not be confused with non-dissemination of nuclear technology'.[38]

The thesis that proliferation can be curbed through technical constraints has been dismissed on two related grounds. First, those countries which have sought to develop the nuclear fuel cycle seek energy independence. The Brazilian Government White Paper on Nuclear Energy states:

To avoid what happened in the case of oil, it was imperative that the solution in the case of nuclear energy be one that enabled the country to reach the indispensable autarky in the medium term. The economic growth of the country or its mere subsistence cannot be dependent upon third country decisions as to prices and supplies of essential fuels.[39] Pakistan states that its position on reprocessing was non-negotiable, since a 'country buying expensive nuclear technology must insist on having all the elements in the fuel cycle under its control'.[40] Second, all Third World states have affirmed the sovereign right of all states to develop atomic energy for civil use. Their position has hardened considerably since the Organization of Petroleum Exporting Countries (OPEC) oil price increases in 1973. The result has been that countries like Mexico support the Brazilian case[41] and reject the American and Nuclear Suppliers Group policies.

At the forty-one nation conference on nuclear energy in Iran in April 1977 a resolution was adopted opposing President Carter's policy on breeder reactors, because these states believe breeders can offer energy independence.[42] At the International Fuel Cycle Conference held in Washington in October 1977, not one of the forty national participants would cancel or defer reprocessing, enrichment or the use of plutonium as fuel.[43] A Finnish draft resolution before the UN in October 1977, proposing a series of restrictive technological measures, was effectively amended by the developing countries to affirm the right of all nations to unimpeded access to the peaceful benefits of nuclear energy.[44] A Pakistani draft resolution linking nuclear technology to development and declaring the freedom of all states to acquire such technology was adopted by the General Assembly in December 1977.[45]

The Third World demand for a greater voice in nuclear energy policy poses a more serious problem: the clear divergence of interest and opinion regarding proliferation. The very attempts by the nuclear exporters to strengthen the NPT may actually weaken its status by heightening its imbalance. The consensus essential to curb further proliferation is wanting. How can this rapidly hardening divergence of interest be reconciled?

ACCEPTABLE COMPROMISES

The proliferation of nuclear weapons is a complex and dynamic problem. To suggest that the problem of arriving at agreement on means to restrict proliferation will necessarily involve a reconciliation of interest is an understatement, for it will require a consensus on values. While the nuclear suppliers have rediscovered a relatively recent principle, the myth of a purely peaceful atom, the Third World has learned a far older lesson, that technology is political. Any future measures to curb proliferation that will be acceptable to both groups will have to recognize both technical and political interests.

The Third World response to the suppliers' technical initiatives poses an immediate question. Can technical measures be imposed which are politically acceptable to the Third World? The states of the Third World have affirmed the ideal of effective IAEA safeguards, but the problem is to turn the principle into practical application. A system in which the IAEA is not merely an accounting but a managerial body controlling the fuel cycle might prove effective. At present this would not be acceptable to either the nuclear suppliers or the nuclear aspirants. If the impasse created by President Carter's initiatives is to be overcome, however, some multi-national means must be sought. The creation of international fuel cycle centres under IAEA auspices could be a viable proposition.

Safeguards could then be reconciled with energy access through co-ownership of these facilities. Such a programme would require a considerable re-evaluation of the nuclear policies of the weapons countries, not only America's but those of countries like Britain interested in commercial reprocessing. But the prize of more effective non-proliferation should be worth the costs.

A major problem that confronts any comprehensive safeguard system is the PNE. The PNE represents an ambiguity in nuclear status that has not been lost on the Third World. Pakistan had no doubts about the implications of the Indian test. As one Pakistani official stated simply, 'The barrier to nuclear proliferation interposed by the non-proliferation treaty has been abolished'.[46] Yet India and other countries regard the PNE as part of the peaceful uses of the atom. The validity of either argument is best tested by determining the validity of the PNE itself. The initiative to do so rests with the superpowers, who have not reached a consensus. While the 'Plowshare' programme of the United States has not produced evidence of commercial benefit, the Soviet Union continues nominal support for PNEs, and thus maintains legitimacy for countries interested in blurring their nuclear intentions.[47]

The technical approach to the proliferation problem is ultimately limited, since safeguards cannot be placed against the power of decision. The Third World's view that proliferation is a political problem is fundamentally right; it is a question of security, power, and prestige. The reason the Third World has become the focus of the problem is that the majority of these states are not protected by alliance systems and do not possess influence commensurate with their aspirations.

Among the political incentives to exercising the nuclear option, security is paramount and is based on both global and regional strategic considerations. Globally, vertical proliferation is the common threat to all non-nuclear weapon states. The importance of measures to curb proliferation lies not merely in the principle of arms control but in the linkage of vertical to horizontal proliferation encapsulated in the NPT. Maintaining the NPT depends upon the Third World's conception of the Treaty's balance, whereby under Article VI, the weapon states were committed to ending vertical proliferation and under Article IV, to the transfer of technology. An immediate problem facing the superpowers is to enhance the credibility of their commitment to arms control and to communicate to the Third World the political and technical difficulties of the Strategic Arms Limitations Talks.

It is difficult to envisage any means which could increase the weight of Security Council Resolution 255. A juridical undertaking by the United States and the USSR would necessarily imply a degree of harmony that does not yet exist in détente and could not in consequence be regarded as credible. The inadequacy of the global solutions to proliferation which have been offered points to the potential success of regional methods. Nuclear weapon-free zones along the lines of the Treaty of Tlatelolco could provide valuable complements to the NPT. Unfortunately, attempts to establish such zones have met with particular regional problems. India, for example, considers the Pakistani proposition for a South Asian nuclear weapon-free zone too restrictive. Debate has persisted over the role nuclear weapon states are to play in free zones, further complicating their establishment. Until the strategic direction of China is clarified, the Asian stalemate will probably continue.

The purpose of the NPT is to maintain stability in international relations by preventing a world of nuclear powers. Stability has many facets, encompassing not only arms but economic and political relations. Stability also cannot be construed as static. Stability cannot be attained by imposing the status quo, however appealing that may be, since imposition of any state of affairs is likely to foster conflict.

The clearest implication of the Third World attitude towards proliferation is that the debate must be widened not only in the sense of participation but in the sense that the problem must be countered on political and economic, as well as technical fronts.

NOTES AND REFERENCES

1. *The Hindu*, 19 October 1977. The frustration of Third World NPT signatories has been directed to the failure in their eyes of the superpowers to fulfill the obligations under Article VI of the NPT which requires that Parties to the Treaty 'undertake to pursue negotiations in good faith on measures relating to the cessation of the arms race'.
2. *The Hindu*, 21 June 1968.
3. *The Egyptian Gazette*, 14 April 1968.
4. *Guardian*, May 1968.
5. *Japan Times*, 8 June 1968.
6. *DAWN*, 2 May 1968.
7. *The Hindu*, 21 June 1968.
8. Ibid.
9. *DAWN*, 28 May 1968.
10. *DAWN*, 21 June 1968.
11. UN General Assembly Official Records 14th session, 880th meeting, 30 September 1960, paragraph 85.
12. *International Herald Tribune*, 17 August 1977.
13. UN General Assembly Official Records 15th session, 1961.
14. *DAWN*, 2 May 1968.
15. J. Araujo, *The Times*, 9 February 1968.
16. *International Herald Tribune*, 6 February 1968.
17. *The Hindu*, 26 July 1968.
18. *New York Times*, 27 May 1974.

19. *The Hindu*, 10 March 1977.
20. The following is taken from the Final Document of the Conference reprinted in *DAWN*, 21 December 1968.
21. Resolutions F-M.
22. Failure was not for the rejection of a security need but on the grounds of who would guarantee whom.
23. Resolution D.
24. Resolution C.
25. Resolution E.
26. Resolution F.
27. The idea being a progressive transfer of nuclear facilities from military to civil use under Resolution D.
28. Only in late 1981 did the United States sign Protocol I to the Treaty which requires powers outside the region to accept its conditions for areas in the zone under their jurisdiction. The Soviet Union has not signed Protocol II which requires nuclear-weapon states to respect the free zone and not to use or threaten to use nuclear weapons against Treaty members. The US signed Protocol II in the 1970s.
29. Resolution B.
30. Indeed, American companies lost the Brazilian contract because the West Germans spiced a reactor deal with the full fuel cycle. The West Germans further granted considerable export finance. (See *Financial Times*, 22 December 1977.)
31. South Africa announced on 3 May 1977 that she was ready to export enriched uranium. (See *Guardian*, 4 May 1977.)
32. *International Herald Tribune*, 13 January 1978.
33. The principal difficulty in Nuclear Suppliers Group negotiations has been French and West German attitudes to exports of reprocessing for they claim they cannot violate agreements but have apparently said there would be no further sales.
34. From Official Text, 'The Administration's Nuclear Non-Proliferation Act of 1977.'
35. *The Times*, 9 April 1977.
36. *Financial Times*, 13 April 1977.
37. Mr Munir Ahmad Khan, Chairman of the Pakistan Atomic Energy Commission, *DAWN*, 8 October 1977.
38. *The Hindu,* 20 October 1977.
39. *New York Times*, 28 March 1977.
40. *DAWN*, 13 May 1977.
41. *Guardian*, 19 January 1978.
42. *The Hindu*, 15 April 1977.
43. *International Herald Tribune*, 24 October 1977.
44. *DAWN*, 1 November 1977.
45. *DAWN*, 11 December 1977.
46. *The Times*, 24 May 1974.
47. J. Maddox, *Prospect for Nuclear Proliferation, Adelphi Paper*, 113 (London: International Institute for Strategic Studies, 1975) p. 29.

12 Nuclear Overkill: the Commercialization of Nuclear Power in the Developing Countries

BIJAN MOSSAVAR-RAHMANI

There exists a tendency among Western analysts to characterize nuclear weapons proliferation in the developing countries as a problem emanating from either a political or a technological process within the developing countries themselves. In one scenario, a 'garrison' or 'pariah' country takes a conscious and deliberate decision to seek a nuclear weapons capability to meet perceived security needs and requirements. Accordingly, it is argued, such a country might be dissuaded from doing so by a combination of political incentives and disincentives including, for example, security guarantees against external threats, if the nuclear weapons option is dropped, or sanctions, if it is not.

The potential threshold countries, on the other hand, initially start out with strictly civilian nuclear power programmes, but, through the acquisition of reactors and particularly the sensitive fuel cycle facilities, may eventually reach a level of technological competence and acquire the necessary fissile material to manufacture nuclear weapons. This might be prevented, it is argued, by denying these countries access to uranium enrichment and spent fuel reprocessing facilities that produce not only reactor fuel but fissile material, and offering them instead guarantees and assurances of adequate non-weapons-grade fuel.

During the past several years, prompted in large part by the Indian 'peaceful nuclear explosion' of 1974, efforts have intensified in various fora to reach international consensus on how actually to implement non-proliferation strategies along these lines.

The international nuclear community now appears to be preparing to move cautiously, and with some misgivings, toward what might emerge as a fragile and delicate balance between non-proliferation and civilian nuclear power. But the effort to achieve that balance and retain it promises to be complicated by what has long been a third, albeit frequently and conveniently ignored, dimension to the proliferation problem: the process of premature and indiscriminate promotion – even oversell – of nuclear power in the developing countries; a process appropriately dubbed the 'vulgarization' of nuclear power.

NUCLEAR POWER: PROMISE AND PERFORMANCE

For nearly three decades, the industrialized countries have had great hopes and expectations for harnessing heat from nuclear fission to produce steam to operate machinery to generate electrical power cheaply, reliably, and abundantly. The first sustained and controlled nuclear fission chain reaction was achieved in 1942, and the first civilian nuclear reactors became operational over a decade later. By the end of the 1960s, orders for hundreds of new reactors had been placed in rapid succession in nearly 20 countries around the world.

But, despite early expectations, in many instances the nuclear reactors, once operational, proved at best to be only marginally cost-competitive, if at all, with traditional fossil-fuelled plants. Widespread hopes for nuclear-generated electrical power 'too cheap to meter' were frustrated in large part by rapidly rising capital costs for reactors. In fact, it was becoming increasingly evident that the cost estimates and hence the economic rationale that had prompted earlier nuclear plant construction were critically flawed.

Had the world energy picture not changed in the early 1970s, it is conceivable that the costly experience of the 1960s might have substantially slowed down plant construction. However, the oil embargo imposed by the Organization of Arab Petroleum Exporting Countries (OAPEC) in 1973-4 and the concomitant quadrupling of oil prices enhanced once again the perception of the commercial feasibility of nuclear power. Furthermore, a growing realization that fossil fuels, particularly oil and natural gas, might be in short supply in the longer term induced state-owned and private utilities in many industrialized, developing, and Eastern Bloc countries to assign greater weight to fuel diversification. Specifically, the concern over securing access to and controlling prices of fossil fuels increased the attraction of the nuclear option, and a sudden and marked increase in nuclear reactor orders followed, despite the past experience in cost overruns.

But the renewed perception of nuclear power as a commercially and technologically viable alternative to fossil fuels was not to last long; it was again shaken by a changing plant-construction and operation-cost picture, a closer look at uranium availability, growing international awareness of proliferation and security risks, and a growing public concern over safety and environmental hazards posed by the reactors and radioactive waste products from the nuclear fuel cycle. A number of key industrialized countries including the United States, Great Britain, the Federal Republic of Germany, and France began to reassess and cut back orders for new reactors. Projections of nuclear power capacity in these countries still indicate large increases to 1985, but much of this is accounted for by earlier orders for plants that are now in the construction phase. The future of nuclear power in the industrialized countries beyond that period remains highly uncertain.

The developing countries, however, have been slower to alter their earlier nuclear power targets. The perception of nuclear reactors as sources of almost infinite, secure, and cheap electrical power has tended to persist in these countries, perhaps because of the comparatively greater impact on their fragile economies of the oil price rise. Clearly, under the present circumstances at least, nuclear power is none of these.

The present generation of light-water reactors – which comprise the largest share of all reactors in operation, under construction, or in the planning phase – use low-enriched uranium as fuel. However, availability of uranium ore worldwide is limited; in fact, it is becoming increasingly recognized that proven reserves of uranium are no more plentiful, in relation to potential demand, than those of such traditional fossil fuels as crude oil. Furthermore, for a variety of economic, political, and technical reasons, even those limited reserves may not actually be produced or, if produced, necessarily made available to the developing countries.

Given the potential link between the spread of civilian nuclear hardware, fuel, and know-how, on the one hand, and nuclear weapons proliferation, on the other, three principal uranium-rich countries – the United States, Canada, and Australia – have already sought to impose strict conditions on the export of uranium to satisfy their respective safeguards concerns.

The uranium market is expected to remain a highly politicized one, and, given the likelihood of even greater intervention by the principal producers on political grounds, will continue to be both unstable and unpredictable. Where security of fuel supply is concerned, nuclear power, particularly insofar as the developing countries outside of the present nuclear club are concerned, is no more reliable than, for example, crude oil.

The problem is further compounded by the fact that the bulk of the world's limited uranium resources will continue to be produced by only a handful of countries; the four largest present-day producers together account for nearly 90 per cent of the non-communist world output. Moreover, the world uranium market is expected to be dominated by these countries into the latter part of the next decade, even with the entry of several other important producers such as Niger, Gabon, and Spain.

The existence of such concentration, if not actual cartelization, in the uranium market has important ramifications for uranium prices. It is uncertain, for example, whether prices will remain constant in real terms over the coming years or whether they will be hiked substantially, as was the case in the period between 1973 and 1978 when prices jumped five-to six-fold as a result of artificial market manipulation.

In addition to the uranium producers' cartel, moreover, the developing countries face a second highly politicized, unstable, and cartelized market for uranium enrichment services. The United States continues to hold a virtual monopoly over enrichment services at present, although the Soviet Union has been making some inroads into that market. Two European enrichment projects will soon come on stream: one, the URENCO joint venture among Great Britain, the Federal Republic of Germany, and the Netherlands; and the other, the French-led EURODIF consortium, including Spain, Italy, Belgium, and, indirectly, Iran. But Iran's indirect participation in EURODIF notwithstanding, Brazil will be the only developing country with direct access to its own enrichment facilities, if the planned facility supplied by West Germany is constructed.

Because of the decision by the nuclear suppliers to restrict severely, if not to ban altogether, any further sale of sensitive enrichment technologies that could be used to produce weapons-grade uranium, the developing countries with light-water reactors will necessarily continue to be highly dependent on the suppliers of enrichment services for reactor fuel. Even if the enrichment facilities were available for sale, economies of scale would preclude any commercial operation in the smaller developing countries.

While the suppliers have indicated some willingness to offer enriched uranium under agreed terms as part of a non-proliferation bargain, such past events as the temporary moratorium on the new enrichment contracts that was in effect in the United States in the mid-1970s and the contentious domestic debate over uranium production in Australia raise questions about the long-term credibility of these guarantees.

On the other hand, plutonium from the back end of the fuel cycle is unlikely to be available as a hedge against the unreliability of the suppliers of uranium and enrichment services. Spent fuel from light-water reactors can be reprocessed to retrieve still unused uranium and also fuel-grade plutonim transformed from part of the original heavy uranium isotopes. Both can then be recycled back into reactors as fresh fuel. However, plutonium recovered through reprocessing is both highly toxic and weapons-grade, making reprocessing extremely controversial. One key country, the United States, has indefinitely postponed commercial reprocessing of spent fuel and has urged others to do the same; many, in fact, are expected to follow suit.

But even if several countries, such as France and Great Britain, continue to operate their existing commercial reprocessing facilities, the terms under which reprocessing services might be offered to the developing countries remain unclear and unpredictable. The actual sale of the facilities themselves will undoubtedly be barred for many years to come, given the concerns about safeguarding against their misuse. Considering its high costs, reprocessing, like enrichment, makes very little commercial sense in developing countries with small nuclear programmes anyway.

Finally, the developing countries face yet another highly concentrated group of nuclear hardware suppliers, which supply not only reactors but importantly, spare parts as well as trained technicians to build, operate, maintain, and eventually dismantle the nuclear facilities and dispose of their spent fuel.

The reactor market is presently dominated by about a half dozen major conglomerates, which, despite some competition in overseas sales, are highly interconnected. The two predominant US nuclear manufacturers, Westinghouse and General Electric, which together share some two-thirds of the domestic market in that country, have been deeply involved in the European and Japanese nuclear power programmes as well. For example, the principal West German domestic nuclear reactor now in operation is virtually identical to the General Electric boiling water reactor, while the principal export reactor is of the Westinghouse pressurized water reactor design. In France the Framatome conglomerate produces pressurized water reactors under licence from Westinghouse, both for domestic and export uses. In fact, until several years ago, Westinghouse held a substantial share in the ownership of Framatome itself. In the Japanese market, of the three principal nuclear reactor manufacturers, Mitsubishi holds a Westinghouse licence and Hitachi and Toshiba hold General Electric ones.

While several other countries, such as the Soviet Union, Canada and Sweden, have more or less independent nuclear industries, all have grouped together in the so-called London Nuclear Suppliers Group, primarily to set ground rules and restrictions for the export of nuclear technology. Such interconnection and collusion will significantly affect prices. Moreover, while it lasts, collusion may result in joint embargoes against a particular country or group of countries, on the sale of hardware or other services necessary to the construction and operation of nuclear facilities. This could be in response to legitimate safeguards concerns or even in pursuit of other commercial or foreign policy objectives, but in any case could significantly reduce the long-term reliability and security of supplies from the perspective of the developing countries.

NO CHEAP ENERGY

As for the myth of cheap nuclear power, the figures tell a different story. Rapidly increasing costs throughout the 1970s, for capital investment in plant and equipment and operating costs, including fuel, have whittled down, if not totally eliminated, any competitive edge over fossil-fuelled plants – particularly coal-fired ones – within the industrialized countries themselves. Between 1967 and 1977, published estimates of capital costs for new light-water reactors in the industrialized countries in current dollars per kilowatt-electric (KWe) installed grew nearly 10-fold to over $1000 for a reactor of the standard 1000 megawatt-electric (MWe) size.

Reactor manufacturers, and even the utilities, have persistently underestimated these costs; indeed, capital costs have outpaced expectations in nearly all instances because of large overruns. The cost increases have been attributed to increased escalation and interest due to longer construction and licensing time requirements; more stringent safety and environmental criteria; additional engineering; labour, equipment, and materials costs; and general inflation.

The commercial attraction of nuclear power is even more suspect in the developing countries. In Iran, for example, the capital costs in current mixed dollars per KWe installed for four reactors (two French and two German) in the 1000 MWe class presently under construction are over $3000, or some three to four times higher than those of similarly sized reactors in the principal industrialized countries.[1] Precise figures for the other developing countries are not publicly available. In all likelihood, the figures will not be as high as the Iranian ones, but higher than comparable facilities in the supplier countries themselves, and certainly higher than original expectations and initial estimates on which basic decisions were made. For example, the former chief of Brazil's government electricity monopoly, ELECTROBRAS, was recently quoted as saying that the original 1974 decision to purchase reactors was based on cost estimates of some $550 per KWe installed; but in practice, costs to date have tripled in that country.[2]

The developing countries are further burdened by the substantial foreign exchange component of total reactor costs, a problem that is not faced in the industrialized countries where most of the equipment is manufactured locally. Finally, the developing countries face important infrastructural bottlenecks to the implementation of large-scale nuclear power programmes. The total size of a country's inter-councted electrical power grid imposes clear limits on the size of any

TABLE 12.1

Installed capacity must be at least	To accommodate a single plant of
850 MWe	100 MWe
3300 MWe	300 MWe
9200 MWe	600 MWe
20000 MWe	1000 MWe

(Data taken from a study by the International Atomic Energy Agency.[3])

one single generating plant that the system can reasonably accommodate, while still functioning reliably, if that largest unit accidentally fails or is shut down for repairs, maintenance, or refuelling. (See Table 12.1)

Following these guidelines and using projections of electrical power demand in individual developing countries, which may well have been overstated, the International Atomic Energy Agency (IAEA) estimated that the numbers of developing countries shown in Table 12.2 might be able to accommodate nuclear reactors of given sizes in the course of the next two decades:[4]

TABLE 12.2

Plant sizes of	*By 1980*	*By 1985*	*By 2000*
1000 MWe or larger	2	6	11
600 MWe to 1000 MWe	3	7	9
300 MWe to 600 MWe	11	10	9

However, despite potential demand, smaller reactors, particularly those below 600 MWe installed capacity, are not presently offered commercially, nor are they expected to be in the foreseeable future, as can be seen from Table 12.3. In recent years, the manufacturers have increasingly turned to the 1000 MWe-class reactors apparently to capture economies of scale in the construction and operation of these larger reactors. To go back to smaller reactors now, they argue, would entail costly design changes and other initial fixed charges so high that there would be no commercial markets for such reactors, either at home or abroad.

UNREALISTIC PROMISES

Yet despite the specific misgivings about the economic and technical viability of large nuclear reactors in the developing countries and the general considerations that have led to a reassessment and substantial down-scaling of nuclear power programmes in the industrialized countries, the developing nations have been slower to reassess their own nuclear targets. Why?

It has sometimes been argued that developing countries have sought

TABLE   Reactors operating and under construction[a] in developing countries
as of January 1979

	Operating reactors		Under construction		Total by 1985	
	No.	MWe	No.	MWe	No.	MWe
Argentina	1	345	1	600	2	945
Brazil	–	–	2	1871	2	1871
India	3	602	5	1087	8	1689
Iran	–	–	2	2380	2	2380
Mexico	–	–	2	1308	2	1308
Pakistan	1	126	–	–	1	126
Philippines	–	–	1	621	1	621
South Korea	1	564	2	2134	3	2698
Turkey	–	–	1	620	1	620
Total Developing	6	1637	16	10621	22	12258

[a] Or in advanced planning stage but expected to be operational by 1985.

nuclear reactors not out of any serious interest in commercial power
generation, but rather to enhance national prestige, to gain access to
nuclear technology and training in order to rise on the nuclear technology 'learning curve', or even to build nuclear weapons. Some
countries have based decisions to start a small nuclear programme on
such considerations. But this does not explain the decision by several
other countries, such as Iran and Brazil, for example, to seek to
purchase and install substantial commercial nuclear power-generating
capacities. Those decisions have indeed been based on a perception,
now increasingly challenged, that nuclear reactors offer cheap and
plentiful electrical power.[5]

This myth of nuclear power as the energy panacea of the developing
countries was created and nurtured – consciously in some cases,
inadvertently perhaps in others – in large part by the international
companies that manufacture or provide a wide range of nuclear hardware and services, by their respective governments in support of these
vendors' export efforts, and even by the Vienna-based IAEA. All have
applied hard-sell tactics to create on artificial and premature demand
for nuclear power in developing countries. The nuclear vendors, faced
with declining sales at home in the mid-1970s, increasingly turned
instead to what promised to be a very lucrative overseas export
market.

With each contract for a 1000 MWe-class reactor expected to run into the billions of dollars, the commercial stakes have been high indeed, prompting the companies to move rapidly and aggressively into overseas markets. Several companies, in fact, have viewed this opportunity as their only change for commerical survival. In the process, the vendors exaggerated the promise of nuclear power and understated its risks. The developing countries were often told, for example, that the breeder reactor would usher in an era of cheap and literally unlimited electrical power. They were thus encouraged to prepare themselves by installing light-water reactors, not only to gain experience with nuclear technology generally, but to build up stockpiles of plutonium for subsequent use as fuel in their breeders. What the developing countries were not told was that even if the lagging technical and political problems facing the breeder were resolved soon, the economies of scale in breeder construction would necessitate a unit so large – perhaps as much as twice the size of the largest present-generation reactors – that breeders could not be technically integrated into their electrical power grids (with the possible exception of one or two countries,) before the turn of the century.

But it has not been industry alone that has pushed nuclear hardware sales in the developing countries. The nuclear supplier governments, too, despite periodic misgivings about the export of sensitive technologies, have actively promoted such sales.

Nuclear exports, it was held, would not only serve the national interest by keeping the domestic manufacturers afloat and thereby helping to maintain an independent nuclear industry, but would also mean billions of dollars in foreign exchange earnings through the export of reactors as well as a wide range of related technical and fuel services. Reactor sales, furthermore, would help spread some of the research and development costs (largely borne by the governments in the past), help the vendors achieve economies of scale in reactor production (thus reducing unit costs for reactors installed domestically), preserve thousands of jobs in the nuclear sector, and so on.

Given these seemingly strong economic incentives to export, as well as the prestige associated with such sales, the governments cooperated extensively in the sales effort, at times intervening on behalf of the vendors with the developing countries, even 'sweetening' deals by offering concessionary loans, substantial export credits, barter arrangements, and even less stringent proliferation-proof packages including enrichment and reprocessing facilities, as in the West German-Brazilian deal.

Even the international nuclear 'watchdog' agency, the IAEA, has urged on the buyers. The IAEA had its origins in post-Second World War US efforts to establish an international system to check the proliferation of nuclear weapons by regulating the development of civilian nuclear power programmes worldwide. However, the plan was widely viewed – and criticized – as an attempt by the United States to control, if not to restrict, the spread of nuclear know-how in a manner consistent with its own political and commercial interests. In order to make the plan more palatable both to other industrialized countries eager to export nuclear hardware and to those developing countries anxious to gain access to nuclear technology generally, the IAEA's responsibilities were expanded to include facilitating and promoting the spread of civilian nuclear use worldwide.

Article II of the IAEA statute directs the agency to 'seek to accelerate and enlarge the contribution of atomic energy in peace, health and prosperity throughout the world'. This promotional role rather than the original safeguards role has characterized much of the IAEA's activities over the past 22 years. In seeking to commercialize and internationalize nuclear power, moreover, the IAEA has proceeded in a negligent and indiscriminate fashion, particularly in the developing countries.[6]

The IAEA, for example, has tended to promote nuclear power in much of the developing world without first assuring that the nuclear option is well chosen for specific developing countries, given the wide range of differences that exist in such important areas as infrastructure and indigenous energy resource base.[7] The IAEA has repeatedly erred in its analyses of nuclear power economics in the developing countries and has systematically underestimated costs and overestimated nuclear potential.[8] Importantly, these over-optimistic IAEA studies were used by a number of developing countries in drawing up their nuclear programmes in the early to mid-1970s.

It should be noted, moreover, that the international promoters had natural allies within the developing countries themselves in the form of a burgeoning nuclear sector consisting of government nuclear authorities and private, usually highly placed and influential, contractors, pursuing institutional and personal interests respectively.

Aggressive salesmanship coupled with the misrepresentation of information about the nuclear power option on the part of industrialized countries, hardware vendors, the IAEA, and even the domestic promoters have helped to create artificial demand for nuclear power in countries that were not prepared for it and that could have more effectively and economically utilized alternative, even indigenous, sources of energy instead.

IMPLICATIONS FOR NON-PROLIFERATION POLICIES

But in addition to perpetuating wrong judgments about energy choices in the developing world, commercial nuclear overkill has and will continue to have important ramifications in the area of nuclear weapons proliferation as well. Admittedly, the spread of civilian nuclear power does not necessarily correspond to an actual increase in weapons proliferation. Indeed, there are at pesent some serious and well-recognized disincentives – political, security, and economic – that outweigh the incentives for going nuclear in developing countries. But a civilian nuclear programme could increase the potential or the ability to build weapons, both on shorter notice and at little extra economic cost. Already, a number of additional countries have, by starting up civilian nuclear programmes, moved down the path to a nuclear weapons capability without having decided to do so in advance. For such countries, the 'distance remaining will be shorter, less arduous, and much more rapidly covered. It need take only a smaller impulse to carry them the rest of the way'.[9]

That impulse could conceivably come in the wake of a failure of nuclear reactors either to meet exaggerated performance standards or to provide cheap or at least competitive electrical power, as promised by the nuclear promoters. Indeed, if nuclear reactors do prove to be major technical or financial fiascoes – and this likelihood cannot be ruled out – a frustrated developing country could conceivably be prompted to consider a weapons programme as a means of justifying the substantial investment in civilian reactors and human resources.

The international nuclear regime of the past 20 years has been built on an *a priori* judgement that civilian nuclear power should not only be made accessible but also actively and indiscriminately promoted in the developing countries. This vulgarization of nuclear power must be slowed down and ultimately reversed.

First, the IAEA's responsibilities in the area of nuclear power commercialization should be dropped totally. The agency's promotional role, which has included clear exaggeration of the attraction of nuclear power, has facilitated sales of hardware by the industrialized countries at the cost of rational and informed energy planning in a number of developing countries and, possibly, at the cost of an increased drift toward proliferation as well.

The agency should be restructured into a strong, impartial regulatory authority focusing on the enforcement of universally applied safeguards against possible diversion of nuclear materials to weapons uses, as originally envisaged. Perhaps it is time, too, to resurrect the original proposal for the creation of an International Fuel Bank under IAEA auspices, into which spent fuel would be deposited in return for equivalent low-enriched uranium fuel.

Second, a new international institution, separate from the IAEA and nuclear industry interests generally, should be established to collect, evaluate, and disseminate objectively a wide range of information about nuclear energy and its applications, including such questions as uranium availability, nuclear power economics, safety and environmental considerations, plant performance, and so on, all with particular application to the developing countries. Moreover, its scope of work should be broadened to look at nuclear power in the context of total energy needs and options in these countries.

Presently, the sources of information and data available to assist the developing countries in nuclear power decision making are limited to supplier country nuclear energy bodies, vendors, and other national and international promotional organizations. Information provided by these traditional sources has been misrepresentative, irrelevant, and in many instances misleading for planners in the developing countries.

Third, the supplier countries should cease to oversell nuclear power on behalf of their vendors in the developing countries. This will be a bitter pill to swallow given the extensive commercial stakes for these countries in the export of nuclear hardware. Nonetheless, acceptance of a reduction in sales, if it occurs, is a small price to pay to achieve professed non-proliferation objectives.

A supplier government cannot reasonably expect both to promote and to safeguard nuclear power objectively. The two roles are not consistent and compatible, as intense commercial competition is not conducive to non-proliferation measures. In the past, at least promotional considerations seem to have won out in many instances where tensions did arise.

Presently, of course, there is a US-led attempt to reconcile the two through such fora as the International Nuclear Fuel Cycle Evaluation. Even if this effort had succeeded in reaching consensus, it would have proven short-lived while the industrialized countries continue to flirt with a dual role. For as the competition among the vendors intensifies with a shrinkage of the international nuclear market, non-proliferation objectives may once again be dominated by commercial ones.

NOTES AND REFERENCES

1. The capital costs of the two French reactors per KWe were reportedly originally quoted at $200 in 1975. Iran has recently announced cancellation of further construction work on these two reactors.
2. Norman Gall, 'Nuclear Setbacks', *Forbes*, 27 November 1978, p. 105.
3. International Atomic Energy Agency, *Market Survey for Nuclear Power in Developing Countries*, 1974 (Preliminary Report), IAEA-165 (Vienna, 1974) cited in Richard J. Barber Associates, *LDC Nuclear Power Prospects, 1975-1900: Commercial, Economic and Security Implications*, ERDA-52 (Washington, DC 1975) p. II-8.
4. Ibid., p. II-9.
5. Brazil and Iran have recently begun to reconsider their large-scale commitment to nuclear power and instead are looking more carefully at indigenous hydro and natural gas resources, respectively. On the other hand, several developing countries, most notably India, continue to view some dependence on nuclear power as both necessary and desirable. Clearly, under very special circumstances, such as total absence of indigenous sources of fossil fuels, the nuclear option may well prove to be an attractive one over the longer term.
6. For a critique of IAEA's assessment of the potential of nuclear power in developing countries, see the Barber study, op. cit.
7. For example, of the four countries judged by the IAEA to have the greatest potential for nuclear power in the developing world (and which would together account for over 50 per cent of the total installed nuclear megawatts), two – Iran and Mexico – have substantial indigenous oil and natural gas reserves, one – Brazil – has substantial unused hydro potential, and one – India – has large coal and lignite reserves.
8. In the mid-1970s, for example, IAEA experts were estimating capital costs for light-water reactors in developing countries at several hundred dollars per KWe installed for 1000 MWe class reactors, using a cost base developed for the industrialized countries. This approach was erroneous because not only was the cost base of questionable relevance to the developing countries, but it was in fact not even indicative of actual costs in the industrialized countries themselves. Certainly the cost experience in Brazil and Iran (where capital costs per KWe are now estimated to run between $1500 and $3000) have borne out the inadequacies of the IAEA estimates.
9. Albert Wohlstetter, 'Spreading the Bomb Without Quite Breaking the Rules', *Foreign Policy*, no. 25 (Winter 1976) p. 148.

Appendix 1
Status of the
Non-proliferation Treaty

PARTIES

Afghanistan
Australia
Austria
Bahamas
Bangladesh
Belgium
Benin
Bolivia
Botswana
Bulgaria
Burundi
Cambodia
Cameroon
Canada
Central African Empire
Chad
Costa Rica
Cyprus
Czechoslovakia
Denmark
Dominican Republic
Ecuador
El Salvador
Ethiopia
Fiji
Finland
Gabon
Gambia
Germany (East)
Germany (West)
Ghana
Greece

Grenada
Guatemala
Guinea
Haiti
Holy See
Honduras
Hungary
Iceland
Indonesia
Iran
Iraq
Ireland
Italy
Ivory Coast
Jamaica
Japan
Jordan
Kenya
Korea
Laos
Lebanon
Lesotho
Liberia
Libya
Liechtenstein
Luxembourg
Madagascar
Malaysia
Maldive Islands
Mali
Malta
Mauritius ·

Mexico
Mongolia
Morocco
Nepal
Netherlands
New Zealand
Nicaragua
Nigeria
Norway
Panama
Paraguay
Peru
Philippines
Poland
Rumania
Rwanda
San Marino
Senegal
Sierra Leone
Singapore
Somalia
Sri Lanka

Sudan
Surinam
Swaziland
Sweden
Switzerland
Syrian Arab Republic
Taiwan
Thailand
Togo
Tonga
Tunisia
Union of Soviet
   Socialist Republics*
United Kingdom*
United States of America*
Upper Volta
Uruguay
Venezuela
Vietnam
Western Samoa
Yugoslavia
Zaire

SIGNATORIES (HAVE SIGNED THE TREATY, BUT HAVE NOT COMPLETED THE PROCESS OF RATIFICATION)

Barbados
Columbia
Egypt
Kuwait

Trinidad and Tobago
Turkey
Yemen Arab Republic (Sana)
Yemen (Aden)

NON-SIGNATORIES (HAVE NEITHER SIGNED NOR RATIFIED THE TREATY)

Albania
Algeria
Argentina
Bahrain
Brazil
Burma
Chile

China*
Congo
Cuba
France*
Guinea-Bissau
Guyana
India

* Nuclear weapon state. India has detonated a 'peaceful nuclear device'.

Israel
Korea (North)
Malawi
Mauritania
Nauru
Niger
Oman
Pakistan
Portugal

Qatar
Saudi Arabia
South Africa
Spain
Tanzania
Uganda
United Arab Emirates
Zambia

Appendix 2
A Non-proliferation
Bibliography

Atlantic Council, Nuclear Fuels Policy Working Group, *Nuclear Fuels Policy*, (Washington, DC: Atlantic Council, 1976).

Atlantic Council, Nuclear Fuels Policy Working Group, *Nuclear Power and Nuclear Weapons Proliferation*, 2 vols (Washington, DC.: Atlantic Council, 1978).

Auton, Graeme P., 'Nuclear Deterrence and Medium Powers: A Proposal for Doctrinal Change in the British and French Cases', *Orbis*, xx, 2 (Summer 1976).

Bader, William B., *The United States and the Spread of Nuclear Weapons* (New York: Pegasus, 1968).

Baker, Steven J., *Commercial Nuclear Power and Nuclear Proliferation, Peace Studies Program Occasional Paper*, 5 (Ithaca, NY: Cornell University, May 1975).

Baker, Steven, 'Nuclear Proliferation: Monopoly or Cartel?', *Foreign Policy*, 23 (Summer 1976).

Barnaby, Frank, *Preventing Nuclear-Weapons Proliferation* Stockholm International Peace Research Institute, 1975).

Barton, John H. and Lawrence C. Weiler (eds), *International Arms Control: Issues and Agreements* (Stanford University Press, 1976).

Bebbington, William P., 'The Reprocessing of Nuclear Fuels', *Scientific American* (December 1976).

Beecher, William, 'The Rush is on to Join Nuclear Club', *Boston Globe*, 25 May 1979.

Bellany, Ian, 'Nuclear Non-proliferation and the Inequality of States', *Political Studies*, xxv, 4 (December 1977).

Bertram, Christoph, *Arms Control and Technological Change, Adelphi Paper*, 146 (London: International Institute for Strategic Studies, 1978).

Betts, Richard K., 'A Diplomatic Bomb for South Africa?', *International Security*, iv, 2 (Fall 1979).

Betts, Richard K., 'Nuclear Proliferation and Regional Rivalry: Speculations on South Asia', *Orbis*, xxiii, 1 (Spring 1979).

Betts, Richard K., 'Paranoids, Pygmies, Pariahs and Non-proliferation', *Foreign Policy*, 26 (Spring 1977) 157-83.

Bibliography: Nuclear Proliferation (Washington, DC: Library of Congress, Congressional Research Service, 1978).

Blackett. P.M.S., *Atomic Weapons and East-West Relations* (Cambridge University Press, 1956).
Blackett, P.M.S., *The Military and Political Consequences of Atomic Energy* (London: Turnstile Press, 1949).
Bloomfield, Lincoln P., 'Nuclear Spread and World Order', *Foreign Affairs*, LIII, 4 (July 1975).
Bloomfield, Lincoln P. and A.C. Leiss, 'Arms Control and the Developing Countries', *World Politics*, XVIII, 1 (1965).
Bray, Frank and Michael L. Moodie, 'Nuclear Politics in India', *Survival*, XX, 3 (May/June 1977).
Brenner, Michael, 'Carter's Bungled Promise', *Foreign Policy*, 36 (Fall 1979).
Brenner, Michael, 'Carter's Non-proliferation Strategy: Fuel Assurances and Energy Security', *Orbis*, XII, 2 (Summer 1978).
Burt, Richard, 'Fears Rising in Washington that an India-Pakistan Nuclear Race is Inevitable', *New York Times*, 24 August 1979.
California Seminar on Arms Control and Foreign Policy, *Nuclear Policies: Fuel Without the Bomb* (Cambridge, Mass.: Ballinger, 1978).
Cervanka, Z. and B. Rogers, *The Nuclear Axis* (London: Friedman, 1978).
Chayes, Abram and W. Bennet Lewis (eds), *International Arrangements for Nuclear Fuel Reprocessing* (Cambridge, Mass.: Ballinger, 1977).
Clausen, Peter, 'Nuclear Conference Yields Potential New Consensus,' *Arms Control Today* (June 1979).
Conference on Energy and Nuclear Security in Latin America, Proceedings (Muscatine, Iowa: Stanley Foundation, 1978).
Cubie, James, *Myths and Realities: Nuclear Power, Nuclear Bombs* (Washington, DC: Center for the Study of Responsive Law, 1977).
Dahlberg, Richard C., 'Weapons Proliferation and Criteria for Evaluating Nuclear Fuel Cycles', Bulletin of the Atomic Scientists (January 1978).
Donnelly, Warren H., 'Control of Proliferation of Nuclear Weapons', reprinted in *Congressional Record*, 18 June 1976.
Donnelly, Warren H. and Donna S. Kramer, *Nuclear Weapons Proliferation: Legislation for Policy and Other Measures* (Washington, DC: Library of Congress, Congressional Research Service, 1977).
Dowty, Alan, 'Nuclear Proliferation: The Israeli Case', *International Studies Quarterly*, XXII, 1 (March 1978).
Duffy, Gloria, 'Soviet Nuclear Exports', *International Security*, III, 1 (Summer 1978).
Duffy, Gloria and Gordon Adams, *Power Politics: The Nuclear Industry and Nuclear Exports* (New York: Council on Economic Priorities, 1978).
Dunkel, Winfried M., 'Nuclear Proliferation – A German View', *Military Review* (November 1977).
Dunn, Lewis A., 'Half Past India's Bang', *Foreign Policy* 36 (Fall 1979).
Dunn, Lewis, *India, Pakistan, Iran... A Nuclear Proliferation Chain?* (Croton-on-Hudson, NY: Hudson Institute, 1976).
Dunn, Lewis, 'Nuclear Gray Marketeering', *International Security*, I, 3 (Winter 1977).
Dunn, Lewis, *The Role of Sanctions in Non-proliferation Strategy* (Croton-on-Hudson, NY: Hudson Institute, 1977).
Dunn, Lewis and Herman Kahn, *Trends in Nuclear Proliferation, 1975–1990:*

Projections, Problems and Policy Options (Croton-on-Hudson, NY: Hudson Institute, 1976).

Epstein, William, *The Last Chance: Nuclear Proliferation and Arms Control* (New York: The Free Press, 1976).

Epstein, William, 'Nuclear Proliferation in the Third World', *Journal of International Affairs*, 29, 2 (Fall 1975).

Falk, Richard A., *Nuclear Policy and World Order: Why Denuclearization?* (New York: Institute for World Order, 1979).

Falk, Richard, 'The Nuclear Teaser', *Alternatives*, 3, 2 (December 1977).

Falk, Richard, 'A World Order Problem,' *International Security*, I, 3 (Winter 1977).

Faltermayer, Edmund, 'Keeping the Peaceful Atom from Raising the Risk of War', *Fortune*, 9 April 1979.

Faulkner, Peter (ed.), *The Silent Bomb: A Guide to the Nuclear Energy Controversy* (New York: Random House, 1977).

Ford-Mitre, Nuclear Energy Study Group, *Nuclear Power: Issues and Choices* (Cambridge, Mass.: Ballinger, 1977).

Franko, Lawrence G. and A. Javier Ergueta, *US Regulation of the Spread of Nuclear Technologies Through Supplier Power: Lever or Boomerang?* (Washington, DC: Carnegie Endowment for International Peace, 1978).

Freedman, Lawrence, 'Israel's Nuclear Policy', *Survival*, XVII, 3 (May/June 1975).

Frye, Alton, 'How to Ban the Bomb: Sell It', *New York Times Magazine*, 11 January 1976.

Gall, N., 'Atoms for Brazil, Dangers for All', *Foreign Policy*, 23 (Summer 1976).

Gall, Norman, 'Nuclear Setbacks', *Forbes*, 27 November 1978.

Garris, Jerome, *Sweden's Debate on the Proliferation of Nuclear Weapons* (Santa Monica, Ca.: California Seminar on Arms Control and Foreign Policy, 1972).

Gati, Toby Trister, *Soviet Perspectives on Nuclear Non-proliferation* (Santa Monica, Ca.: California Seminar on Arms Control and Foreign Policy, 1976).

Gelber, Harry, *Nuclear Weapons and Chinese Policy, Adelphi Paper*, 99 (London: International Institute for Strategic Studies, 1973).

Gilinsky, Victor, 'The Military Potential of Civil Nuclear Power', in Mason Willrich (ed.), *Civilian Nuclear Power and International Security* (New York: Praeger, 1971).

Goldschmidt, Bertrand, 'A Historical Survey of Non-proliferation Policies', *International Security*, II, 1 (Summer 1977).

Gorman, Stephen M., 'Security, Influence, and Nuclear Weapons: The Case of Argentina and Brazil', *Parameters*, IX, 1 (March 1979).

Greenwood, Ted, *et al., Nuclear Power and Weapons Proliferation, Adelphi Paper* 130 (London: International Institute for Strategic Studies, 1976).

Greenwood, Ted, *et al., Nuclear Proliferation: Motives, Capabilities, and Strategies for Control* (New York: McGraw-Hill, 1977).

Groom, A.J.R., *British Thinking about Nuclear Weapons* (London: Frances Pinter, 1974).

Hafemeister, David W., 'Non-proliferation and Alternative Nuclear Technologies', *Technology Review* (December 1978-January 1979).

Halstead, Thomas A., 'The Spread of Nuclear Weapons – Is the Dam About to Burst?', *Arms Control Today* (November 1974).

Hamilton, Michael P. (ed.), *To Avoid Catastrophe: A Study in Future Nuclear Weapons Policy* (Grand Rapids, Mich.: Eerdmans, 1977).

Harkavy, Robert E. 'The Pariah State Syndrome', *Orbis*, XXI, 3 (Fall 1977).

Herz, John, *International Politics in the Atomic Age* (New York: Columbia University Press, 1967).

Hiroharu, Seki, 'Nuclear Proliferation and Our Option', *Japan Quarterly*, XXII, 1 (January-March 1975).

Hoffman, Stanley, 'The Hell of Good Intentions', *Foreign Policy*, 29 (Winter 1977-78).

Hoffman, Stanley, 'Nuclear Proliferation and World Politics', in A. Buchan (ed.), *A World of Nuclear Powers?* (Englewood Cliffs, NJ: Prentice Hall, 1966).

Huck, Arthur, *The Security of China* (New York: Columbia University Press, 1970).

Husbands, Jo L., 'Nuclear Proliferation and the Inter-American System', in Thomas J. Farer (ed.), *The Future of the Inter-American System* (New York: Praeger, 1979).

Imai, Ryukichi, 'Non-proliferation: A Japanese Point of View', *Survival*, XXI, 2 (March/April 1979).

Ikle, Fred C., 'The Second Nuclear Era', *Department of State Bulletin*, 19 May 1975.

Jaipal, Rikhi, 'The Indian Nuclear Situation', *International Security*, I, 4 (Spring 1977).

Joskow, Paul L., 'The International Nuclear Industry Today', *Foreign Affairs*, LIV, 4 (July 1976).

Kaiser, Karl, 'The Great Nuclear Debate', *Foreign Policy*, 30 (Spring 1978).

Kapur, Ashok, *India's Nuclear Option: Atomic Diplomacy and Decision Making* (New York: Praeger, 1976).

Kemp, Geoffrey, *Nuclear Forces for Medium Powers, Adelphi Papers*, 106, 107 (London: International Institute for Strategic Studies, 1974).

Kennan, George F., *The Cloud of Danger* (Boston: Little, Brown, 1977).

Kincade, William H., 'Banning Nuclear Tests: Cold Feet in the Carter Administration', *Bulletin of the Atomic Scientists* (November 1978).

Krell, Gert, 'Military Doctrines, New Weapons Systems, and Arms Control', *Bulletin of Peace Proposals* (January 1979).

Krishna, Raj, 'India and the Bomb', in K.K. Sinka (ed.), *Problems of Defense of South and East Asia* (Bombay: Maraktalas, 1969).

Lefever, Ernest W., *Nuclear Arms in the Third World: US Policy Dilemma* (Washington, DC: Brookings Institution, 1979).

Lellouche, Pierre, 'France in the International Nuclear Controversy: Giscard's New Foreign Nuclear Policy', *Orbis*, XXII, 4 (Winter 1979).

Lellouche, Pierre and Richard K. Lester, 'The Crisis of Nuclear Energy', *Washington Quarterly*, II, 3 (Summer 1979).

Long, Clarence D., 'Nuclear Proliferation: Can Congress Act in Time?', *International Security*, I, 4 (Spring 1977).

Lopes, J. Leite, 'Atoms in the Developing World', *Bulletin of the Atomic Scientists* (April 1978).

Lowrance, William W., 'Nuclear Future for Sale: To Brazil from West Germany, 1975', *International Security*, I, 2 (Fall 1976).

Maddox, John, *The Spread of Nuclear Weapons* (London: Chatto & Windus, 1962).

Maddox, John, *Prospect for Nuclear Proliferation, Adelphi Paper*, 113 (London: International Institute for Strategic Studies, 1975).

Marder, Murrey and Don Oberdorfer, 'How West, Soviets Moved to Head Off S. African A-Test', *Washington Post*, 28 August 1977.

Marwah, Onkar, 'India's Nuclear and Space Programs: Intent and Policy', *International Security*, II, 2 (Fall 1977).

Marhaw, Onkar and Ann Schultz (eds), *Nuclear Proliferation and the Near-Nuclear Countries* (Cambridge, Mass.: Ballinger, 1975).

Meckoni, Vinay, 'Regional Nuclear Fuel Cycle Centres', *International Atomic Energy Agency Bulletin* (February 1976).

Mendl, Wolf, *Deterrence and Persuasion* (London: Faber & Faber, 1970).

Miller, Marvin, 'The Nuclear Dilemma: Power, Proliferation, and Development', *Technology Review* (May 1979).

Moniz, Ernest J. and Thomas L. Neff, 'Nuclear Power and Nuclear-Weapons Proliferation', *Physics Today* (April 1978).

Morawiecki, Wojciech, 'The IAEA's Role in Promoting Physical Protection of Nuclear Materials and Facilities', *International Atomic Energy Agency Bulletin*, 3 (June 1978).

Müller, Harald, 'Nuclear Exports and Nuclear Weapons Proliferation', *Bulletin of Peace Proposals*, 1 (1979).

Myrdal, Alva, *The Game of Disarmament* (New York: Pantheon Books, 1976).

Myrdal, Alva, 'The High Price of Nuclear Arms Monopoly', *Foreign Policy*, 18 (Spring 1975).

Myrdal, Alva, *The Right to Conduct Nuclear Explosions: Political Aspects and Policy Proposals* (Stockholm International Peace Research Institute, 1975).

NPT: Paradoxes and Problems (Washington, DC: Arms Control Association, 1975).

Neff, Thomas L. and Henry D. Jacoby, 'Non-proliferation Strategy in a Changing Nuclear Fuel Market', *Foreign Affairs*, 57, 5 (Summer 1979).

Nye, Joseph S., 'Balancing Non-proliferation and Energy Security', *Technology Review* (December 1978-January 1979).

Nye, Joseph S., 'Non-proliferation: A Long-Term Strategy', *Foreign Affairs*, LVI, 3 (April 1978).

Nye, Joseph S., 'Time to Plan for the Next Generation of Nuclear Technology', *Bulletin of the Atomic Scientists* (October 1977).

Nye, Joseph S., 'We Tried Harder (And Did More)', *Foreign Policy* 36 (Fall 1979).

Oberdorfer, Don, 'Arms Sales to Pakistan Urged to Stave Off A-Bomb There', *Washington Post*, 6 August 1979.

Palsokar, R.D., *Minimum Deterrence: India's Answer to China* (Bombay: Thacker, 1969).

Pendergast, William R., 'US Foreign Policy and Nuclear Proliferation', *Naval War College Review*, XXXI, 1 (Summer 1978).

Perry, William and Sheila Kern, 'The Brazilian Nuclear Program in a Foreign Policy Context', *Comparative Strategy*, I, 1 (1978).

Pillsbury, Michael, 'A Japanese Card?', *Foreign Policy*, 33 (Winter 1978-79).

Ping, Hsin, 'Utilization of Nuclear Energy and the Struggle Against Hegemony', *Peking Review*, 15 (1978).

Power, Paul F. 'The Indo-American Nuclear Controversy', *Asian Survey*, (June 1979).

Pranger, Robert and Dale Tahtinen, *Nuclear Threat in the Middle East* (Washington, DC: American Enterprise Institute, 1975).

Quester, George, *The Politics of Nuclear Proliferation* (Baltimore: The Johns Hopkins University Press, 1973).

Rathjens, G. *et al.*, *Nuclear Arms Control Agreements: Process and Impact* (Washington, DC: Carnegie Endowment for International Peace, 1974).

Ray, Dixie Lee, 'Multinational Nuclear Power – Peaceful Use or International Terror?', *Pan American Magazine* (October 1974).

Redick, John R., *Military Potential of Latin American Nuclear Energy Programs* (Beverly Hills: Sage, 1972).

Redick, John R., 'Nuclear Proliferation in Latin America', in Roger Fontaine and James D. Theberge (eds), *Latin America's New Internationalism: The End of Hemispheric Isolation* (New York: Praeger, 1976).

Redick, John R. 'Regional Restraint: US Nuclear Policy and Latin America', *Orbis*, XXII, 1 (Spring 1978).

Ribicoff, Abraham A., 'A Market Sharing Approach to the World Nuclear Sales Problem', *Foreign Affairs*, 54, 4 (July 1976).

Rose, David J. and Richard K. Lester, 'Nuclear Power, Nuclear Weapons and International Stability', *Scientific American* (April 1978).

Rosenbaum, David, 'Nuclear Terror', *International Security*, I, 3 (Winter 1977).

Rotblat, J., 'Controlling Weapons-Grade Fissile Material', *Bulletin of the Atomic Scientists* (June 1977).

Schelling, Thomas, 'Who Will Have the Bomb', *International Security*, I, 1 (Summer 1976).

Scherr, Jacob and Thomas Stoel, 'Atoms for Peace?', *Amicus*, I, 1 (Summer 1979).

Singh, Sampooran, *India and the Nuclear Bomb* (New Delhi: S. Chand, 1971).

Smart, Ian, 'Janus: The Nuclear God', *World Today* (April 1978).

Stilwell, Richard, 'Commentary – The US, Japan and the Security of Korea', *International Security*, II, 2 (Fall 1977).

Stockholm International Peace Research Institute, *The Near-Nuclear Countries and the NPT* (Stockhom: Almqvist & Wiksell, 1972).

Stockholm International Peace Research Institute, *Nuclear Proliferation Problems* (Cambridge, Mass.: MIT Press, 1974).

Stockholm International Peace Research Institute, *Postures for Non-proliferation: Arms Limitation and Security Policies to Minimize Nuclear Proliferation* (New York: Crane, Russak, 1979).

Subrahmanyam, K., 'The Nuclear Issue and International Security', *Bulletin of the Atomic Scientists* (February 1977).

Symington, Stuart, 'Controlling the Cancer of Nuclear Proliferation', *Congressional Record*, 13 March 1975.

Symington, Stuart, 'Nuclear Proliferation and Counterforce', *Congressional Record*, 22 October 1975.

Symington, Stuart, 'The Washington Nuclear Mess', *International Security, I, 3 (Winter 1977)*.

US Comptroller General, *An Evaluation of the Administration's Proposed Nuclear Non-proliferation Strategy* (Washington, DC: GPO, 1977).

US Congress, House Committee on Foreign Affairs, Subcommittees on International Economic Policy and Trade, *Progress in US and International Non-proliferation Efforts*, 96th Cong., 1st Sess. (Washington, DC: GPO, 1979).

US Congress, House International Relations Committee, Subcommittee on International Economic Policy and Trade, *Nuclear Proliferation Factbook 95th Cong., 1st Sess. (Washington, DC: GPO, 1977)*.

US Congress, House International Relations Committee, *Nuclear Proliferation: Future US Foreign Policy Implications*, 94th Cong., 1st Sess. (Washington, DC: GPO, 1975).

US Congress, House Committee on Science and Technology, Subcommittee on Fossil and Nuclear Energy Research, Development and Demonstration, *Alternative Breeding Cycles for Nuclear Power: An Analysis*, 95th Cong., 2nd Sess. (Washington, DC: Library of Congress, Congressional Research Service, 1978).

US Congress, Office of Technology Assessment, *Nuclear Proliferation and Safeguards* (New York: Praeger, 1977).

US Congress, Senate Committee on Foreign Relations, Subcommittee on Arms Control, International Organizations, and Security Agreements, Hearings: *Nuclear Reduction, Testing, and Non-proliferation*, 94th Cong., 2nd Sess. (Washington, DC: GPO, 1976).

Van Praagh, David, 'India's Bomb', *Asian Affairs: An American Review* (July-August 1974).

Warnecke, Steven J., 'Non-proliferation and INFCE: An Interim Assessment', *Survival*, XXI, 3 (May/June 1979).

Weiss, Leonard, 'Nuclear Safeguards: A Congressional Perspective', *Bulletin of the Atomic Scientists* (March 1978).

Williams, Frederick, *et al.* 'The Nuclear Non-proliferation Act of 1978: Reactions from Germany, *International Security*, III, 2 (Fall 1978).

Willrich, Mason, 'The Non-proliferation Treaty: Nuclear Technology Confronts World Politics', *Yale Law Journal*, 77, 8 (July 1968).

Willrich, Mason, 'A Workable International Nuclear Energy Regime', *Washington Quarterly*, II, 2 (Spring 1979).

Willrich, Mason and Philip M. Marston, 'Prospects for a Uranium Cartel', *Orbis*, 19, 1 (Spring 1975).

Wilson, Richard, 'How to Have Nuclear Power Without Weapons Proliferation', *Bulletin of the Atomic Scientists* (November 1977).

Wohlstetter, Albert, 'Spreading the Bomb Without Quite Breaking the Rules',

Foreign Policy, 25 (Winter 1976-77).
Wohlstetter, Albert, *Moving Towards Life in a Nuclear Armed Crowd* (Los Angeles: Pan Heuristics, 1976).
Wonder, Edward, 'Nuclear Commerce and Nuclear Proliferation: Germany and Brazil', *Orbis*, XXI, 2 (Summer 1975).
Young, Elizabeth, *A Farewell to Arms Control* (Harmondsworth, UK: Penguin, 1972).
Zablocki, Clement J., 'Nuclear Proliferation: Future US Foreign Policy Consideration', *Congressional Record*, 3 May 1976.
Zablocki, Clement J., 'Talking Pakistan Out of the Bomb', *Washington Post*, 28 August 1979.

Index